ROYAL HISTORICAL SOCI

STUDIES IN HISTORY

New Series

THE IRISH REBELLION OF 1641
AND THE WARS OF THE THREE KINGDOMS

A Prospect of bleeding IRELANDS miseries: Presented in a Brief

Recitement to the eyes and hearts of all her commiserating friends in *England* and *Scotland*, as one maine Motive to move their Christian courage for her assistance, when we consider there hath been at the least two hundred thousand Protestants slain and most inhumanely massacred by the barbarous and blood-thirsty Rebels, putting them to the most cruell kinds of death that they could invent, as you may read by this following Relation. Diligently Collected from the most certain Intelligence.

Recompence unto them double what they have done unto others.

Reader what passages of cruelty thou shalt here peruse thou hast not the least cause to suspect of truth, they being such as by clear evidence have bin made manifestly true by faithfull Intelligence of eye and eare witnesse.

1. Within the County of Fermanagh great cruelties have been acted upon the poor English Protestants where multitudes of men women and children have been kill'd in cold blood.

2. In the Castle of Lisgoole there were above one hundred and fifty men, women, and children, burnt there when that Castle was set on fire.

3. At the Castle of Moneah about one hundred English were slain by the Barbarous Rebels.

4. The Castle of Tullah being yeelded upon composition with promise of fair quarter from the Rebells, but as soon as ever they entred the same they put all to the sword without exception.

5. At Lissenskeah they murthered near one hundred of the Scotch Protestants, which they use in every place as cruelly as the English.

6. One Mr. Middleton they compeld to heare Mass and afterward they caused him his wife and children to be hanged up and murthered.

7. In the Countys of Armagh and Tirone great and Barbarous cruelties have been exercised.

8. At one place there were carried out at severall times in Troops one thousand Protestants, which were drowned at the bridg of Portnedown, which for that purpose was broke down in the midst.

9. And within the County of Armagh foure thousand Protestants have in severall places been drowned.

10. The Protestants have been driven naked before these Barbarous Butchers in severall companies like sheep appoynted for the slaughter, to the places of execution.

11. And if any fayned or grew weary on the way, they prickt them forward with their sword poynts whereby they killed many on the way.

12. With their Pikes and swords they thrust the poor stript Christians into the waters, or off the Banks, or Bridges.

13. Those that assay by swiming to save their lives, they shoot or beat out their brains.

14. Sir Phellim Oneal hath proved the cheif actor of these Barborous and bloody massacres.

15. He having caused all the Protestants in Armagh and there abouts under pretence of conducting them murthered of young and old five hundred persons.

16. He caused the Town of Armagh, and Cathedrall Church to be fired which were burnt down.

17. At a town called Killaman, fourty and eight families were Murthered by his direction.

18. In the same town there were twenty too English Protestants Burnt in one house.

19. Within two miles of the same the Rebels murthered of English two hundred Families.

20. They have been so eager at their prey, that they would not suffer the poor Protestants to say their prayers before they murthered them.

21. They have imprisioned some in noysome dungeons of dirt and mire, with bolts on their leggs where they were starved to death by Leasure.

22. At Cassell the Rebels cruelly murthered fifteen English Protestants using the rest most barbarously.

23. They have most Barbarously mangled many Protestants and left them languishing in their payn in the high ways half dead accounting it to favourable to end them of their payn by a suddain death.

24. They have buried many alive both men women and poor harmless infants.

25. At one time at a town called Clownis, they buried seventeen persons which they had half hanged which were heard to send forth Lamentable groans.

26. After they had cruelly wounded some they hung them upon tenter hooks.

27. Others when they had put rops about their necks they dragged through the water.

28. Some they dragged through the woods and Boggs till they dyed.

29. They have put ropes about the necks of many and cast them several times into the water, wherby to cause them to confess where their moneys were.

30. They have hanged up some a small time, and then taken them down again, to make them confess where their money was, which when they told them, then they hanged them outright.

31. When they have stript the Protestants naked, they bid them go look for their God, and bid him cloth them again.

32. They have hung up English by the armes and then hackt them with their swords to try how many blows they would indure before they dyed.

33. Some have had their bellys ript up and so left with their Intrails taken out.

34. They have ript up women big with child, and the young Infants hath falled out, which the Rebells have often given to doggs, and swine to eat or cast into ditches.

35. The Rebells robb'd, stript, and murthered a great company of Protestants in the County of Armagh, some they burnt, some they slew by the sword, and some they hanged, others they starved and put to death more cruelly.

36. After they had cruelly wounded some they hung them upon tenter hooks.

37. They have hanged some by the heels, and then with their skeans cut them in peeces.

38. Some young Infants have been found in the feild, Sucking the Brests of their murthered Mothers.

39. A great number of Protestants especially of women and children, they have slisht & mangled in many places of their bodies, and not kill'd outright, but left them wallowing in their blood.

40. Denying to kill them outright, till two or three days after, and then they would dash out their brains with stones.

41. A woman that leapt out of a window to save her self from burning was murthered by the Rebels, and the next morning her child found sucking at her breast which they also murthered.

42. The Rebels stabb'd one Jane Addis, left her sucking child alive by her, & putting the breast into its mouth said Each English bastard, so the child perisht for want, of which Act they bragg'd.

43. Many young Infants have been stifled in vaults and cellers, or starved in caves which have cryed to their mothers rather to send them out to dye by the Rebels then to starve so miserably there.

44. Multitudes of men, women, and children were drowned, cast into ditches, boggs, and turf-pits.

45. Many have been inclosed in their houses which have been set on fire and burnt with their houses to ashes in a most miserable manner, and if any attempted to escape they threw them into the fire again.

46. They have dragg'd out some from their sick beds to the place of execution.

47. In the parish of Loghgall to the river of Toll they forced children to carry their aged parents out of their beds to drown them in that river.

48. They have enforced children to execute their parents, and wives their own husbands by hanging and other ways.

49. The wife of Florence Fitz Patrick was outragious with her husbands souldiers because they brought not the grease of a Protestant woman whom they had cruelly murthered for her to make caudls withall.

50. The Irish men some of them detest not the cruelty of those bloody queans that follow their camp, that cry our spare neither man woman nor child.

51. They have boyld children to death in Cauldrons.

52. They hanged a woman and her daughter in the hair of her own head.

53. In a frosty night they stript a woman big with child which presently after fell in labour, and both child and she dyed at the instant.

54. The Rebels often utter threatnings out to cut off all that have a drop of English blood in them, and their women cry out that the English are only meat for doggs.

55. Neare the Town of Monaghan, they most cruelly murthered one Mr. Foord in his own Garden, most inhumanely tortured his wife, Laying hot Tongs to her hands and feet (to make her tell where his money was) that with the payn thereof she died.

56. They have most villanously ravished Virgins and women, and afterwards have bin so bloody and hard-harted, as to dash their childrens brains out.

Thus have you heard of some part of the miseries and tortures inflicted upon the poor Protestants in Ireland, by the bloody Rebels; many more inhumane murthers they have committed, which I forbeare for brevity sake: But such is the care and wisdom of the Parliament to put an end to the bleeding miseries of Ireland, that they have chosen that renowned, faithfull, and valiant Commander Major General SKIPPON to be Field-Marshal over their Forces, and Major General MASSEY is chosen Lieutenant General of the horse, the Lord crown their endeavours with victory over those inhumane blood-thirsty Rebels, that so dying Ireland may yet live to praise him.

Aprill 16. London, Printed for *J. H.* and are to be sold in *Popes head Alley.* 1647.

A prospect of bleeding Irelands miseries, London 1647.
© The British Library Board, 669. f. 11 (4)

THE IRISH REBELLION OF 1641
AND THE WARS
OF THE THREE KINGDOMS

Eamon Darcy

THE ROYAL HISTORICAL SOCIETY
THE BOYDELL PRESS

First published 2013
Paperback edition 2015

A Royal Historical Society publication
Published by The Boydell Press
an imprint of Boydell & Brewer Ltd
PO Box 9, Woodbridge, Suffolk IP12 3DF, UK
and of Boydell & Brewer Inc.
668 Mt Hope Avenue, Rochester, NY 14620–2731, USA
website: www.boydellandbrewer.com

ISBN 978 0 86193 320 4 hardback
ISBN 978 0 86193 336 5 paperback

ISSN 0269–2244

A CIP catalogue record for this book is available
from the British Library

The publisher has no responsibility for the continued existence or accuracy of
URLs for external or third-party internet websites referred to in this book,
and does not guarantee that any content on such websites is,
or will remain, accurate or appropriate

TO MY PARENTS

Contents

Contents

Acknowledgements

This book would not have been possible without the generous assistance of the Irish Research Council for the Humanities and Social Sciences, the Huntington Library, California, and the Folger Shakespeare Library, Washington DC. Staff in the various archives that I have visited over the last few years have been exceptionally kind and helpful. I would like to thank the archivists at Trinity College, Dublin; the National Library of Ireland; the Royal Irish Academy; Marsh's Library; the Representative Church Body Library; Dublin City Library and Archive; the House of Lords Record Office; the British Library; the Bodleian Library; the Huntington Library; and the Folger Shakespeare Library. In particular I would like to thank, Mary Higgins, Pamela Hilliard, Jenny Horner, Bernard Meehan, Paula Norris, Felicity O'Mahony and †Ann Walsh. Furthermore, everybody at the Royal Historical Society and Boydell & Brewer have been most helpful in seeing this manuscript through to publication. In particular, I would like to thank Christine Linehan for all her help with the copy editing and indexing.

While researching and writing this book I have incurred numerous intellectual debts to fellow researchers at Trinity College Dublin and other institutions as well. I would like to thank Charlene Adair, Robert Armstrong, Ciaran Brady, Ian Campbell, Stephen Carroll, Aidan Clarke, Joseph Clarke, David Dickson, David Ditchburn, Anne Dolan, Barbara Fennell, Kevin Forkan, Edda Frankot, Patrick Geoghegan, John Gibney, Raymond Gillespie, Crawford Gribben, Caitlín Higgins Ní Chinnéide, Annaleigh Margey, Bríd McGrath, Graeme Murdock, Elaine Murphy, Ethan Shagan, Scott Spurlock, Trish Stapleton, Justin Dolan Stover, Alexandra Walsham and John Walter. Ian Campbell, Aidan Clarke, John Gibney, John Morrill, Micheál Ó Siochrú, Jane Ohlmeyer and Ethan Shagan all read parts of this book in draft form and made numerous helpful suggestions as to how it could be improved. John Walter helped me to tease out aspects of chapter 2 and has been a great help with my work in general. I am particularly indebted to John Morrill, Micheál Ó Siochrú and Jane Ohlmeyer who read the entire manuscript prior to publication; their input was invaluable. Professor Ohlmeyer, needless to say, has always been on call if I needed any help with my work, or my career, which is much appreciated. Professor Morrill helped to see this book through to publication with the Royal Historical Society and for that I am eternally grateful.

To all my friends from college and at home, who provided me with many helpful distractions when necessary, thank you! The extended Ó Coigligh family were very generous, particularly Alma who provided a roof over my head and James who provided me with his copy of Spenser's *View* from 1633 (great bedtime reading) while I was researching in London. Similarly, the Ó Catháins were very helpful and good fun; in particular I would like to thank Úna for all her endless support and helpful advice. Finally, to my family – I am forever grateful to my siblings, Maeve and Eoghan, and to the extended Darcy and Keogh clans. Sadly, there are some who are no longer here with whom I would have liked to share this and who are never far from my thoughts. This book is dedicated to my parents, Niamh and Peter, who have been fantastic since I embarked on this journey. Your advice, encouragement and support have been ceaseless. Murach an aire agus an tacaíocht a fuair mé uathu, ní bheadh an obair seo curtha i gcrích agam.

Eamon Darcy
July 2012

Abbreviations

BL   British Library, London
HMC   Historical Manuscripts Commission
IMC   Irish Manuscripts Commission
NLI   National Library of Ireland
TCD   Trinity College Dublin

CSPD *Calendar of state papers, domestic series, 2nd ser.* London 1858–97
CSPI *Calendar of state papers relating to Ireland,* London 1860–1911
DIB   James McGuire and James Quinn (eds), *Dictionary of Irish biography: from the earliest times to the year 2002,* Cambridge 2009: dib.cambridge.org
HJ   *Historical Journal*
JBS   *Journal of British Studies*
ODNB *Oxford Dictionary of National Biography*
P&P   *Past & Present*

Introduction: The 1641 Rebellion and the Wars of the Three Kingdoms

What began on 23 October 1641? Was it a rebellion? An uprising? A nationalist rising? A Catholic plot? A pre-meditated massacre? An indiscriminate slaughter? A fabrication? An exaggeration? A response to the wider pressures of 'Britain' and an integral part of the Wars of the Three Kingdoms? Contemporaries, scholars and historians alike have debated and contested the causes and course of what is now known as the 1641 rebellion in Ireland. Like any military event there were participants (both losers and winners), survivors, victims and witnesses. The records and testimonies left behind are fraught with difficulties for researchers. Memories of 1641 justified a range of controversial policies such as land confiscations, penal laws and the Union of Great Britain and Ireland. Historians have had to consider the course of wider Anglo-Irish history and politics when attempting to understand what unfolded in Ireland during the 1640s. Accounts were highly partisan, divided along Catholic and Protestant, and later nationalist and unionist, lines. These passionate debates meant that the main body of evidence for the rebellion of 1641, now known as the 1641 depositions, has been decried as lies by Catholics and exalted by Protestants as evidence of Catholic perfidy. As a result, historians have been reluctant to engage with the depositions to any great detail. They are a problematic source due to their highly partisan nature: they are the product of a commission comprising eight Church of Ireland clergymen who recorded the testimonies of thousands of mainly Protestant deponents, the majority of whom believed that the 1641 rebellion was a Catholic plot to destroy the Irish Protestant community.

Take as an example the deposition of Robert Maxwell, who was the rector of Tinon in Armagh and was imprisoned by the rebels shortly after the outbreak of rebellion. He managed to escape and would later provide an account of his experience on 22 August 1642. Maxwell testified that during the beginning of the rebellion Sir Phelim O'Neill, MP for Dungannon and leader of the Ulster rebels, along with his brother, Turlogh Óg O'Neill, and half-brother, Robert Hovenden, taunted English settlers calling them 'base degenerate cowards'. O'Neill and his followers had followed closely events which took place in Scotland in the preceding years. In 1637 Charles I attempted to streamline the Calvinist Scottish Church into English (Anglican) practices. In response, the Scots formed the National Covenant and took arms against the king, desiring greater political and religious privileges. According to Maxwell, this gave hope to Phelim O'Neill that Irish

Catholics would also take up arms to defend their religious beliefs and rallied Catholic Ireland to the cause. There were 'frequent and extraordinary meetings of preists and ffriars almost everywhere' who provided the main organisational backbone of the rebellion. Rumours abounded that Hugh O'Neill, the earl of Tyrone, would return from Spain with thousands of Spanish troops to spearhead the rebellion. Hugh O'Neill left Ireland in 1607 as part of the Flight of the Earls and had in fact died in 1616. Maxwell claimed that most of the Catholic nobility, both the native Irish and Old English (descendants of the first English settlers in Ireland – who had now 'degenerated' into Irish customs) had all resolved to rebel. To fund the rebellion they had duplicitously borrowed as much as they could from the 'Brittish'. Maxwell also claimed that two prominent members of the Irish nobility, the earl of Antrim, Randal MacDonnell, and the baron of Slane, Thomas Fleming, had, along with numerous other nobles, been enlisted by Catholic clerics to support the rebellion as had Catholics across England and Europe. One friar declared to Maxwell that he hoped to 'say masse in Christchurch Dublin'. Maxwell, eager to understand why rebellion broke out, pressed Phelim O'Neill to reveal his motives. O'Neill acknowledged that aside from his desire to fight for Catholicism, he wished for the reversal of the plantations and for Catholics to be granted control of all fortifications, while all 'strangers' were to be expelled from Ireland.

How would Sir Phelim O'Neill gain support from lesser nobles, gentry and the lower social orders for his rebellion? O'Neill's opinion, as recounted by Maxwell, was that Irish Catholics lived in fear of the English parliament. O'Neill alleged that MPs plotted to 'bring them all to Church, or to cutt off the papists in the Kings dominions'. Playing on the tensions between the king, covenanters (those who adhered to the National Covenant) and the English parliament, O'Neill forged a commission from Charles I ordering the lower social orders to enlist in the Irish rebellion. 'In all wars', O'Neill claimed, 'rumors and lyes served many tymes to as good purpose as armes.' His kinsmen and clan boasted of a prophecy that he would lead an army into England to expel the king. Aggrieved by religious persecution and spurred on by Catholic nobles, the native Irish attacked their Protestant neighbours and killed thousands of settlers. The Old English also partook in this violence and killed 'British Protestants'. O'Neill ordered the execution of Maxwell's brother and sister-in-law, while other soldiers tortured English animals and killed prominent members of settler society, such as the local school teacher and several landowners. The killings spread as settlers from the lower social orders were attacked. Such was the scale of death and destruction that corpses were left unburied in ditches and on the streets and began to 'stinke and infest the ayre'. Maxwell attested to the fact that he had heard of various slaughters committed in the province of Ulster, such as the murder of roughly 1,000 Protestants in Antrim, the burning of twenty-four English settlers in a house in Lisnagarry in Armagh and the killing of 600 more at Garvagh in Derry. The most horrific of these incidents

2

occurred when Irish rebels forced 190 people to their deaths in the river Bann at Portadown bridge.[1]

Although he declared that the rebels 'never dreamt the deponent should live to tell it again', Maxwell escaped to Dublin. He attributed his survival to two factors. First, he recalled that one night outside his house 'a light was observed, in manner of a long pillar, to shine for a long way through the air, and ... gave so great a light about an hour together, that divers of the watch read both letters and books of a small character thereby'. Maxwell's family, upon viewing this sign, 'interpreted the same to be an immediate expression and token of Divine providence'. This, subsequently, led them to believe that God spared them, as the rebels 'had a purpose to destroy the deponent and his family, but were always hindered and interrupted'. In typical God-fearing manner, 'the deponent, with the rest of his family, gave themselves to fasting and prayer, expecting each hour that universal cutting off which fell out very shortly after'. Secondly, Maxwell was protected by prominent members of the native Irish community. Phelim O'Neill's mother, Katherine Hovenden, 'preserved twenty-four English and Scots in her own house' and sympathised with their plight. For example, upon hearing of the drowning of fifty-six prisoners, 'she swooned twice'. Aghast at Phelim's actions, she denounced her son: 'she used often to say she had never offended the English, except in being mother to Sir Phelemy'. In his deposition, Maxwell contrasted O'Neill's behaviour with that of his other half-brother, Alexander, who safely conducted thirty-five English prisoners out of Armagh and prevented the rebels from torching the town after Maxwell pleaded with him to save the inhabitants.[2] Alexander Hovenden refused to take any further part in the rebellion after O'Neill had allegedly signed a warrant allowing for the execution of innocent settlers.[3]

Maxwell's testimony is illustrative of both the problems and potential of looking at the 1641 depositions to investigate the causes and course of the 1641 rebellion. First, he believed that the rebels were motivated primarily by religious grievances with economic and political considerations being only secondary concerns. Historians in more recent times, however, have argued that the rebellion broke out as a result of the gradual decline of Catholic political influence and economic strength.[4] Secondly, Maxwell blamed members of the Catholic nobility for the murders of British settlers, which

---

[1] This will be discussed in greater detail in chapter 2 below.

[2] For other accounts of how Protestant settlers survived among the native Irish during the 1640s see Joseph Cope, 'The experience of survival during the 1641 Irish rebellion', *HJ* xlvi (2003), 295–316.

[3] Unless otherwise stated all quotations are taken from the deposition of Robert Maxwell: TCD, MS 809, fos 5–12.

[4] Nicholas Canny, *Making Ireland British, 1580–1650*, Oxford 2001; Aidan Clarke, 'Ireland and the general crisis', *P&P* xlviii (1970), 79–99; Michael Perceval-Maxwell, *The outbreak of the Irish rebellion of 1641*, London 1994.

has been strongly contested by scholars.[5] Maxwell's deposition provides evidence for his worldview, that of a Protestant minister imbued with a strong belief in divine providence. Living in a polarised community there is some sense that Maxwell was suspicious of Catholics living nearby. Yet, Maxwell's deposition tentatively suggests some form of interaction between natives and newcomers prior to the 1641 rebellion. Katherine Hovenden, a leading figure within the native Irish social hierarchy in Armagh, assisted settlers in their attempts to escape and survive the rebellion. What were relations between native and newcomer societies like prior to the rebellion? What motivated the Irish rebels? Did they take arms to defend the Catholic faith as alleged by Maxwell? Is this why popular violence erupted in 1641? What did contemporaries believe had occurred and why? Before addressing any of these issues it is necessary first to look at life in Ireland in the years leading up to 1641.

The polarisation of Irish society

Prior to the Reformation in the mid-sixteenth century, the Old English were seen as the powerbrokers in Ireland at the expense of the native Irish. After the Reformation, with the polarisation of Irish society along sectarian lines, newly-arrived Protestant, English settlers (the New English) began to label the native Irish and Old English ethnic groups as one Catholic or 'papist' community. Catholic firebrands (in colonists' eyes) such as James Fitzmaurice in the 1570s and 1580s and Hugh O'Neill in the 1590s began to appeal across ethnic divides to an ideology of common faith and fatherland and to shared identity among the native Irish and Old English.[6] Their 'rebellions' were a response to the fact that in the late sixteenth century Ireland witnessed an unprecedented level of bloodshed and violence during the vast expansion of Tudor power. In fact, the entire reign of the Tudors in Ireland was exceptionally violent even in moments of relative 'peace', which has only recently been acknowledged by historians.[7] From the 1570s onward, in particular, through scorched earth policies, 'the native population was starved and terrorised into submission' and surrendered their authority to the Tudor monarchy.[8] Such cycles of violence would dominate Irish politics in the early modern period.

[5]   Canny, *Making Ireland British*, 472; Perceval-Maxwell, *The outbreak of the Irish rebellion*, 228.

[6]   Hiram Morgan, 'Hugh O'Neill and the Nine Years War in Tudor Ireland', *HJ* xxxvi (1993), 21–37.

[7]   David Edwards, Padraig Lenihan and Clodagh Tait, 'Early modern Ireland: a history of violence', in David Edwards, Pádraig Lenihan and Clodagh Tait (eds), *Age of atrocity: violence and political conflict in early modern Ireland*, Dublin 2007, 9–33, esp. pp. 12–19.

[8]   David Edwards, 'The escalation of violence in sixteenth-century Ireland', in Edwards,

Fears of further persecution, particularly when religion became the main indicator of disloyalty after the succession of James VI and I to the English crown in 1603, caused some of the leading Irish nobility to flee for Europe in 1607. At a local level in Ulster, the composition of Irish society in Ireland radically changed over the first half of the seventeenth century. Protestant, New English settlers took the place of absent Irish lords. These settlers viewed the native Irish and Old English Catholics with suspicion. This led to considerable tensions between the two religious communities in Ireland. To impose their new-found authority on the island, these newly-enriched English planters frequently used excessive force. Furthermore, they denied Irish Catholics the opportunity to use English common law structures.[9] Tense relations between natives and newcomers led to misunderstandings and, sometimes, violent conflict erupted.[10] At a high political level, policies pursued by colonial administrators further threatened and alienated Ireland's Catholic population. For example, after the suppression of Cahir O'Doherty's rebellion in 1608, O'Doherty's lands were divided out amongst the New English. Arthur Chichester, lord deputy of Ireland (1605–15), benefited most from this land grab, much to the chagrin of the dispossessed. Chichester's vision for the plantation of Ulster involved the segregation of the native Irish and the preferential treatment of New English settlers, particularly those who served in the Nine Years' War. In his first year as lord deputy, Chichester challenged the loyalty of the Old English and issued 'mandates' requiring them to attend the services of the established Church. Westminster, alarmed at this attack on the Old English, lambasted Chichester for acting without their authority. In his attempts to call an Irish parliament in 1613 he first met with members of the Old English community. They were appalled at his refusal to listen to their petitions and so canvassed the royal court for his removal.[11] From a Catholic perspective (i.e. the perspective of both the native Irish and Old English) it was clear that a new Protestant and English order was emerging in Ireland.

The ascendancy of the royal favourite, George Villiers, duke of Buckingham, as James VI and I's key minister in Ireland dramatically altered the composition of the Irish peerage and further diluted Catholic influence in the upper echelons of Irish political life. In 1603 89 per cent of peers were Catholic (twenty-four out of twenty-seven peers)) but by 1628, after Buckingham's death, the Catholic share of power had been diluted to 54 per

Lenihan and Tait, *Age of atrocity*, 34–78.

9   Idem, 'The plight of the earls: Tyrone and Tyrconnell's "grievances" and crown coercion in Ulster, 1603–7', in Thomas O'Connor and Mary Ann Lyons (eds), *The Ulster earls and baroque Europe: refashioning Irish identities, 1600–1800*, Dublin 2010, 53–76.

10   Darren McGettigan, 'O'Doherty, Cahir', *DIB*; Raymond Gillespie, *Conspiracy: Ulster plots and plotters in 1615*, Belfast 1987.

11   Raymond Gillespie, 'Chichester, Arthur', *DIB*; John McCavitt, *Sir Arthur Chichester: lord deputy of Ireland, 1605–1616*, Belfast 1998.

cent.[12] The influx of Protestant men of less noble standing and less noble breeding to the uppermost ranks of Irish political society can only have alarmed Ireland's Catholic population. According to Aidan Clarke's masterly study of the Old English in the early seventeenth century, these descendants of the original invaders of Ireland maintained a distinct identity, aloof from the native Irish. Clarke's undeniably seminal work, however, overlooked a key context in seventeenth-century Irish history: Europe. After the Flight of the Earls and the establishment of Irish colleges to educate native Irish and Old English students as Catholic clerics in France, Italy and Spain, exiles and students fashioned a new identity for Ireland that transcended ethnic differences. Geoffrey Keating's 'Foras Feasa ar Éirinn', a popular manuscript, offered the shared designation of 'Irishmen' to the Catholics of Ireland. They created this new identity with the Spanish king in mind. Aware of tensions between England and Spain in the 1620s, Irish Jesuits in Spain campaigned for Spanish intervention in Ireland and 'began to present themselves as religious crusaders against a heretical English monarchy'. Despite this, Anglo-Spanish relations were prioritised ahead of Hiberno-Spanish, for Spain feared antagonising a powerful English enemy.[13]

During the Counter-Reformation, the Catholic Church laid strong foundations that survived the haphazard attempts of generations of reformers to convert Catholics.[14] In Armagh, priests downplayed ethnic differences between the native Irish and the Old English and in Ulster it appears that a broad knowledge of the nuances of the Catholic faith existed across the social orders.[15] Priests catered for their flocks' increasing dissatisfaction with the new Protestant and English order emerging in Ireland. Catholic polemics linked Protestantism with the devil and argued that Luther was the fallen son of Lucifer. 'Consequently, in the popular mind the rites and personnel

[12] Jane Ohlmeyer, Making Ireland English: the Irish aristocracy in the seventeenth century, New Haven 2012, 27–63 at p. 42; Victor Treadwell, Buckingham and Ireland, 1616–1628: a study in Anglo-Irish politics, Dublin 1998.

[13] Bernadette Cunningham, The world of Geoffrey Keating: history, myth and religion in seventeenth-century Ireland, Dublin 2007; Aidan Clarke, The Old English in Ireland, 1625–1642, Dublin 2000; Brendan Kane, 'A dynastic nation? Re-thinking national consciousness in early seventeenth-century Ireland', in David Finnegan, Éamonn Ó Ciardha and Marie-Claire Peters (eds), The flight of the earls: Imeacht na nIarlaí, Derry 2010, 124–31; Óscar Recio Morales, Ireland and the Spanish empire, 1600–1825, Dublin 2010; quotation from Igor Perez Tostado, Irish influence at the court of Spain in the seventeenth century, Dublin 2008, 23.

[14] Colm Lennon, 'The Counter Reformation in Ireland, 1542–1641', in Ciaran Brady and Raymond Gillespie (eds), Natives and newcomers: essays on the making of Irish colonial society, 1534–1641, Woodbridge 1986, 75–92.

[15] Tadhg Ó hAnnracháin, 'The survival of the Catholic Church in Ulster in the era of the flight of the earls and the Ulster plantation', in Finnegan, Ó Ciardha and Peters, The flight of the earls, 221–6.

of the Church of Ireland became tainted with diabolical overtones.'[16] At the same time, public pronouncements by English commentators that the Irish should be converted were not met with enthusiasm on the ground. By the 1620s, the established Church in Ulster had effectively abandoned the conversion of Irish natives in favour of adopting a more anglocentric Church that had little appeal to the Irish. Tellingly, in 1640 only five native Irish people were enrolled at Trinity College Dublin, the university founded to promote the Church of Ireland.[17] This religious polarisation caused much resentment in Ireland during the reign of the Stuart monarchs in Ireland and led to the outbreak of sectarian violence in 1641. In fact, religion is a vital component of the events of 1641. Fears of religious persecution mobilised the lower social orders and some of the rebels consequently targeted Protestant people and artefacts. These religious grievances became one of the most contested aspects of the rising during the 1640s. Catholic nobles vehemently denied that religion was the main cause of their quarrel, while the Protestant administration poured scorn on their protestations. Furthermore, religious beliefs provided a lens through which deponents could understand and rationalise their experience.

While other historians have argued that in the 1630s, Ireland, much like England, was relatively at peace, the central premise of this work is that throughout the early seventeenth century an uneasy equilibrium existed between the various religious and ethnic communities that could be upset at any moment. This is not to deny that the economic downturn of the late 1630s, the tenure of Thomas Wentworth as lord lieutenant, and the policy of plantation (both proposed and implemented), and the wider crisis of the three kingdoms were contributing factors. The sustained persecution and alienation of native Irish and Old Catholics for their faith, however, was at the root of all the problems that led to the 1641 rebellion.[18] The Catholic elites lost their land and many of their economic and political liberties because of their religious beliefs. Meanwhile, the majority of those from the lower social orders who fought were roused by the elites into an anti-Protestant and anti-English frenzy. What united rebels of all social strata was their shared faith and fatherland.

---

[16] Brian Mac Cuarta, *Catholic revival in the north of Ireland, 1603–41*, Dublin 2007, 90; Nicholas Canny, 'Religion, politics, and the Irish uprising of 1641', in Judith Delvin and Ronan Fanning (eds), *Religion and rebellion: the proceedings of the Twenty Second Irish Conference of Historians*, Dublin 1997, 40–70.

[17] Aidan Clarke, 'Bishop William Bedell, 1571–1642 and the Irish Reformation', in Ciaran Brady (ed.), *Worsted in the game: losers in Irish history*, Dublin 1989, 61–70; Alan Ford, *The Protestant Reformation in Ireland, 1590–1641*, Frankfurt 1987, 66.

[18] For the clearest assessment of how Ireland was at peace see Canny, *Making Ireland British*, 455–60.

The 1641 rebellion and the Wars of the Three Kingdoms

While Irish Catholic nobles felt threatened by religious persecution, English and Scottish nobles witnessed the gradual expansion of the Stuart monarchy's power. King Charles I attempted to impose an Anglican Church on Scotland causing considerable controversy among the Calvinist ecclesiastical hierarchy. The Scots' recourse to arms sparked a series of interconnected and complex wars across England, Ireland and Scotland, now known as the Wars of the Three Kingdoms. This included the 1641 rebellion, the confederate wars (1642–8), the execution of Charles I and the Cromwellian conquest of Ireland.

Numerous accounts of the troubled decades of the mid-seventeenth century have located events in England, Ireland and Scotland in this wider 'British' and Irish framework. There are benefits to this approach. A successful war in Scotland for religious liberties gave hope to Irish Catholics. Irish rebels followed the covenanters' example in taking up arms in defence of their faith and political liberties. Irish Protestant politicians, aware of the wider crisis that Charles faced, had to compete for the king's attention now that the English parliament also wished for greater religious and political autonomy. News sent by the Irish colonial authorities after the outbreak of rebellion on 23 October 1641 exacerbated tensions between king and parliament, particularly in the tumultuous spring and summer of 1642. This led to the outbreak of the English civil wars, which pitted the king against parliament. Without war in Scotland it is unclear whether rebellion would have broken out in Ireland when it did. The title of this book is deliberately provocative. This book draws upon events in Scotland when necessary but Scotland receives little attention, for one simple reason: the colonial administration in Ireland naturally looked to the king and the English parliament for aid. When private letters did not achieve the desired result, they resorted to London printers to canvass English support for their efforts. The Irish confederates also looked to England for help. They pledged loyalty to the king and lobbied for his support by branding Protestant politicians as parliamentarians. So perhaps another title could have been *The Irish rebellion of 1641 and the English civil wars.*

Are there other methodological models that might be appropriate to this discussion of the 1641 rebellion? When looking at this issue from the perspective of English colonists, Ireland fitted into the broader colonial/imperial framework of the Atlantic world. Without doubt, Ireland provided a training ground for English colonists in their conquest of America. Plantations in Leinster and Munster provided a blueprint for later English colonisation in America, particularly in Virginia. Historians have, however, debated whether Ireland fits into this model of American colonisation.[19] Aside from

---

[19] Thomas Benjamin, *The Atlantic world: Europeans, Africans, Indians and their shared*

offering a chance to experiment with plantation, Ireland and its inhabitants provided another opportunity for English people to forge their own
identity at the expense of natives. Were English colonists' attitudes toward
the native Irish similar to their views on Native Americans and Highland
Scottish communities, all of which were deemed barbaric peoples? News
reports from Ireland in the 1640s, subsequently printed in England, lent
further credence to the existence of an international Catholic conspiracy
against English Protestants. Other crises also captured Protestants' imaginations. The St Bartholomew's Day massacre in France on 24 August 1572 and
the Thirty Years' War in Germany (1618–48) were commonly described to
English audiences as manifestations of this popish threat. Readers sought out
works that narrated these massacres as a moral tale.[20] Massacre pamphlets
depicted not only sectarian atrocities in the three kingdoms and Europe,
but also events in the New World such as the Virginia Massacre of 1622
and the indiscriminate murder of Native Americans by Spanish soldiers in
the sixteenth century. Such pamphlets were composed with clear biblical
allusions that assisted the reader in understanding and interpreting the text.
This book will locate reports on the 1641 rebellion in these wider contexts
and will consider English cultural constructions of violence.

That there was a growing appetite for news from distant lands suggests
an awareness of a widening world boundary as a result of exploration and
colonisation, and England's enhanced role in international politics during
the seventeenth century. The printing of massacre pamphlets and news from
foreign lands also reflected the development of an interest in Britain's imperial ambitions.[21] James VI and I, Charles I, Oliver Cromwell and Charles II
all presided over the expansion of Britain's overseas colonies. Each carefully
outlined how their dominions should be ruled, largely in a peaceful manner.
In times of colonial war and rebellion, however, English colonists and rulers
adopted a more belligerent stance toward natives. They took pains to justify
armed conquests. Another goal of this book, therefore, is to examine how

history, 1400–1900, Cambridge 2009, 236–7; Nicholas Canny and Philip Morgan (eds),
The Oxford handbook of the Atlantic world, 1450–1850, Oxford 2011; Nicholas Canny,
Kingdom and colony: Ireland in the Atlantic world, 1560–1800, Baltimore 1988; Andrew
Hadfield, Literature, travel, and colonial writing in the English Renaissance, 1545–1625,
Oxford 2007; Jane Ohlmeyer, 'A laboratory for empire? Early modern Ireland and English
imperialism', in Kevin Kenny (ed.), Ireland and the British Empire, Oxford 2004, 26–60.

20 Raymond Gillespie, Devoted people: belief and religion in early modern Ireland, Manchester
1997; Peter Lake, 'Deeds against nature: cheap print, Protestantism and murder in early
seventeenth century England', in Peter Lake and Kevin Sharpe (eds), Culture and politics
in early Stuart England, London 1994, 257–84; Alexandra Walsham, Providence in early
modern England, Oxford 2001.

21 John Speed, The theatre of the empire of Great Britaine: presenting an exact geography
of the kingdoms of England, Scotland and Ireland, London 1611; Mark Netzloff, England's
internal colonies: class, capital, and the literature of early modern English colonialism, London
2003.

English rulers legitimised the use of excessive force in English colonies. A key element in early modern colonial policy is revenge. English colonisers called for vengeance and re-colonisation when natives rebelled against their overlords. This has important implications for a proper understanding of 1641 and the subsequent Cromwellian invasion in 1649.

To consider the perspective of Ireland's Catholic population, scholars of the native Irish have captured their views on the Stuart monarchy.[22] Bardic poets began to link the kingdom of Ireland to the Stuart dynasty and promoted a shared identity with James VI and I.[23] Studies of the confederation of Kilkenny, the administrative and political wing of the Irish rebels, have illustrated the importance of Europe to the identity of Irish Catholics. The Catholic powers of Europe all received confederate diplomats eager to press the necessity of their cause and the need for a pan-Catholic alliance against the English parliament. Eventually, the confederation itself would become a microcosm of wider Counter-Reformation debates on the nature of Church reforms.[24] Engaging studies of the Irish diaspora in Europe have shown how influential these continental links were in Ireland and as such the 1641 rebellion needs to be understood within wider events in Europe.[25] This book will only scratch the surface of Irish-language material and other materials from Europe in order to offer some consideration of what the Catholics of Ireland said about the causes, course and nature of the Irish rebellion. It is important to point out here that the term 'Catholic' refers both to the native Irish and Old English communities. After the formation of the confederation of Kilkenny both ethnic groups were officially united as one 'Catholic' community. There are moments in this book where it is necessary to refer to each community by their ethnic denomination. Native Irish refers to the indigenous population while Old English refers to descendants of the original invasion of Ireland by Henry II. Over the course of the mid-seventeenth century, however, contemporaries were less inclined to distinguish between their ethnicities and so, for the most part, they were labelled, and called themselves, simply 'Catholic'.

[22] Marc Caball, *Poets and politics: continuity and reaction in Irish poetry, 1558–1625*, Cork 1998; Michelle O'Riordan, *The Gaelic mind and the collapse of the Gaelic world*, Cork 1990.
[23] Bernadette Cunningham, 'Seventeenth-century constructions of the historical kingdom of Ireland', in Stephen Forrest and Mark Williams (eds), *Constructing the past: writing Irish history, 1600–1800*, Woodbridge 2010, 9–26.
[24] Jane Ohlmeyer, 'Ireland independent: confederate foreign policy and international relations during the mid-seventeenth century', in Jane Ohlmeyer (ed.), *Ireland from independence to occupation, 1641–1660*, Cambridge 1995, 89–111; Tadhg Ó hAnnracháin, *Catholic Reformation in Ireland: the mission of Rinuccini, 1645–1649*, Oxford 2002.
[25] O'Connor and Lyons, *The Ulster earls and baroque Europe*; Thomas O'Connor and Mary Ann Lyons (eds), *Strangers to citizens: the Irish in Europe, 1600–1800*, Dublin 2008.

Evaluating the evidence

How did the participants in the 1641 rebellion portray their actions to the wider world? How important were initial interpretations of the rebellion to later historiography? To answer these questions, the following chapters are an investigation of the construction of the historical memory of the 1641 rebellion from 1641 to 1662. During the mid-seventeenth century combatants on either side offered vastly differing perspectives on what happened, and set the parameters for subsequent debate. Before such matters can be addressed, it is first necessary to understand what literary frameworks were in place for English colonists to draw upon in order to describe the native Irish. When the colonial administration chronicled the rebellion, did they draw upon these historical constructs of the native Irish? Historians and literary theorists have investigated the tomes of colonial writings on Ireland and its inhabitants, composed by Giraldus Cambrensis, John Davies, Fynes Moryson, Barnaby Rich and Edmund Spenser among others.[26] Nicholas Canny and David Edwards have shown how these prominent authors shaped English policies in Ireland.[27] But these scholarly works were hardly read by the ordinary planters who arrived in Ireland, looking to create a new life for themselves and their families. The purpose of this book, therefore, is to build upon this work and look at accounts that spoke to a popular audience. Those of the lower social orders who arrived in Ireland from England were more likely to have encountered more accessible texts. Pamphlets and ballads were tailormade for such audiences. They were cheap, could be read aloud to larger groups of people and provided practical advice for settlers on how to survive in Ireland.[28] These sources are just as important as writings composed by the elites for an understanding of how the New English viewed the native Irish in their daily interactions and in revealing English attitudes toward the Irish at local level. As a laboratory for empire, furthermore, are there simi-

[26] Jacqueline Hill, 'Politics and the writing of history: the impact of the 1690s and 1790s on Irish historiography', in D. G. Boyce, R. Eccleshall and V. Geohegan (eds), *Political discourse in seventeenth- and eighteenth-century Ireland*, New York 2001, 222–39; John McGurk, 'The pacification of Ulster, 1600–3', in Edwards, Lenihan and Tait, *Age of atrocity*, 119–29; Ohlmeyer, 'A laboratory for empire', 26–60; Hiram Morgan, 'Giraldus Cambrensis and the Tudor conquest of Ireland', in Hiram Morgan (ed.), *Political ideology in Ireland, 1541–1641*, Dublin 1999, 22–44; Andrew Murphy, *But the Irish sea betwixt us: Ireland, colonialism, and Renaissance literature*, Lexington 1999.

[27] Canny, *Making Ireland British*; David Edwards, 'Ideology and experience: Spenser's *View* and martial law in Ireland', in Morgan, *Political ideology*, 127–57.

[28] Adam Fox, *Oral and literate culture in England, 1500–1700*, Oxford 2000; Rab Houston, *Literacy in early modern Europe: culture and education, 1500–1800*, London 2002; Ethan Shagan, 'Rumours and popular politics in the reign of Henry VIII', in Tim Harris (ed.), *The politics of the excluded*, Basingstoke 2001, 30–66; Margaret Spufford, *Small books and pleasant histories: popular fiction and its readership in seventeenth-century England*, London 1981.

larities between representations of the native Irish and of Native Americans? Historians are in disagreement as to whether the native Irish were portrayed in a similar manner.[29] Chapter 1 will therefore analyse representations of violence in scholarly tomes and 'popular' texts and compare cultural depictions of the native Irish with depictions of the Native Americans. More important, it will investigate how English colonists portrayed massacres in colonial settings and show that they drew upon an established lexicon to describe such events and to frame their proposals for further conquest in these colonies. Finally, it will ask whether ordinary planters viewed their Catholic neighbours with suspicion and *vice-versa*.

As will be shown in chapter 1, inter-community tensions were never far from the surface of Irish life. When rebellion broke out in 1641, the state authorities quickly noted the nature and course of the movement. They established a 'Commission for the Despoiled Subject' (the deposition commission) which recorded 8,000 witness testimonies from Protestant settlers and a small number of Irish Catholics. The commission was mandated to investigate cruelties and robberies committed against the settler community, and were uninterested in attacks on Irish Catholics. Thus, the largest archive on the 1641 rebellion is one-sided. Without a doubt, the 1641 depositions are a very controversial source to use when investigating the outbreak of popular violence in Ireland.[30] As deponents fled their homes, fearing for their lives, they encountered other settlers fleeing the violence and shared stories of their woe. Some were subjected to further tortures *en route* to Dublin. Due to the trauma of what they experienced – being attacked and forced out of their homes – and the spread of horror stories amongst the settler community, it is fair to say that they were in no fit state to provide an accurate and unbiased account. Deponents may have exaggerated the extent of the cruelties that they faced or experienced due to trauma, or because they wished to demonise/implicate a neighbour whom they disliked. The depositions, therefore, are fraught with contradictions and infused with inconsistencies. What they accurately capture, however, are the fears of the settler population. It is for this reason that they are so valuable. Hearsay may be inadmissible as evidence for the atrocities of 1641, but when investigating such testimonies historians can capture cultural constructs of

[29] Murphy, *But the Irish sea*, 4–5; Bernard Sheehan, *Savagism and civility: Indians and Englishmen in colonial Virginia*, Cambridge 1980.

[30] For detailed methodological surveys of the depositions see Nicholas Canny, 'The 1641 depositons as a source for the writing of social history: County Cork as a case study', in P. O'Flanaghan and C. Buttimer (eds), *Cork history and society: interdisciplinary approaches to the history of an Irish county*, Cork 1993, 249–308; Aidan Clarke, 'The 1641 depositions', in Peter Fox (ed.), *Treasures of the Library, Trinity College Dublin*, Dublin 1986, 111–22, and 'The Commission for the Despoiled Subject, 1641–7', in Brian Mac Cuarta (ed.) *Reshaping Ireland, 1550–1700: colonization and its consequences*, Dublin 2011, 241–60; Canny, *Making Ireland British*, 461–9; Walter Love, 'Civil war in Ireland: appearances in three centuries of historical writing', *Emory University Quarterly* xxii (1966), 57–72.

violence and what people believed had occurred, or expected to occur, in times of war and conflict. Nicholas Canny and Micheal Perceval-Maxwell have provided detailed overviews of the outbreak of violence in the 1641 rebellion.[31] The remit of their works did not include an investigation of the forms of violence that were adopted by the rebels, nor did they consider the value of hearsay testimonies for understanding settler fears after the outbreak of rebellion. Chapter 2, therefore, will examine the outbreak of the rebellion and the patterns of popular violence in order to illustrate why such butchery occurred and to consider its effect on the wider population.

The deposition commission liaised closely with the colonial authorities throughout the 1640s. It gathered intelligence on the rebel movement and subsequently sent edited copies of the original testimonies to leading political figures across the three kingdoms, while also compiling detailed reports on the rebellion which were then printed in London. The manipulation of the depositions provides today's historian with a fascinating glimpse of how state authorities perceived the rebellion and deliberately portrayed its course to the wider public. This marked the advent of print as the primary tool in Irish statecraft. Raymond Gillespie and Colm Lennon have examined the fledgling stages of Irish print culture during the early modern period and have shown how the English administration in Ireland adopted print to communicate with the population and to strengthen its own authority.[32] Research by Robert Armstrong and Micheál Ó Siochrú has deftly captured the political machinations of the confederation of Kilkenny and the colonial administration in Ireland.[33] This book will build upon their work, looking at the confederates' printed output and that of the colonial order in Ireland and locate it in the context of the wider crisis in the three kingdoms. In an English context Jason Peacey has demonstrated the intricate relationship between politicians, printers and booksellers in the 1640s, and quite rightly has argued that historians need to pay greater attention to the use of the polemic and its centrality to the Wars of the Three Kingdoms. He has shown, for example, how political groups patronised and endorsed writers

---

[31] Canny, *Making Ireland British*, 461–550, and 'What really happened in Ireland in 1641?', in Ohlmeyer, *Ireland from independence to occupation*, 24–42; Perceval-Maxwell, *The outbreak of the Irish rebellion*, 213–39.

[32] Raymond Gillespie, 'The circulation of print in seventeenth-century Ireland', *Studia Hibernica* xxix (1995–7), 31–58; *Reading Ireland: print, reading and social change in early modern Ireland*, Manchester 2005, and 'Print culture, 1550–1700', in Raymond Gillespie and Andrew Hadfield (eds), *The Oxford history of the Irish book: the Irish book in English, 1550–1800*, Oxford 2006, iii. 17–33; Colm Lennon, 'The print trade, 1550–1700', in Gillespie and Hadfield, *The Oxford history of the Irish book*, iii. 61–73.

[33] Robert Armstrong, *Protestant war: the 'British' of Ireland and the Wars of the Three Kingdoms*, Manchester 2005; Micheál Ó Siochrú, *Confederate Ireland, 1642–1649: a constitutional and political analysis*, Dublin 1999.

and printers to compose favourable accounts to garner public support.[34] Furthermore, Peacey argued that news from Ireland was stage managed by English politicians to stoke popular fears of Catholicism.[35] The purpose of chapter 3, therefore, is to show how Irish politicians manipulated the news and intelligence that they sent to England and the effect of this on the outbreak and course of the English front in the Wars of the Three Kingdoms. Chapter 3 does not focus on the accuracy or otherwise of what the colonial authorities said about the rebellion. Rather it will forensically investigate the transfer of the depositions from manuscript into print.

Chapters 1 and 3 will argue that portrayals of atrocities in the New World mirrored those of massacres in the 1641 rebellion. Pamphlet news printed in London, therefore, is vital to our understanding of how a conflict could be portrayed to the wider world. They reveal contemporary values, how people expected combatants to behave and the ways in which wars could be portrayed as exceptionally brutal. Ethan Shagan has argued that literary constructs from John Foxe's *Book of Martyrs* shaped the portrayal of the Irish rebellion among English printers.[36] Certainly, news of the rebellion was modified to suit the tastes of the English public in London, but there were other factors at play. Throughout the early modern period European military leaders attempted to enforce new rules of war. It became increasingly unacceptable for armies to target civilians, particularly women and children. Such social values infused printed literature that described conflicts across the early modern world as well as the literary constructs outlined by Shagan. The 1641 rebellion took place at a time when war was rife throughout Europe. In the 1620s and 1630s stories of atrocities that occurred during the Thirty Years' War in Germany spread through the English countryside due to the publication of news from the battlefront. Both conflicts were seen as exceptionally violent. Some historians have suggested that there were similarities in representation of the 1641 rebellion and the Thirty Years' War.[37] Indeed, printed literature on the 1641 rebellion has led others to view the battlefield in Ireland as apparently exempt from these emerging codes of conduct.[38] One of the goals of this book is to situate the Irish rebellion in a wider Atlantic world context, where codes of conduct were also impor-

[34] Jason Peacey, *Politicians and pamphleteers: propaganda during the English civil wars and interregnum*, Aldershot 2004, 1–30.

[35] Ibid. 240–1.

[36] Ethan Shagan, 'Constructing discord: ideology, propaganda, and English response to the Irish rebellion of 1641', *JBS* xxxvi (1997), 4–34.

[37] Joseph Cope, *England and the 1641 rebellion*, Woodbridge 2009, 89–103; Barbara Donagan, 'Codes and conduct in the English civil war', *P&P* cxviii (Feb. 1988), 65–96.

[38] Donagan, 'Codes and conduct', 65–96; Micheál Ó Siochrú, 'Atrocity, codes of conduct and the Irish in the British civil wars, 1641–1653', *P&P* clxxxxv (May 2007), 55–86; Geoffrey Parker, 'The etiquette of atrocity: the laws of war in early modern Europe', in Geoffrey Parker (ed.), *Empire, war and faith in early modern Europe*, London 2002, 143–68.

tant, particularly in the light of Spanish excesses there. Thus the purpose of chapter 4 is to understand how English and Irish propagandists portrayed the 1641 rebellion in print. Did they draw upon existing cultural frameworks of violence, atrocity and war? It will argue that contemporary values invested in military conduct were more influential in shaping the portrayal of the rebellion.

Chapters 3 and 4 will illustrate why and how the colonial authorities and English pamphleteers portrayed Ireland as an arena of anarchy after 1641. They maintained this stance when the rebellion and confederate wars had been successfully crushed by the Cromwellian conquest of Ireland. As the fledging commonwealth regime took stock of its newly-conquered territory, those involved in the deposition commission and the Protestant war effort campaigned for strict laws against participants in the rebellion. They claimed that a premeditated massacre of Protestant settlers had occurred, organised by prominent members of the Catholic nobility. These allegations were addressed by the confederation of Kilkenny during the 1640s and by prominent Irish Catholics in the 1660s, but this version of events was drowned out by the multitude of pamphlets that described the 'massacres' of 1641. While work by Toby Barnard, John Gibney, Micheal Perceval-Maxwell and Deana Rankin have looked at later 'memories' of the 1641 rebellion, their works do not provide a detailed analysis of debates that occurred about the nature of the 1641 rebellion during the early years of the Restoration.[39] Chapter 5 will therefore draw extensively upon accounts written by combatants in the Wars of the Three Kingdoms and show how they defended their cause. There will be little discussion of later historical memories of 1641, for the 'memory' of 1641 in the 1650s and 1660s closely followed party lines established in the 1640s. Rather, the purpose of chapter 5 is to illustrate how the parameters of debate (and the sides taken) have changed little in subsequent historiography.

The eminent nineteenth-century historian William Lecky argued that 'the Irish massacre of 1641 seems to me one of the great fictions of history'; however, the narrative itself is central to any study of Ireland since the seventeenth century.[40] Lecky's choice of the word 'fiction' is telling, for it reveals his views on the record that has survived about the 1641 rebellion. Later historians would talk about how narratives of the 1641 rebellion grossly exaggerated the scale of violence and accused the colonial administration

---

[39] Toby Barnard, "'Parlour entertainment in an evening?': histories of the 1640s', in Micheál Ó Siochrú (ed.), *Kingdoms in crisis: Ireland in the 1640s: essays in honour of Donal Cregan*, Dublin 2001, 20–43; John Gibney, *Ireland and the Popish Plot*, Basingstoke 2009, 99–114; Michael Perceval-Maxwell, 'Sir Robert Southwell and the duke of Ormond's reflections on the 1640s', in Ó Siochrú, *Kingdoms in crisis*, 229–47; Deana Rankin, *Between Spenser and Swift: English writing in seventeenth-century Ireland*, Cambridge 2005.

[40] Quoted in John Ranelagh, *A short history of Ireland*, Dublin 1999, 62.

of deliberately misrepresenting the nature of the conflict. These imagined events became an integral part of subsequent identities. For example, in 1800, during parliamentary debates on the Act of Union, which brought an end to Irish legislative independence, Patrick Duigenan, a vocal supporter of the Union pointed to the rebellions of 1641 and 1798 as examples of 'the unappeasable enmity of the Irish Romish clergy to their Protestant countrymen'.[41] In 1817 John Graham, an ecclesiastical historian, hailed the Protestant version of events as 'indisputable' while denouncing Catholic accounts as either 'cursory' or 'uninteresting'.[42] Catholic and nationalist authors criticised their Protestant counterparts for appropriating historical events for political ends. In 1896 Charles Gavan Duffy, a well-known newspaper editor and advocate of Irish independence, argued that 1641, like all of Irish history, had been misconstrued: 'Ireland and Irishmen suffer wrong from systematic misrepresentation.'[43] Thus, any history of 1641 must consider not just the facts but also the fabrications that coloured Ireland's subsequent political, cultural and social experience. As Lecky eloquently put it, 'a faithful historian is very largely concerned with the fictions as well as with the facts of the past ... the facts of history have been largely governed by its fictions'.[44] This book, therefore, is just as concerned with the imagined events of the 1640s as with the real and offers a study of the beginning, the narration and the effect of the story of the 1641 rebellion.

[41] Patrick Duigenan, *The nature and extent of the demands of the Irish Roman Catholics fully explained*, London 1810, 209.

[42] John Graham, *Annals of Ireland, ecclesiastical, civil and military*, London 1817, 5–6.

[43] Charles Gavan Duffy, 'Books for the Irish people', in *The revival of Irish literature*, London 1896, 38.

[44] William Lecky, *Historical and political essays*, London 1908, 20.

1

Representing Violence and Empire: Ireland and the Wider World

Barnaby Rich, an Essex-born soldier and amateur poet, wrote extensively of his life on the Munster plantations and of his military encounters with Irish natives. Like many other English settlers, Rich wondered why the conquest of Ireland had failed after four hundred years. He blamed Catholic priests who educated Irish natives 'in the disciplines of the Popes Church'. Now the indigenous population vowed 'obedience and subiection to his holinesse'. Consequently, native Irish congregations were trained 'to hate ... and despise their Prince'.[1] Across the Atlantic Ocean a colonial contemporary of Rich based in Virginia, Robert Gray, recorded his views on the newly colonised Native Americans. They were profane heathens – 'they worship the diuell', had no manners – 'differ[ing] very little from beasts' – and lacked a culture, 'hauing no art'. There was one glimmer of hope, however, in that the Native Americans were 'by nature louing and, gentle, and desirous to imbrace a better condition'.[2] The comments of Rich and Gray indicated their sense of superiority over what they termed 'barbarous' peoples and reflected intellectual values invested in the term 'civility' – a byword for English social, cultural and political supremacy.

Both commentators believed that Irish and American natives under the English crown could be civilised. Rich argued that Irishmen blindly imitated those imbued with a corrosive hatred of English and Protestant rule, while Gray's gut feeling was that 'it is not the nature of men, but the education of men, which make them barbarous and vnciuill'. The solution, according to Gray, was simple: 'Chaunge the education of men, and you shall see that their nature will be greatly rectified and corrected.'[3] Education, however, was only one aspect of English perceptions of civility.[4] In early modern English eyes civility was built on a foundation of law, the administration of justice and the provision of education and religion. All foreign peoples, not just

---

[1] Barnaby Rich, A souldiers vvishe to Britons welfare: or A discourse, fit to be read of all gentlemen and souldiers, London 1604, 39.

[2] Robert Gray, A good speed to Virginia, London 1609, [16].

[3] Ibid. [15].

[4] For an investigation of the evolution of ideas of civility across medieval and early modern Europe see John Gillingham, 'From civilitas to civility: codes of manners in medieval and early-modern England', Transactions of the Royal Historical Society 6th ser. xii (2002), 267–89.

Native American and Irish societies, were measured against these standards. If a country consisted of an educated and a pious Christian population, this was indicative of a polity that administered law and order fairly and catered for the spiritual welfare of its inhabitants. Both went hand in hand. Uncivilised societies were therefore portrayed as akin to the animal kingdom, lacking the central tenets of civility. The people were duplicitous (having no knowledge of manners or social decorum), violent (as laws were not executed properly), heathen (having no religion) and under the thumb of tyrants who exercised their power arbitrarily. As increasing numbers of English and Scottish people began to explore the world it was this framework of civility that shaped their perceptions of newly-encountered communities and fashioned their own communal identity and their sense of place in the wider world.

A key historiographical problem in dealing with the representation of the Irish rebellion of 1641 is that historians have not located the rebellion in the context of the Atlantic world and reportage of the Nine Years' War (1594–1603). First, in respect of the Atlantic world, similarities exist between representations of atrocities and rebellions under English imperial control in America. While historians have debated whether Ireland was a kingdom or colony (which is beyond the remit of this book), there is evidence to suggest that certain cultural protocols influenced how colonial rebellions were presented by printers and pamphleteers and understood by the wider public.[5] Such accounts provide a valuable insight into contemporary attitudes toward state-sponsored violence.[6] Secondly, did pamphlet reports on the Irish rebellion of 1641 echo descriptions of the Nine Years' War? A consideration of both these issues will reveal that the portrayal of 1641 rebellion relied on both traditional Anglo-Irish prisms, but also on a growing awareness among Englishmen of their burgeoning empire in the Atlantic world.

Expanding the empire: English perceptions of colonial conquest

In the first half of the seventeenth-century Stuart monarchs portrayed their rule as benign and explained in great detail how their policies were benefi-

---

[5] For an introduction to the wider debate on whether Ireland was a kingdom or colony see Canny, *Kingdom and colony*, and Jane Ohlmeyer (ed.), *Political thought in seventeenth-century Ireland: kingdom or colony?*, Cambridge 2000.

[6] Bruce P. Lenman, *England's colonial wars, 1550–1688: conflicts, empire and national identity*, London 2001, 23–71, 168–72; Jane Ohlmeyer, '"Civilisinge of those rude partes": colonization within Britain and Ireland, 1580s–1640s', in Nicholas Canny (ed.), *The origins of empire: British overseas enterprise to the close of the seventeenth century*, Oxford 1998, 124–47; Sheehan, *Savagism and civility*.

cial to all of their subjects as a means to negotiate their authority.[7] James VI
and I in particular was keen to promote his government as just and to praise
English people as the apex of 'civility'. In stark contrast to his English
subjects, Scottish Highlanders in the north and Irish Catholics to the west
lived in barbaric obscurity and were descended from the most violent and
barbarous peoples known to man: the Scythians. In order to examine how
the 1641 rebellion came to be understood by English printers, the monarchy
and the houses of parliament it is necessary first to investigate representations of violence, and violent people, and to consider how such tropes were
adopted in contemporary commentaries on colonial America, Ireland and
Scotland.

Scythians provided the literary guidebook for English commentators to
describe uncivil people. The regions in which they lived were unsafe for
travel and commentators were quick to stress their undesirable characteristics, such as their: 'food, apparell and armour, ... their vnmercifull lawes,
their fond superstitions, their bestiall liues, their vicious ma[n]ners, their
slauish subiection to their owne superiours, and their disdainfull and brutish
inhumanitie vnto strangers'.[8] Literary representations of Scottish Highlanders and native Irish people were constructed within these parameters of
barbarity. '*Highland-men* (the naturall *Scot* indeed) are supposed to descend
from the *Scythians*, who with the *Getes* infesting *Ireland*, left both their Issue
there, and their manners, apparant in the *Wild-Irish* euen to this day.'[9] In
contrast, Samuel Purchas, who compiled geographical descriptions of foreign
territories, claimed that England did not 'degenerate from nature'.[10] Nature,
in this sense, referred to civilised society as opposed to the animal and plant
kingdom as it would be understood in the modern era. By referring to the
growth of the English state as natural (in the early modern meaning of the
word) it portrayed the non-civilised as unnatural. For example, John Barclay
described how Native Americans 'forsaked nature' and were 'incapable of

[7] Michael Braddick and John Walter, 'Introduction: grids of power: order, hierarchy
and subordination in early modern society', in Michael Braddick and John Walter (eds),
*Negotiating power in early modern society: order, hierarchy, and subordination in Britain and
Ireland*, Cambridge 2001, 1–42; John Walter, *Understanding popular violence in the English
revolution*, Cambridge 1999, 4–5, and *Crowds and popular politics in early modern England*,
Manchester 2006, 9–10.

[8] Richard Hakluyt, *The principal nauigations, voyages, traffiques and discoueries of the
English nation*, London 1599–1600, i, 'To ... Lord Charles Howard'. Lord Inchiquin
described Ireland as a place 'unsafe to travel' due to the violence of the natives: Richard
Cox, *Hibernia anglicana, or, The history of Ireland, from the conquest thereof by the English*,
London 1689, appendix XVI, 67.

[9] John Speed, *A prospect of the most famous parts of the vvorld*, London 1646, 131.

[10] Samuel Purchas, *Purchas his pilgrimes in fiue bookes*, London 1625, 'To the reader', no
pagination.

our civility', prior to the first plantation of English settlers in America.[11] The behaviour of the natives, however, depended upon those who exercised authority over them.

In contemporary English political discourse, the English state exemplified a fair political system that administered justice in a fair manner over a civil and religious populace. Violent punishments inflicted by those in positions of power in other countries, by contrast, seemed akin to uncivil and animalistic behaviour. Purchas related how oppressed Native Americans under Spanish dominion 'seeme to haue learned the sauage nature of the wilde Beasts' and as a result 'doe great hurt, and will not, by either cunning or force of the Spaniards, be reduced to any other course'.[12] In an Irish context, rather than blame the excessive use of force by the Tudors, commentators stressed how Gaelic Irish chieftains and nobles (or Catholic clergymen) ruled by force and concluded that the natives became violent through living under such repressive conditions. Contemporaries placed a moral, social and political obligation on the ruling classes to provide a space where 'civilitie' could take root and flourish. To achieve this, authorities had to maintain a 'just' legal system and needed to educate the natives in the Protestant faith. They believed that this would sustain peaceful societies. The rhetoric of civility, therefore, also informed political theories on the role of the monarch and the state.

In an intimate and revealing tract entitled *Basilikon doron*, James VI and I elucidated the correct forms of government for his eldest son, Henry, to follow. James warned Henry that should he become king he might have to secure his domain by using 'severe justice' in the beginning of his reign to establish his authority. Once his position of authority was firmly secured, the repressive use of power was best avoided. The king advocated the restrained and balanced execution of law: 'All the dayes of your life mixe justice with mercie, punishing or sparing.' Indeed, James later hoped to unify England and Scotland by encouraging consensus. Should a king act 'tyrannically', using draconian punishments, 'the number of them to be punished would exceede the innocent'. As the weak in society were oppressed by those more fortunate, James asked his son to 'embrace the quarrel of the poore and distressed' and argued that 'it is your greatest honour to represse the oppressors'. The king's rhetoric on the need for the moderate exercise of state violence, however insincere, illustrates how prevalent contemporary notions of violence and civility permeated political discourse within Stuart Britain and Ireland.[13]

---

[11] John Barclay, *The mirrour of mindes, or, Barclay's Icon animorum, Englished by T. M.*, London 1631, 63.

[12] Samuel Purchas, *Purchas his pilgrimage*, London 1613, 660.

[13] James VI, *Basilikon doron*, London 1682, 24–6; J. G. A. Pocock, 'Two kingdoms and three histories? Political thought in British contexts', in Roger Mason (ed.), *Scots and*

A civilised society consisted of non-violent, pious members, governed by a just monarch.[14] The developing rhetoric of restraint prompted many in the early Stuart era to believe that they lived in relative peace and civility in comparison to earlier times.[15] The desire to export 'civility' allegedly underpinned early colonial ventures and, in light of the highly charged confessional context of early modern Europe and the continuing expansion of European influence in America, it became clear that colonial powers viewed their mission (or at least portrayed their mission) as one of divine necessity. When speaking of the Native Americans a short grammar book explained this concept clearly: 'God hauing ordained schooles of learning to be a principall meanes to reduce a barbarous people to ciuilitie, and thereby to prepare them the better to receiue the glorious Gospel of Iesus Christ.'[16] A key responsibility of English colonists, therefore, was the conversion of heathen populations.

English commentators poured scorn on their Spanish imperial rivals for failing to achieve this objective in their colonisation of the Americas.[17] Thomas Gainsford, a veteran of the Dutch revolts (1565–1609), criticised the Spanish for their arbitrary use of violence against the Native Americans. He claimed that Spanish soldiers were like 'prying and raging wolues ouer silly sheepe, either with a couetous minde of intrusion, or tyrannous desire of deuouring'.[18] Such behaviour prompted extremely violent reactions from the natives: 'The cruelties of the Spaniards were such, as the Indians, when they got any of them, would binde their hands and feete, and laying them on their backes, would poure gold into their mouthes, saying in insultation, Eate gold, Christian.'[19] One author even suggested (rather optimistically) that Spanish cruelties in the Americas persuaded Irish natives to abandon their long-held connections with Spain: 'I doubt not they ye Irish are so foolish to entertain such proud guestes knowing their tyrannie, & hauing not so well desereued [deserved] at their hands as those simple soules whom they

---

Britons: Scottish political thought and the union of 1603, Cambridge 1994, 293–312 at pp. 303–4; Johann Sommerville, *King James VI and I: political writings*, Cambridge 1994, pp. xvi–xix.

[14] William Camden, *Annales the true and royall history of the famous empresse Elizabeth queene of England France and Ireland*, London 1625, bk I, 92; *The statutes at large, passed in the parliaments held in Ireland: from the third year of Edward the Second, A. D. 1310, to the first year of George the Third, A.D. 1761 inclusive*, Dublin 1765, i. 329–38.

[15] Henry Barrow, *Mr Henry Barrowes platform*, London 1611, EEBO image number 54; John Gordon, *Enotikon or A sermon of the vnion of Great Brittanie*, London 1604, 48.

[16] John Brinsley, *A consolation for our grammar schooles*, London 1622, no pagination.

[17] J. H. Elliott, *Empires of the Atlantic world: Britain and Spain in America, 1492–1830*, New Haven 2007, 3–28, 117–52.

[18] Thomas Gainsford, *The glory of England*, London 1618, 222–3.

[19] Purchas, *Purchas his pilgrimage*, 688–9.

so cruelly murdered.'[20] The restrained exercise of state violence, therefore, was a key responsibility of colonists, at least in contemporary accounts that justified English colonial enterprises.

News of the murders of the Native Americans by Spanish soldiers spread throughout Europe through translations of a text first written by Bartholomé de las Casas, the bishop of Chipas in Mexico. De las Casas described the range of barbaric acts that they committed in a tract entitled 'A short account of the destruction of the Indians'. It became a bestseller across Europe for it provided a testimony on the extent of Spanish and Catholic barbarity and cruelty, written by someone from within their ranks. The English translation of de las Casas's tract, first published as *The Spanish colonie* in 1583, drew parallels with the Turkish attacks on early Christians and compared the Spanish to Pontius Pilate.[21] Condemnations of Spanish tyranny in the Americas prompted other authors to frame their own theories on empire and to discuss the legitimate use of violence. Commentators pointed to the excessive use of force by Spanish soldiers as an example of how not to build an empire. Robert Gray assured his audience that 'farre be it from the nature of the English, to exercise any bloudie crueltie amongst these people'. Gray even framed the colonial mission as a chance to do good in the eyes of God: 'Oh how happy were that man which could reduce this people from brutishnes, to ciuilitie, to religion, to Christianitie, to the sauing of their soules.'[22]

How did Stuart monarchs attempt to expand English influence and export civility? Did they justify this desire as a godly mission? James VI and I had considerable experience of trying to facilitate the growth of civility in his own kingdoms – most notably in the Scottish Highlands, which proved one of the more problematic regions. In *Basilikon doron*, James claimed that two types of people lived there, 'the one, that dwelleth in our maine land, that are barbarous for the most part, and yet mixed with some shewe of civility'. The other, who lived in the islands off Scotland, 'are all uterlie barbares, without any sort or shew of civilitie'. In order to civilise the Highlanders, James opted to 'plant colonies among them' so 'that within short time may reforme and civilize the best inclined among them'. For those that did not conform, James planned to 'root out or transport the barbarous and the

---

[20] Robert Payne, *A briefe description of Ireland: made in this yeare, 1589 by Robert Payne, vnto xxv of his partners for whome he is vndertaker there: truly published verbatim, according to his letters, by Nich Gorsan one of the sayd partners, for that he would his countreymen should be partakers of the many good notes therein contained*, London 1589, 7.

[21] Bartholomé de las Casas, *The Spanish colonie, or Briefe chronicle of the acts and gestes of the Spaniardes in the West Indies, called the newe world, for the space of xl. yeeres: written in the Castilian tongue by the reuerend Bishop Bartholomew de las Cases or Casaus, a friar of the order of S. Dominicke: and nowe first translated into English*, by M. M. S, London 1583, 'To the reader'; Anthony Pagden, 'Introduction', in Nigel Griffin (ed.), *Bartolomé de las Casas: a short account of the destruction of the Indies*, London 2004, pp. xiii–xlii, xliv.

[22] Gray, *Good speed to Virginia*, no pagination.

stubborne sort, and plant civilitie'.[23] To do this, ministers would preach the Gospel there, as well as build schools to educate the people in the ways of the established Church. Alongside the provision of education, James hoped to eradicate barbarous communities in Scotland through the correct execution of justice. Restraint was the key, for it was necessary to honour those 'that are obedient to the law'.[24] Violence, therefore, was only to be used as a last resort. He advised his son Henry that if he decided to attack the Scottish Highlanders, he should 'be slow in making war' and to make sure that 'the justnesse of your cause be your greatest strength'.[25] In their public rhetoric the Stuart monarchy vowed only to use violence when provoked. None the less, nobles in England and Ireland complained about their excessive imposition of martial law.[26]

The main aim of early modern 'British' imperial expansion, aside from obvious financial gain, was commonly expressed in the desire for the propagation of Scriptures and the Christian fertilisation of pagan minds in foreign territories. In 1609 Robert Gray outlined the godly destiny of the first Virginian planters: 'God hath made you instruments for the inlarging of his Church militant here vpon earth.' The reward for the colonists' efforts was expressed in suitably religious terms: 'When the period of your life shall be finished, the same God [will] make you members of his Church triumphant in Heauen.'[27] Commentators were keen to highlight planters' success in converting the natives. Three years later, William Strachey praised the first Virginian colonists for allowing God's truth 'in [the] blackest [of] nations [to] shine'.[28] To maintain this effort Virginian colonists constantly expressed the need for ministers to 'perpetuate the Plantation'. Fifty men were therefore employed by 1620 to 'beare vp the charge of bringing vp Thirty of the *Infidels* children in true Religion and ciuility'.[29] The spread of English law and the Protestant faith underpinned the successful colonisation of any polity by English adventurers. The English and Scottish architects of the British empire believed that the planting of colonies was the most effective way to export civility.[30] The close relationship between colonisation and confes-

---

23 James VI, *Basilikon doron*, 26–7.

24 Ibid. 33–6.

25 Ibid. 42–5.

26 Edwards, 'The escalation of violence', 34–78, and 'The plight of the earls', 53–76; Austin Woolrych, *Britain in revolution*, Oxford 2004, 57–9.

27 Gray, *Good speed to Virginia*, sig A3v.

28 William Strachey, *For the colony in Virginea Britannia*, London 1612, 'To the right honorable, the lords of the councell of Virginea'.

29 Edward Waterhouse, *A declaration of the state of the colony and affaires of Virginia*, London 1620, 3, 7.

30 Peter Heylyn, *Mikrokosmos: a little description of the great world: augmented and reuised*, Oxford 1625, 503.

sionalisation shaped depictions of violence in the Atlantic world, which in turn aimed to shape readers' responses.

Early Stuart political discourse emphasised the necessity of fair and restrained use of state-sponsored violence both at home and abroad. Barbarous peoples to the north and west of England jeopardised the colonial project. The rhetoric of civility allowed English adventurers to condemn the actions of the Spanish as indicative of tyrannical and uncivil government. As a result of excessive use of force by the Spanish, Native Americans acted in a violent manner. In a similar way so too did the native Irish, although this was the fault of their local (non-English) leaders. English colonists were quick to exonerate themselves whenever natives broke out in rebellion by stressing that they ruled in a just and fair manner. Such attacks were met with calls for retaliation, usually supported with reference to the necessity of conversion to Protestantism. The rhetoric of civility, therefore, provided a cloak through which English colonists could portray their actions and subsequently justify responses to colonial rebellions and violence. What follows is a discussion of these themes in a sample study of the Jamestown massacre in Virginia in 1622.

The Jamestown massacre of 1622

Despite the rhetoric of restraint and promises of proselytisation and anglicisation, the reality of life on the colonial frontier required a form of pragmatism and delicate diplomacy that eluded the first English settlers in North America. Tensions simmered under the surface throughout the first two decades of the 1600s, largely as a result of the inability of early colonists to comprehend the social and cultural norms of Native American society.[31] On 22 March 1622 the natives seized the opportunity to express their dissatisfaction with their new neighbours through a co-ordinated assault on Jamestown, a settlement in Virginia. Perceptions of the Native Americans changed dramatically after they massacred 347 colonists, roughly 25 per cent of the settler population. In response, colonists encouraged the use of excessive force and legitimised their stance by evoking the memory of their comrades lost in the attack. As a direct result of the massacre, later English writers focused on treachery as a salient characteristic of the Native American.[32] The reasons for the attack are beyond the scope of this book; rather it is important to examine how English colonists portrayed a massacre in a colonial setting to English audi-

---

[31] Lenman, *England's colonial wars*, 220–33; Karen Ordahl Kupperman, *Settling with the Indians: the meeting of English and Indian cultures in America, 1580–1640*, London 1980, 140, 169–88; Sheehan, *Savagism and civility*, 55–6.

[32] Karen Ordahl Kupperman, 'English perceptions of treachery, 1583–1640: the case of the American "savages"', *HJ* xx (1977), 263–87; Kupperman, *Settling with the Indians*, 120–1; Sheehan, *Savagism and civility*, 37–64.

ences. This helps to establish how colonists drew upon cultural constructions of violence to describe atrocities in colonial contexts and explains why the 1641 rebellion was portrayed in the way it was.

Edward Waterhouse, an English planter in North America and nephew of Sir Edward Waterhouse, a colonial administrator in Ireland during the 1580s, composed an account of the massacre at Jamestown later printed as the *Declaration of the state of the colony and affaires in Virginia* (1622). While Waterhouse cannot be trusted as a reliable source for the events of 1622, his description of the 'barbarous savageness' and 'incivility' of the Native Americans in their actions against the English colonisers reveals the literary mechanisms adopted to mobilise readers in England to support the civilising mission. To portray the Native Americans as devious assailants, he claimed that they attended breakfast in the houses of their victims before the attack.[33] Then they 'basely and barbarously murthered, not sparing eyther age or sexe, man woman or childe; so sodaine in their cruell execution, that few or none discerned the weapon or blow that brought them to destruction'.[34] Colonists were slaughtered as they conducted their 'seuerall workes and husbandries on the fields, and without their houses, some in planting Corne and Tobacco, some in gardening, some in making Bricke, building, sawing, and other kindes of husbandry'.[35] After the massacre corpses suffered 'barbarous despights and foule scornes' which Waterhouse assured 'are vnbeffiting to be heard by any ciuill eare'.[36] Such evocative language, designed to shock readers, shared many characteristics with accounts of atrocities committed across early modern Europe.

The *Declaration* was a manifesto for revenge and conquest: 'This Massacre must rather be beneficiall to the Plantation then impaire it.'[37] The loss of 347 soules was not in vain: as they died in the name of a godly cause they became 'glorious martyrs' in the eyes of contemporaries at home in England. Now the English 'may now by right of Warre, and law of Nations, inuade the Country, and destroy them who sought to destroy us'; thus the protocols of civil English and colonial government were invoked.[38] The author's emotional account of the massacre was a clear attempt to arouse sympathy among English readers for their brethren in the colonies. Waterhouse was careful to remind his readers that the colonists' values and way of life were those of true, Christian Englishmen.[39] While colonists had earlier tolerated the natives' incivility, now Waterhouse demanded their complete subjuga-

---

33 Waterhouse, *A declaration of the state of the colony*, 11–14.
34 Ibid. 14.
35 Ibid.
36 Ibid. 15.
37 Ibid. 33.
38 Ibid. 23.
39 Ibid. 15–17.

tion. A total conquest would prove 'much more easie then of ciuilising them by faire meanes, for they are a rude and barbarous, and naked people', in short, 'hinderances to Ciuilitie'.[40] Through focusing on the martyrdom of his fallen commrades and praising the native convert who warned settlers of the attack ('such was the good food of an Infidell conuerted to Christianity') Waterhouse subtly reminded his readers of the necessity of spreading God's word to this heathen population.[41]

English colonies, in order to continue converting and civilising Native Americans, needed a regular supply of English labourers to work the land. Waterhouse hoped to stimulate interest in investment in the colony through the publication of the *Declaration*. A list of the murdered colonists was included to encourage their heirs to emigrate and continue the work of their kinsmen. Waterhouse's own description of the land, and the annexed treatise by Fretum Hudson describing the Virginian countryside in great detail, emphasised the profitablity of American lands. Potential investors were therefore continually reminded of the prospects for improving their financial lot. Signficantly, the pamphlet included a comprehensive list of tools, provisions and other household goods necessary for new settlers to sustain themselves.[42] Waterhouse's publication, therefore, stood as both a mandate for, and means to, securing the colony. The inventory of suitable items to carry over to America was fleshed out with details of the bountiful Virginian soil, 'capable of the richest commodities of most parts of the earth'.[43] From farmyard animals and game, to natural resources such as wood, flax and hemp, and food like fruit, berries and corn, Virginia 'paralleth the most opulent and rich Kingdomes of the world' as proven by her booming economy.[44] Waterhouse subtly emphasised the profitable nature of the colony, and the practicalities of investing in it. Profit, however, was not the sole motivation behind these calls for revenge, which suggests that a range of strategies were employed to mobilise people to support the colonial project in Virginia. Profit and proselytization were the twin arms of the colonial mission: while harnessing American land for financial gain provided a motive, civilising and converting Native Americans furnished Englishmen with the rationale for subjugating a people and its territories.[45]

Despite his best efforts Waterhouse's *Declaration* did not achieve the required levels of investment in the Virginia colony. Years later, John Smith, a colonial governor, would blame the lack of 'good order and government'

[40] Ibid. 24.
[41] Ibid. 20.
[42] Ibid. front matter.
[43] Ibid. 3.
[44] Ibid. 4–5, 7.
[45] Ibid. 11.

for the failure of the Virginian colony.[46] Fears that 'Christians' were being targeted were assuaged by his belief that the Native Americans 'did not kill the English because they were Christians, but for their weapons and commodities'.[47] Prior to the Virginian massacre English colonists rarely described Native Americans as monstrous, only those with whom they had little contact.[48] Afterward, however, colonists rarely referred to the natives in a favourable light. Smith's subsequent report on the Virginia colony highlighted the colonists' military superiority and recorded his encounters with the 'savages': 'I had but 18 to subdue them all.' As contacts between natives and newcomers in the immediate aftermath of the massacre became less frequent colonists depicted the Native Americans as animals: 'They seldome see any salvages, but in the woods.'[49] This was indicative of the sense of fear the colonists believed the Native Americans felt due to their actions at Jamestown: 'They feare we may beate them out of their dens.'[50] Depictions of the American community mirrored discussions of other uncivilised people known to Englishmen. True to form they did not farm animals properly, and thus had eaten their store of 'wild hogs'. Colonists turned their noses up at Native American cuisine: 'They never regard any food from the savages.'[51] Earlier promises to act in a peaceful manner were forgotten as colonists defended the use of force as just vengeance: 'Some few there are, that upon their opportunitie have slaine some few [Native American] stragglers, which have been revenged with the death of so many of themselves.'[52] When natives rose up against English colonists, calls for vengeance were a common response from those who survived.

Smith subjected Native Americans to the spectacle of revenge. Describing how he took the Native American king, Opchanacanough, 'by the long locke on his head, with my pistole at his breast, I led him among his greatest forces'; Smith subsequently killed the king before some of the natives.[53] Others involved in the attack on Jamestown were gathered to face their punishment: 'I made all the country pay contribution, hauing little else whereon to liue'.[54] Smith now warned his readers 'let all men be assured ... what those savages are that thus strangely doe murder and betray our country men'.[55] Like Waterhouse, Smith believed that the colony would

---

46 John Smith, *The true travels, adventures*, London 1630, 42.
47 Idem, *New Englands trials*, London 1622, sig. C2.
48 Kupperman, *Settling with the Indians*, 43–4.
49 Smith, *The true travels, adventures*, 42.
50 Idem, *New Englands trials*, sig. C2.
51 Idem, *The true travels, adventures*, 42–3.
52 Ibid. 42.
53 Idem, *New Englands trials*, sig. C2.
54 Ibid.
55 Ibid. sig. C3.

survive as men of noble rank (i.e. more civilised), as opposed to 'vagabonds and condemned men', were arriving in Virginia.[56] None the less, the purpose for the new adventurers was clear: 'Take heart, and fill your veynes; the next that bleed Shall be those Fiends: and for each drop of ours I strongly hope, we shall shed theirs in showers.'[57] After a massacre in a colonial context, therefore, bloodletting and revenge became a key aspect of the colonisers' discourse.

While the rhetoric of English imperial expansion preached moderation, this merely reinforced English perceptions of civility and correct government. The Virginian frontier, however, was much more violent and 'uncivil' than this. The guerrilla-type assault on Jamestown provided the justification that English colonists needed to use violence to secure their settlements. An unexpected massacre against the colonial order could, therefore, have disastrous consequences for colonial relations and drastically alter English perceptions of natives under their imperial domain. It must be stressed that, despite the rhetoric of restraint that circulated in English society, the simple fact was that the English state used excessive means to crush rebellions both in the Atlantic archipelago and in the American colonies. The literary constructs of civility became the model through which Englishmen could invent a favourable record of their actions, portraying themselves in the best possible light. In a colonial context, by constantly blaming the barbarity and incivility of the natives, the colonists absolved themselves from culpability. In this way, the superiority of English political, judicial and legal systems were reinforced as the benchmark for civility.

Civilising Ireland: violence and empire

Ireland served as a training camp for colonists who intended to travel to America. This has led one historian to dub Ireland 'a laboratory for empire'.[58] Many colonial adventurers served in multiple colonies within the Stuart empire and scholarly investigations have suggested how the Irish, Scottish and American colonial experiences informed imperial discourse.[59] English cultural values invested in the term 'civility' shaped the representation of Irish, Scottish and American natives within the framework of wider European discourses on education, law and order. Torn between the desire to portray their government as restrained, just and peaceful, English accounts

---

[56] Ibid. sigs C2v–C3.

[57] Christopher Brooke, 'A poem on the late massacre in Virginia', *Virginia Magazine of History and Bibliography* lxxii (July 1964), 259–92, quotation at p. 262.

[58] Ohlmeyer, 'A laboratory for empire?', 26–60.

[59] David Harding, 'Objects of English colonial discourse: the Irish and Native Americans', *Nordic Irish Studies* iv (2005), 37–60; Lenman, *England's colonial wars*, 23–71, 168–72; Ohlmeyer, '"Civilisinge of those rude partes"', 124–47; Sheehan, *Savagism and civility*, 54.

of Ireland oscillated between preaching restraint and calling for revenge – depending on the political climate.[60]

Colonial discourse on Ireland evolved from the writings of the twelfth-century chronicler Giraldus Cambrensis, whose *Topography of Ireland* set the agenda for subsequent colonial writers. Cambrensis portrayed the Irish natives as bestial, violent (they all carried a hidden axe about their person) and as pagans. Early modern treatises that spoke of Ireland and Irish natives sometimes touched on themes originally developed by Giraldus Cambrensis, most notably Edmund Spenser, Sir John Davies, John Derricke and Barnaby Rich. This is evident in their descriptions of Irish natives, which closely resemble the image of the indigenous population that had been harnessed since the twelfth century. By the early modern period, commentators drew comparisons between the Highlanders and Irishmen:

> These [Highlanders] after the Irish fashion were accustomed to be cloathed with a mantle, and a shirt coloured with Saffron, and to goe bare legged as high as their knees. Their weapons are Bow and Arrowes, with a very broad Sword & Dagger, sharpe but on one edge. They all speake *Irish*, and feed upon fish, milke, cheese, and flesh, and have great store of cattell.[61]

A collection of cattle implied a nomadic lifestyle, one outside a walled domain; in short, an uncivilised lifestyle. Parallels were also drawn between Welsh laws and Irish laws.[62] Such subtle critiques of the cultural, social and political nuances of the Celtic fringes reinforced the superiority of the emerging English state.

The Reformation, and the polarisation of communal identities in Ireland along religious lines, added another dimension to the trope of colonial writings on Irish society. Authors subsequently focused more on the striking differences between their two forms of Christianity and the belief that Catholics (largely based on the actions of the Spanish in the Americas) were untrustworthy, violent subjects. Throughout the early modern period people believed that Catholic clerics had duped the native Irish and prevented them from participating in civil practices or engaging with God's word. Explanations for primitive practices such as 'praying for the dead … damnable pestiferous Stewes of Nunnes and Whores' and the 'ill husbandry

---

[60] Ethan Shagan, *The rule of moderation: violence, religion and the politics of restraint in early modern England*, Cambridge 2011, 1–4.

[61] Quotation from Giovanni Botero, *Relations of the most famous kingdomes and common-wealths thorowout the world*, London 1630, 115. See also William Camden, *Britain, or A chorographicall description of the most flourishing kingdomes, England, Scotland, and Ireland*, London 1637, 3.

[62] John Davies, *A discoverie of the state of Ireland: with the true causes why that kingdom was neuer entirely subdued, nor brought vnder obedience of the crowne of England, vntill the beginning of his maiesties most happie raigne*, London 1613, 129.

of the Irish' lay in their religious beliefs and ethnicity.[63] According to Robert Payne, an agricultural entrepreneur and pamphleteer, some of the indigenous population recognised the opportunities presented by civil life according to English customs. As a result there were three types of Irish people: those who sought to thrive under English rule; 'kerns [and] warlike men'; and 'very idle people, not vnlike our English beggers'. Many paid lip-service to the tried and trusted stereotypes that had characterised the native Irish from Cambrensis's time. For example, in times of treason and revolt Irish people reverted to form and 'imbrued their hands with blood'.[64] Confessional and colonial discourse highlighted the lack of education and primitive agricultural practices, and the Catholic beliefs, of the people, as the main reasons to exploit their bountiful and profitable land. Ireland had 'very riche and plenty of Iron store', 'verie commodious both for Corne and Pasture' and 'fertilitie of the soil', all of which aroused much interest in these works.[65] Such descriptions of both Ireland and its inhabitants (echoing those of other barbarous peoples) provided part of the literary scaffolding for the representation of the 1641 rebellion.

Portrayals of Irish natives contrasted sharply with depictions of civilised Englishmen. John Derricke's *Image of Irelande*, published in 1581, explored the primitive and bestial origin of the Irish and claimed that the 'people [were] sprong from *Macke Swine*, a barbarous offspring' and that this was evident from their 'Doggishe fashion'.[66] What is striking, however, is that Payne's description of the Irish natives was written after the suppression of the Desmond rebellion, which granted the English colonies in Ireland greater security, albeit temporarily. In contrast, a 'View of the present state of Ireland', the most notorious sixteenth-century account of Irish natives, was written by Edmund Spenser as a response to the Nine Years' War, which seriously threatened the colonial order in Ireland. A sense of insecurity shaped Spenser's portrayal of the Irish natives and prompted his call for revenge. This led to the radicalisation of English policy in Ireland as Spenser's writings subsequently influenced some of the most notorious planters in Ireland, such as Sir George Carew.[67] The ongoing state-sponsored violence that followed

---

[63] *The coppie of a letter sent from M Rider, deane of Saint Patricks, concerning the newes out of Ireland*, London 1601, sig. A2r–v; Barnaby Rich, *A newv description of Ireland: wherein is described the disposition of the Irish wherevnto they are inclined: nolesse admirable to be perused then credible to be beleeued: neither vnprofitable nor vnpleasant to bee read and vnderstood, by those worty cittizens of London that be now vndertakers in Ireland*, London 1610, sig. B2v.

[64] Christopher Farewell, *An East-India colation; or A discourse of travels set forth in sundry obseruations, briefe and delightfull*, London 1633, sig. B2v; John Norden, *A prayer for the prosperovs proceedings and good successe of the earle of Essex*, London 1599, [3].

[65] Payne, *A description of Ireland*, 9; Rich, *A newv description of Ireland*, sig. B3, and *A short svrvey of Ireland*, London 1609, 1.

[66] John Derricke, *The image of Irelande*, London 1581, sig. Bii.

[67] Thomas Herron, 'Early modern Ireland and the new English epic: connecting Edmund Spenser and Sir George Carew', *Eolas: The Journal of the American Society of*

contributed to a sense of isolation among Irish noblemen and consolidated the rise of the New English in Ireland.[68] Ten years later, after the brutal suppression of the Nine Years' War, the New English felt increasingly secure as the subjugation of the native Irish was almost complete. Now Sir John Davies, the Irish attorney-general, could argue that the Irish were close to being part of the civil order.[69]

Even though martial law was employed almost continually throughout the late sixteenth and early seventeenth centuries commentators portrayed English rule in Ireland as just and reasonable. English civil courts were representative of the ethnic diversity of the population: 'If any matter be to be tryed there betweene an English man and an Irish, the Jury is half English and halfe Irish.'[70] Furthermore, the Irish had reaped the benefits of English justice. One third of the Irish, 'the better sort are very ciuill and honestly giuen', yet still lacked the means to reach full civility.[71] Aware of the romanticised historical and religious connection between Ireland and Spain, Payne dismissed this 'special relationship' and argued that most Irish natives hated the Spanish:

> Most of ye better sort of ye Irish haue read of their monsterous cruelties in ye west Indians, where they most tiranously [tyrannically] haue murthered many millions more of those simple creatures then now liueth in Ireland, euen such as sought their fauours by offering vnto them al that they had, neuer resisting nor offering them any harme.[72]

Payne's account of Ireland, however, was written with a view to encouraging investment in the Munster plantations, which were to be settled on land recently confiscated from the earl of Desmond. As a result, Payne assured his readers that the Irish people were amenable to English rule.[73]

Representations of native Irish communities ebbed and flowed between positive and negative portrayals according to the political realities and cycles of violence that characterised the course of early modern Irish history. Both Davies and Payne wrote about Ireland after the brutal suppression of rebel-

---

Irish Medieval Studies 1 (2006), 27–52; Edwards, 'Ideology and experience', 127–57. There is some disagreement with this. See Andrew Hadfield, 'Historical witing, 1550–1660', in Gillespie and Hadfield, *The Oxford hstory of the Irish book*, iii. 250–63.

[68] Edwards, 'The plight of the earls', 53–76, and 'The escalation of violence', 34–78.

[69] Davies, *A discoverie of the state of Ireland*, 2.

[70] Payne, *A briefe description of Ireland*, 5.

[71] Ibid. 3.

[72] Ibid. 7. For the latest historiographical reviews of the 'special relationship' between Ireland and Spain in the early modern period see Pérez Tostado, *Irish influence at the court of Spain*, 40–8, and Morales, *Ireland and the Spanish Empire*, 7–15, 29–47.

[73] Raphael Holinshed, *The second volume of chronicles: conteining the description, conquest, inhabitation, and troblesome estate of Ireland*, London 1586, 10–11.

lions, which once again secured the position of English colonies in Ireland. As in American colonies, rebellion and resistance radicalised English perceptions of the Irish natives. To illustrate this, two examples demonstrate the importance of understanding how different contexts shaped colonial literature on Ireland and reveals how literary constructions of civility explain English responses to Irish resistance. The first piece, 'The supplication of blood of the English most lamentably murdered in Ireland, cryeng out of the yearth for revenge' was written by an unidentified Protestant cleric from Cork in 1598, in the midst of the violence of the Nine Years' War. Framed as a personal request to Elizabeth I for more funds and supplies to suppress the native Irish in their attempts to shake off English rule, the tract makes no distinction between Irish natives and the Old English and has a decidedly confessional interpretation of events in Ireland. The author of the 'Supplication' used striking imagery of victimhood to elicit sympathy for Irish Protestants and to mobilise the queen, 'unto whom god hath committed the sword of Iustice, to punishe the offender'. Protestant corpses littered the Irish countryside, 'dismemb[e]red by the tyranie of traytors, devowred by the merciless Iawes [jaws] of ravenous wolves'. Elizabeth was called upon 'to revenge the monstrous rapes of many poore forlorne widdowes, and the bloody murders of many yo[u]re faithfull subiectes'.[74] The 'Supplication' asked her court to 'Weepe England, mourne, lament, not the losse of us, but the losse of thy honor; not o[u]re destruction but thine owne disgrace.'[75] Rather than frame its objectives from the outset as one of conquest, the author focused first on survival: 'Provide for the safetie and securitie of those soules that yet remayne.' The settler population was in a precarious position and lived in constant 'feare of robbinge them of theire goodes, feare of wronginge there persons, feare of murderinge'.[76]

The 'Supplication' compared the behaviour of the rebels with other violent peoples. 'Never shall you read in the stories of the Gothes and Vandalles, in the recordes of the Turkes and Infidells, in the most barbarous and cruel warres that ever were, suche brutishe crueltie, such mounsterous outrage.' Once more, Irish natives were described as animals, or 'savage beasts'.[77] The author reserved his greatest vitriol for the leaders of the insurrection: 'In the Rage of that bastard of Clincartie, wee weare first Robbed, but ore bodies escaped violence, yet weare many of yore Ma[jes]ties lande unpeopled.' Through the use of generalisation, using one incident to exemplify the wider conduct of the war, the author portrayed the Irish as

[74] Willy Maley, 'The supplication of blood of the English most lamentably murdered in Ireland, cryeng out of the yearth for revenge (1598)', *Analecta Hibernica* xxxvi (1995), 1, 3–77 at p.12.

[75] Ibid. 21.

[76] Ibid. 12.

[77] Ibid. 18.

particularly violent. The graphic description of the murder of a man 'being first roasted', then thrust through with a sword could be seen as horrific. The author however, added the following detail:

> Neither did that quinche his [the assailant's] unsatiable desire of blood, until wrappinge the sencelesse corpes in his usuall bedd, he had consumed both bedd and it w[i]th fire. This one horrible murder may geve yore ma[jes]tie a sufficient cause of coniecture what his cruell proceadinges were against many others.

The rebels stole from their English neighbours and attacked English families. Women and children were particularly vulnerable to attack – 'antient women Contempteouslie, savagely, unchristianly, and inhumanely stripped: nothinge lefte them to cover those partes'. No women 'that lighted into their handes escaped their beastly lust'.[78]

Through focusing on the plight of the victims of atrocities, the author of the 'Supplication' could then give voice to his desire for revenge: 'The crye of the fatherlesse orphanes, the crye of the desolate widowes, whoe by his meanes were driven to begge reliefe of the cold devotion of that Countrie, pierce the Cloudes, sound through both the eares of the almighty, crying revenge.'[79] This supported later claims that 'yore estate in Ireland is nowe a bleedinge'.[80] Like Waterhouse's *Declaration*, the 'Supplication' used the victims as the centrepiece in its call for revenge, arguing that God: 'Hath nowe geven you just occation to use such reformation, as before you could not easily have done without suspition of hardenes.'[81] For this commentator, the colonial project in Ireland was more about proselytisation than profiteering. Accusations of the unrestrained use of violence would, of course, contradict English values that constructed literary perceptions of civility. Whereas before there was 'lawe and justice' in Ireland, now the land was 'overawed w[i]th rebellion everywhere'.[82] The 'Supplication' stated however that God gave 'the land to erect the Gospell' and the 'sword to swaye that his word might beare sway amongst them'.[83] The use of restraint in justice ('wicked is that government, and unhappie the subiectes') now in time of war was unsafe.[84] Only martial law, the author argued, would bring the country to peace: 'Lawe uprightly ministred would have helde them in

---

[78] Ibid. 14, 15, 17.
[79] Ibid. 13.
[80] Ibid. 20.
[81] Ibid. 18–19.
[82] Ibid. 21.
[83] Ibid. 21–2.
[84] Ibid, 28.

obedience and awe.'[85] Now therefore, 'lett the sworde spare none that lightes in theire way'.[86]

The graphic descriptions of the cruelties of the Irish rebels and the evocative imagery of the victims of the rebellion must have struck a chord with contemporary audiences. The Irish 'ravenous wolves' and 'savage beastes' tore through the countryside, acting out 'unmercifull' cruelties against 'poore innocent' English victims.[87] The frequent use of 'bloody' imagery highlighted the plight of Protestant English settlers and underlined the extent of Catholic cruelty. While the author may have argued that the failure to implement martial law was the reason behind the massacre of English settlers, the 'Supplication' also portrayed the Nine Years' War as a punishment from God: 'Our sinnes sett up Irishe governm[en]t; plucked downe the English; our sins blinded the eies of understandinge in ore cheefe rules. Instead of Iustice they sett up iniustice.'[88] This reasoning was reinforced by the use of biblical imagery. The central motif deployed in the 'Supplication' was the dashing of children's heads against the rocks by Irish Catholics: 'Younge infants scarce yet seasoned w[i]th the ayre of the world, most lamentably brained: some dashed against the walles.'[89]

Although it is unclear whether children were really killed in such a manner, the dashing of children's heads had profound meaning in the early modern period. In the second book of Kings, the Israelites were punished for being ignorant of their sins. One of their leaders, Hazael, was the loyal follower of King Hadadezer of Syria. Hadadezer fell ill and Elisha, a prophet, ordered Hazael to tell the king he would survive. Upon so doing, Elisha began to weep as he had a premonition that Hazael would destroy Israel. Elisha warned Hazael that he will 'burne the cities of *Israel* with fire, slay the inhabitants, rip vp the women with child, and dash the infants against the stone'. Accordingly, that night Hazael killed the king by smothering him and assumed control of Syria and acted out Elisha's prophecy. This story was used by preachers as a lesson for all those who were unaware of their own sins and the effect that this would have on the wider community.[90] This reinforced settlers' beliefs that they were God's chosen people and defined their enemies as heathens, a standard Protestant interpretation of confessional conflicts, not just in Ireland but also in Europe.

The traditional response to violence against the English colonial order was the appeal for the use of violence in return. In times of relative peace, however, such calls for the adoption of martial law (at least in public rhetoric)

---

[85] Ibid. 65.
[86] Ibid. 73.
[87] Ibid. 13, 18.
[88] Ibid. 24. See also pp. 25, 28.
[89] Ibid. 18.
[90] 2 Kings viii.12.

were tempered with a consideration of the correct forms of civil and colonial government. An example is the tract written by the Irish attorney-general, Sir John Davies, after the Nine Years' War in Ireland. Davies suggested that peace was not the best means of securing the English colony in Ireland, rather: 'A barbarous country must be first broken by a warre, before it will be capeable of good Gouernment.'[91] This would allow the proper exercise of the law and the correct administration of justice 'if theyre be two parts of that Countrey wherein he cannot punish Treasons, Murders, or Thefts, vnlesse he send an Army to do it'. Without the brutal suppression of the Irish menance, Davies confessed that 'I cannot iustly say, that such a Countrey is wholly conquered.'[92]

Admittedly, Davies's motivations differed from those of Giraldus Camb-rensis and Edmund Spenser. Davies, as solicitor- and later attorney-general, was preoccupied with the spread of English law. Like other commentators on uncivilised lands, Davies argued that proper exercise of the law marked a civilised country: 'To giue Lawes vnto a People, to institute Magistrates and Officers ouer them; to punish and pardon Malefactors; to haue the sole authority of making warre and peace, and the like; are the true markes of soueraignetie.'[93] Edmund Spenser also discussed the excessively violent nature of the native Irish, and how their leaders ruled with an iron fist: 'It is then a very unseasonable time to plead law, when swords are in the hands of the vulgare, or to thinck to retaine them with feare of punishments when they loke after liberty and shake of all government.' Irenius, an allegorical figure who represented colonial Ireland, argued in Spenser's 'View' that restraint must be exercised in issues of justice: 'the like regard and moderation ought to be had in tempering and managing of this stubburn nation of the Irish, to bring them from their delight of licensious barbarisme unto the love of goodnesse and civility'.[94] Davies argued a similar point when he claimed that Irish natives had yet to experience the benefits of the English common law, pointing out that Roman emperors neglected one of their responsibilities 'to communicate their Lawes to the rude and barbarous people'.[95]

The failure to implement common law successfully in Ireland meant that colonists recognised a hybrid legal code of common law and Irish Brehon law, much to Davies's chagrin. Those who adopt Irish customs (namely, the Old English) are, he argued, 'rebelles to all good Gouernment, destroy the commonwealth wherein they liue, and bring Barbarisme and desolation vpon the richest and most fruitfull Land of the world'.[96] Whereas English

---

[91] Davies, A discoverie of the state of Ireland, 5.

[92] Ibid. 7.

[93] Ibid. 14–15.

[94] http://www.ucc.ie/celt/published/E500000–001/index.html, accessed 25 Aug. 2010.

[95] Davies, A discoverie of the state of Ireland, 124.

[96] Ibid. 165.

law punished major crimes, such as murder, rape and robbery, by death, Irish law only fined prepetrators, thereby preventing any man from 'enjoy[ing] his Life, his Wife, his Lands or Goodes in safety'. Davies argued, as others had done, that the lack of a civilised legal code meant that the Irish were 'little better then Canniballes, who doe hunt one another, and hee that hath most strength and swiftnes, doth eate and devoure all his fellowes'.[97] It must be pointed out, however, that this was mere rhetoric. Colonial governors in Ireland were keen to exaggerate Irish violence and incivility, particularly when it was politically expedient to do so.

One of the main targets of English criticisms was Irish chieftains, who allegedly exercised their authority illegally. Leaders of Irish families 'did spoyle and impouerish the people at their pleasure'.[98] While such behaviour was a symptom of incivility, Davies argued that the exercise of certain Irish customs was the 'true cause of such Desolation & Barbarism'.[99] Coigne and livery, an early modern extortion racket whereby locals were taxed in return for protection, caused 'depopulation, banishment, & extirpation of the better sort of subiects' and led the Irish natives to become idle.[100] The ubiquity of tyrannical and violent government, dictated by Brehon law, prompted the population to respond in kind: 'They are growne into such a habite of sauage tyranny, that nothing is more pleasing to the greatest number of them, then ciuill warres, murthers and massacres.'[101] Worse than this, apart from the violent, unrestrained exercise of authority by Irish chieftains, Cath-olic priests, Jesuits and friars exerted a poisonous and malign influence over the local population: 'The people are daily seduced, infected and peruerted by Iesuites, Seminaries & other runnagte [renegade] Priests the ministers of Antichirst.'[102] Such sentiments were echoed by others: 'Popish-Priests may vse all violence.'[103]

Justifications for the spread of English civility and the plantations in Laois, Offaly and Munster mirrored the legitimisation put forward for the planting of the Americas. Despite the ideals of civility espoused by colonists, more cynical observers such as Barnaby Rich viewed the English colonisa-tion of Ireland as a failure. English families had become 'degenerate and metamorphosed ... they did not only forget the English language & scorne the use thereof, but grew to bee ashamed of their very English Names, though they were Noble and of great Antiquity; and took Irish *Surnames*

97 Ibid. 165–7.
98 Ibid. 167.
99 Ibid. 168.
100 Ibid. 176.
101 Rich, *A short svrvey of Ireland*, 3.
102 Ibid. sig. A2v.
103 Francis Herring, *Mischeefes mysterie: or, Treasons master-peece*, London 1617, 21.

and *Nick-names*'.[104] More alarmingly, they began to educate the natives in the ways of the barbarian. 'We daily see', Barnaby Rich wrote in 1617, 'the pride, the drunkennesse, the swearing, the bawdery, the bribery, the popery, all the most lewd and idle vices: the beastly and diuellish fashions the one doth vse, the other doth imitate.'[105] While Rich's critique of the natives took aim at what he believed to be the corrupt New English administration,[106] the terms in which his criticisms were expressed were within early modern values invested in 'civility'. Contemporary beliefs that the Old English had reverted to incivility were rooted in the common perception that civility had to be maintained constantly with the just execution of law, order, justice and the provision of religious education.

It must be noted that the arguments of Spenser, Davies, Rich and the 'Supplication' did not, in all probabilty, reach the lower social orders. Historians have gone to great pains to illustrate how these colonial tomes on native Irish behaviour shaped the course of English governance in Ireland. Indeed, Bruce Lenman unceremoniously described this New English literary circle as 'political rapists hoping to leap from nothing to something by a sudden act of possessive violence'.[107] These writers have been cited as proof of the high levels of violence that occurred in early modern Ireland.[108] A distinction must be drawn, of course, between fanciful rhetoric and the reality of the situation in seventeenth-century Ireland. Furthermore, due consideration must be given to the question of audience. These works may not have directly shaped perceptions of the native Irish among the lower social orders from England and Scotland who settled in plantation towns in Ulster.

Cheaper pamphlets served as guidebooks for the hundreds of undertakers and their servants seeking their fortune in the north of Ireland. These texts informed the wider populace of the characteristic traits of the native Irish. Take, for example, Thomas Blenerhasset's *A direction for the plantation in Vlster*, a thirty-two-page pamphlet that spoke to potential planters in Ireland. Blenerhasset, a soldier, planter and amateur poet, described the native Irish as lazy, disorganised and violent. He stressed the need for 'many Castles and fortes well fortified' which 'will restraine the violence of such a scattered people as they are'.[109] Such fears were shared by later planters

---

104 Davies, *A discoverie of the state of Ireland*, 182.

105 Barnaby Rich, *The Irish hubbub*, Dublin 1618, 3.

106 Eugene Flanagan, 'The anatomy of Jacobean Ireland: Captain Barnaby Rich, Sir John Davies and the failure of reform, 1609–22', in Morgan, *Political ideology*, 158–80.

107 Edwards, 'Ideology and experience', 127–57; Lenman, *England's colonial wars*, 122.

108 See Edwards, 'The escalation of violence', 34–78; McGurk, 'The pacification of Ulster', 119–29.

109 Thomas Blenerhasset, *A direction for the plantation in Vlster: contayning in it, sixe principall thinges, viz 1 The securing of that wilde countrye to the crowne of England; 2 The withdrawing of all the charge of the garrison and men of warre; 3 The rewarding of olde seruitors to their good content; 4 The means how to increase the reuenue to the crowne, with a yearely*

such as Thomas Phillips and Thomas Raven. Phillips warned that 'the few British are soe scattered that upon occasion they are not able to succour one another and are daily robbed and spoiled'.[110] Raven, in a review of Derry's defences, anxiously noted how certain sides were exposed to musket shot.[111] Such manifestations of planter fear reveal the source of colonists' anxieties toward the native Irish, attitudes that shaped later interpretations of their actions in 1641.

Blenerhasset's pamphlet is interesting as it did not shy away from the reasons why the plantation of Ulster was 'newly delievered ... from the usurping tyrannie of Traytors, & from a long & most lamentable captiuitie'. According to Blenerhasset, a plantation would 'secure that wilde Countrie any long time', echoing the views of James VI and I on the Scottish High-lands.[112] The *Direction for the plantation in Vlster* was written in an informal style, and is conversational in tone. Blenerhasset informed his readers that they did not pursue the plantations in Ulster previously because of 'the cruell wood-kerne, the deuowring Woolfe, and other suspitious Irish, would so attend on their business'. The main Marshall in Ulster was Sir Toby Caulfield. 'No man', wrote Blenerhasset, 'keppeth better order, as well for the safeguard of himselfe and his neighbours.' As Blenerhasset spoke of the need for defensive fortifications, contemporary maps of Ulster depicted *trace italienne*, the latest military fortifications to embrace Europe.[113] The nature of the Irish people meant that they constituted a clear, consistent, yet invisible danger: 'For although there is no apparent enemy, nor any visible maine force, yet the wood-kerne and many other[s] (who now haue put on the smiling countenance of contentment) doe threaten every houre.' Even in Armagh, the 'scattered plantation' could not restraine the 'violence of the Woolfe'. As is shown by Blenerhasset's calls for more fortifications in Ulster, the aftershock of the Nine Years' War and Cahir O'Doherty's rebellion of 1608 was clearly still being felt.

The key to a successful plantation was its defence, centred in 'a wel forti-fied Towne, to be able at any time at an houres warning with fiue hundred men well armed, to encounter all occasions'. Blenerhasset envisaged these

---

very great somme; 5 How to establish the puritie of religion there; 6 And how the vndertakers may with securitie be inriched, London 1610, [5–6].

[110] Drapers Hall, MS +793. I would like to thank Dr Annaleigh Margey for this reference.

[111] TCD, MS 1209/22.

[112] Blenerhasset, *A direction for the plantation in Vlster*, 'To the prince'.

[113] 'Mountjoy Fort', NLI, MS 2656/VII; 'Map of the province of Ulster', TCD, MS 1209/14; Rolf Loeber and Geoffrey Parker, 'The military revolution in seventeenth century Ireland', in Ohlmeyer, *Ireland from independence to occupation*, 66–88. For further information on the mapping of Ulster during this time see Annaleigh Margey, 'Repre-senting plantation landscapes: the mapping of Ulster, c. 1560–1640', in James Lyttleton and Colin Rynne (eds), *Plantation Ireland: settlement and material culture*, c. 1550–c. 1700, Dublin 2009, 140–64.

towns as a hub for military excursions into the Irish countryside. Soldiers (to the number of one hundred) could search 'all suspitious places, for the Woolfe and the Wood-kerne'. This would, according to Blenerhasset, 'bring such a terror, that the woolfe himself will not dare to continue his haunt'. These measures, and the fact that Blenerhasset proposed that towns would contain 'fiue thousand well armed men, to encounter any forraine enemy, that shall offer arriuall to inuade' would, in Blenerhasset's opinion, discourage native Irish resistance and bring about the demise of bandits such as wood kerne. Such security would allow the plantations to prosper and pave the way for an eventual military withdrawal. The stationing of garrisons across Ulster, however, could not have eased tensions between native and newcomer communities.[114]

The plantations needed people and investment to succeed. Blenerhasset, therefore, warned his audience of potential dangers and to address any possible concerns: 'I doe insure thee, there [are] excellent warriors … [who] in time of need violently abate the violence of any that shall intend any trouble.' At the same time, however, 'the danger [in Ireland], which is nothing so much as amongst good fellowes it is, to be beastly drunke at home'. The Ulster plantations offered those who were down on their luck a chance to 'serve God, be sober' so that 'thou shalt recouer thy selfe'. Blenerhasset made the plantations appeal to all social ranks. Tradesmen and husbandmen were encouraged to go to Ulster to start a new life. Ministers, by partaking in the plantation project, could teach 'poore ignorant vntaught people [who] worship stones and sticks' the true ways of God. Gentlemen were encouraged to settle in Ireland, particularly if they liked to hunt: 'The Fox, the Woolfe, and the Wood-kerne, doe expect thy coming.' With such ambitious people coming over Blenerhasset predicted that 'Ulster, which hath bene hitherto the receptale and very denne of Rebels and deuowring creatures, shall farre excel *Munster*, and the ciuellest part of all that country, and peraduenture in ciuillity and sincere Religion, equal euen faire England herselfe.' Blenerhasset showed how violent Ireland could be, but consistently advertised the profitability of the plantations and their contribution to the spreading of God's word.

Early seventeeth-century ballads and chapbooks constitute another valuable indicator of popular opinion on Irish natives. Chapbooks attracted a large readership as they were priced within the economic reach of the average agricultural labourer. The oral nature of ballads meant that their message could reach much further than those who purchased them.[115] They could be recited (or re-enacted) in the home, the alehouse and at the market place – all vibrant centres of communication. In these songs and poems

---

114 For an example of how the presence of a military garrison contributed to the flight of the earls see Edwards, 'The plight of the earls', 53–76.

115 Fox, *Oral and literate culture*; Spufford, *Small books and pleasant histories*.

Ireland was a war-torn society where honest planters died. The protagonist in *A lanthorne for landlords*, was a 'labouring man' from Lincoln set sail 'to serve in Ireland'. Unfortunately he 'there in Princes wars was slaine/ As doth that Country know/ But left his widow great with child as ever she could goe'.[116] Irishmen allegedly had a voracious sexual appetite – although this may have had something to do with their excessive drinking habits: 'From Ireland I had, a lusty brave lad,/ Each Limbe was proportioned mighty:/ Truth was he was poore yet I gave him o're,/ Cause his breath stunke of Aquavity.'[117] Allusions to their propensity to commit violence meant that Irish men were frequently described as carrying arms, most notably their knives or 'skeanes'.[118] Like the Native Americans, the Irish were described as 'treacherous' and worthy of violent punishment: 'thy vaine and wicked reed:/ Deserues, dislikes, and iustly dooth acquire,/ The swoord'.[119] While such literary depictions of Ireland may have solely entertained, as opposed to informed, English audiences, there is enough evidence to suggest that planters arrived in Ireland with a perception that Irish natives were genetically disposed to commit gruesome cruelties.

It is also possible to trace some aspects of colonial life in Ireland prior to the outbreak of rebellion through looking at the 1641 depositions. They abound with evidence of tensions between the two communities before the rebellion. Such manifestations of settlers' anxieties are unsurprising, particularly since the depositions were made when a climate of terror gripped the Protestant and planter population. George Creichton, a vicar living in Lurgan, Cavan, feared for his life when he learned of the rebellion. Hearing a knock at his door on the evening of 23 October 1641, 'this deponent stepp[ed] to open expecting to meete with a sworde or a skeane to be thrust into his belly'. A native Irish messenger assuaged his concerns: 'be not you afraid, the Irish will doe noe hurt to you'. This messenger had been sent by Captain Turlogh McShane McPhillip O'Reilly specifically to warn Creichton and to urge him to attend O'Reilly. Creichton duly met with O'Reilly, who was accompanied by '20 r 24' men, 'whoe al[l] bidd mee hartily welcome and prayed mee to feare noe evill'. They conversed about the proposed course that the rebellion would take. O'Reilly informed Creichton that he had

---

[116] *A lanthorne for landlords*, London 1630: http://ebba.english.ucsb.edu/ballad/20064/xml, accessed 27 Sept. 2010.

[117] *A merry ballad of a rich maid that had 18 severall suitors of severall countries*, London 1620: http://ebba.english.ucsb.edu/ballad/20114/xml, accessed 27 Sept. 2010.

[118] 'A Scottish lasse ber resolute chusing', in Charles Hindley, *The Roxburghe ballads*, London 1873, 101–6.

[119] *The true reporte of the prosperous successe which God gaue vnto our English souldiours against the forraine bands of our Romaine enemies lately ariued, (but soone inough to theyr cost) in Ireland, in the yeare 1580*, London 1581, [1]; *Later newes from Ireland concerning the late treacherous action, and rebellion, of Sir Carey Adoughertie, and Felli Me Reeah Mack Dauy*, London 1608; Spufford, *Small books and pleasant histories*.

orders to seize all goods and arms of English and Scottish planters and had a commission to kill those who did not subject themselves to his authority. Creichton felt comfortable enough with the rebels to plead with them to shed no blood and he offered to act as an intermediary between O'Reilly and the townspeople of Virginia, County Cavan.[120]

Creichton's pre-1641 connections with leaders of Catholic society allowed him to remain behind enemy lines for a considerable period of time. Other planters and settlers were intimately acquainted with native leaders. Robert Maxwell could identify Phelim O'Neill, the leader of the rebellious forces in the North, as well as members of his family.[121] Quite often, deponents could name those that had robbed, attacked or despoiled them – a clear indication that some degree of familiarity existed between the two communities. Some were robbed by near neighbors whom they could identify.[122] Others had more formal links within the rebel community. Many deponents had loaned money to the rebels.[123] For example, Henry Barnes, a yeoman, reported that Myles O'Reilly the high sheriff of County Cavan, owed him £300.[124] Some planters rented out accommodation and lands to Irish natives who subsequently joined the rebellion.[125] In fact, in 1626, laws had been passed to encourage some Irishmen to dwell among the planters of Laois, Offaly and Westmeath, 'and there mix them among the British and teach their children some trade or profession'.[126] Archaeological evidence suggests that Irish labourers and craftsmen not only aided the construction of English and Scottish settlers' houses, but also built Irish-style buildings for them.[127]

The extent of settler and native interaction can also be measured by the fact that some colonists could speak Irish. Due to the anecdotal nature of the evidence, however, it is difficult to draw firm conclusions. In Ireland, government-sponsored education during the seventeenth century aimed to promote the Protestant faith and to facilitate access to God's word. This

---

[120] Deposition of George Creichton, TCD, MS 832, fos 227–8; Cope, 'The experience of survival', 295–316.

[121] Deposition of Robert Maxwell, TCD, MS 809, fo. 5.

[122] Deposition of John Wheelewright, TCD, MS 832, fo. 272.

[123] For example see the deposition of Robert Southwell, TCD, MS 825, fos 212–13; deposition of Jaruis Erington, MS 820, fo. 292; deposition of Robert Waringe, MS 839, fos 108r–111v.

[124] Deposition of Henry Barnes, TCD, MS 832, fo. 185.

[125] Deposition of Christopher Hampton, TCD, MS 834, fo. 14.

[126] 'Directions to the lord deputy and council for settling the civil affairs of Ireland', CSPI, 1625–32, 185–6.

[127] Colm Donnelly, 'The archaeology of the Ulster plantation', in Audrey Horning and others (eds), The post-medieval archaeology of Ireland, 1550–1850, Dublin 2007, 37–50; Raymond Gillespie, 'The problems of plantations: material culture and social change in early modern Ireland', in Lyttleton and Rynne, Plantation Ireland, 43–60.

contributed to the process of 'anglicising' Ireland.[128] The durability of the Irish language challenged this, however. To encourage Irish Catholics to convert sections of the Bible were published in Irish. The staggered spread of the English language throughout Ireland meant that in local courts some officers had to be bilingual in order to conduct their business more effectively.[129] A skirmish in Cork before the house of Dominick Sarsfield, Viscount Kilmallock and chief justice of Munster, provides some evidence of tensions between native and newcomers, but also suggests how they communicated in both English and Irish. Robert King, a Cork local, accused by Sarsfield of blocking up the highway, called the viscount a 'fool' and a 'knave'. Sarsfield responded by throwing a stone at King's face. This prompted a melee in the town as Irishmen began to berate Sarsfield's soldiers and supporters 'in English', calling them 'rogues and the likes'. One witness in this case could understand the natives as he overheard their intentions to retaliate for this attack on Robert King.[130] Rebel messengers in 1641 were concerned that some planters could understand them if they spoke Irish and were therefore reluctant to discuss sensitive information before them. Joane Constable, a deponent from Armagh, deposed that her sister was threatened with death 'becawse she could speake Irish, & would discover their acts, wants, & words if they suffered her to live'.[131] When deponents named settlers who could speak Irish however, it is more likely that they were the exception rather than the rule.[132]

Planters and natives in the years leading up to the 1641 rebellion were actively encouraged to speak English to one another. In the summer of 1626 directions were given to the plantation towns in Laois, Offaly and Westmeath to secure the town from the threat of idle 'swordsmen'. These were to

---

[128] Toby Barnard, Cromwellian Ireland: English government and reform in Ireland, 1649–1660, Oxford 2000, 183; Helga Robinson-Hammerstein, 'Royal policy and civic pride: founding a university in Dublin', in David Scott (ed.), Treasures of the mind: a Trinity College Dublin quatercentenary exhibition catalogue, London 1992, 1–15; Alan Ford, 'Who went to Trinity? The early students of Dublin University', in Helga Robinson-Hammerstein (ed.), European universities in the age of Reformation and Counter-Reformation, Dublin 1998, 53–74.

[129] John Kearney, Aibidil Gaoidheilge & caiticiosma, Dublin 1571; Tiomna Nuadh ar dTighearnia agus ar Slanaightheora Íosa Criosd, Dublin 1602. The Book of Common Prayer circulated in Irish after John Franke printed it in 1608–9. William Bedell also published an Irish catechism in 1631. See Historical catalogue of the printed editions of Holy Scripture in the Library of the British and Foreign Bible Society, London 1903, ii. 790–1, and Margaret Curtis Clayton, The council book for the province of Munster, c. 1599–1641, Dublin 2008, 183.

[130] 'Examination of divers persons ... 18 April 1626', CSPI, 1625–32, 112–15.

[131] Deposition of Joane Constable, TCD, MS 836, fo. 89.

[132] Examination of Mary Sutton, TCD, MS 813, fo. 115; examination of Roger MacNemarra, MS 816, fo. 308r–v.

be encouraged to wear English clothes, and 'speak, or try to learn, English'.[133] Indeed, native Irish commentators drily noted that if they were to buy tobacco, they only needed money and the ability to speak English.[134] Brian Ó Cuív suggested that one person from every native Irish community could read English.[135] A survey of a group of rebels from outside Dublin, rounded up on the night of 22 October 1641 in the capital city and interrogated in the weeks that followed, suggests a greater awareness of the English language among the indigenous Irish than previously thought. Of the eighty examinations of suspected rebels, only nine needed an English interpreter. Of the remaining seventy-one English-speaking examinants, thirty-two could sign their name. These eighty examinants came from a wide geographical area, Cavan, Carlow, Fermanagh, Kildare, Louth, Meath, Monaghan, Sligo and Tipperary. As these individuals came from diverse locations around Ireland they provide a useful, albeit small, sample for an investigation of literacy levels in Ireland during the seventeenth century. This selection suggests tentatively that 40 per cent of the native Irish population could sign their names comfortably and a rather sizeable 89 per cent could speak English, although a detailed nationwide study must be conducted for greater accuracy.[136] Either way, perhaps more Irish people than previously thought could converse in English.

Many deponents could engage in conversation with their captors in English. Avis Bradshaw, the sixteen-year-old wife of John Bradshaw who had left his wife to defend Drogheda, reported that she heard

> Cahall boy Mc Dermott of Kilrout in the barrony of Clankelly and County aforesaid say that Dublin Castle was taken and that they cold aford the English three or fower barrells of powder and that the Irish wold have a newe kinge within a fortnight after, with words or words to that effect he spoake.[137]

Robert Maxwell described how the rebels called the English 'base degenerate Cowards and the Scotts dishonorabl[e] Bragadochioes who came into England not to fight but to scrap vpp wealth marchandizing theire honors for a summe of money'.[138] Even the use of their term 'braggadocio' reflected a nuanced understanding of the English language, as the word itself only came

---

[133] 'Directions to the lord deputy and council for settling the civil affairs of Ireland', *CSPI, 1625–32*, 185–6.

[134] Gillespie, 'The problems of plantations', 56–7.

[135] Brian Ó Cuív, 'The Irish language in the early modern period', in T. W. Moody, F. X. Martin and F. J. Byrne (eds), *A new history of Ireland*, III: *Early modern Ireland, 1534–1691*, Oxford 1976, 509–45 at p. 529.

[136] This sample of depositions was taken from the two volumes of Dublin depositions. For further details see TCD, MSS 809, 810.

[137] Deposition of Avis Bradshaw, TCD, MS 834, fo. 81.

[138] Deposition of Robert Maxwell, TCD, MS 809, fo. 5.

into popular use in the late sixteenth and early seventeenth centuries.[139] Edward Saltenstal and George Littlefield reported that they 'heard divers of the Rebells often say That if Owen [Roe O'Neill] shold not ere long come out of Spaine Then they wold make Sir Phelim ô Neile their Kinge'.[140] The rebels informed John Brook that they 'are the Quenes soldiers'.[141] Likewise, John Coxee, a Tailor in Fermanagh, reported that: 'One Hugh Ô Ratty (late servant to Henry Manning Esquire) uttering these words (vizt) wee have beene your Slaves all this tyme now you shalbe ours or words to that purpose.'[142]

Coxee informed the commissioners that O'Ratty had been a servant of Manning, suggesting another degree of interaction between the two communities. Some native Irish landlords attacked their Protestant tenants and some native Irish tenants attacked their settler landlords. Indeed, some tenants and neighbours warned their Protestant landlords and friends of the dangers that they faced should they leave their houses.[143] The reality of the situation in some areas might have reflected the estimation of Edward Hyde, earl of Clarendon: 'The Roman Catholick landlords had Protestant tenants & many Protestant landlords Roman Catholick tenants. Friendships & marriages were very frequently contracted betweene them, all passion which followed from their different profession suppressed or laid aside.'[144] That said, Clarendon, who had never visited Ireland, spoke somewhat optimistically on the situation in Ireland prior to the rebellion. Despite the fact that the early stages of the Reformation in Ireland were comparatively peaceful, the 1570s and 1580s witnessed the beginnings of sectarianism in early modern Irish society.[145] Extreme reactions to 'British' and Protestant colonial expansion, namely the Nine Years' War (1594–1603) and the O'Doherty revolt of 1608, prompted new planations in Ulster in 1609 – and strengthened the socio-political position of the settler community in Ireland. The dispossession of native Catholics to make room for Protestant settlers from England and Scotland (who may have been predisposed to view the native Irish as

---

139 *Oxford English dictionary.*

140 Deposition of Edward Saltenstall and George Littlefield, TCD, MS 836, fo. 72.

141 Deposition of John Brook, TCD, MS 835, fo. 85.

142 Deposition of John Coxee, ibid. fo. 95.

143 Information of William Pilsworth, TCD, MS 813, fo. 1; examination of Peter Moore, MS 813, fos 3–4; deposition of Knogher McDermond, MS 824, fo. 5; examination of Daniel O'Hanly, MS 824, fo. 5v; information of Thomas Johnson, MS 816, fo. 12; deposition of Roger Markham, MS 839, fo. 17v; examination of Brian O Cahan, MS 838, fos 29–30; deposition of Henry Boyne, MS 839, fo. 10.

144 Edward Hyde, 'Short view', TCD, MS 658, fo. 4.

145 Alan Ford, 'Living together, living apart: sectarianism in early modern Ireland', and Ute Lotz-Heumann, 'Confessionalisation in Ireland: periodisation and character, 1534–1649', in Alan Ford and John McCafferty (eds), *The origins of sectarianism in early modern Ireland*, 1–23 at p. 5; 24–53.

a threat) as part of the Ulster plantations created further tensions between the two communities in Ireland.[146]

Some historians maintain that the 1641 rebellion caught the colonial authorities by complete surprise due to the peaceful nature of Irish society prior to 1641. In the 'balmier days of 1621' Sir Richard Bolton, lawyer and temporary recorder of Dublin, hinted that colonial attitudes softened towards the native Irish when he argued that 'the Irish are no enemies' and that individuality, not ethnicity, was the main indicator of one's culpability in the eyes of the law.[147] Alan Ford has argued that economic and social ties between Catholics and Protestants moderated confessional tensions.[148] Contemporaries on either side of the confessional divide of 1641 agreed that both communities lived together relatively peacefully prior to the outbreak of the rebellion.[149] Admittedly, there might have been moments when a fragile equilibrium existed between the various identities, factions and communities. Despite this, English writings on Ireland published during this time, such as Sir James Ware's 1633 edition of Spenser's View, reasserted England's right to rule Ireland.[150] Throughout the 1620s and 1630s, in fact, tensions continued to simmer beneath the social and political surface.[151] In more recent times, scholars have demonstrated that the 1630s witnessed much economic hardship, and argued that this, along with the repeated use of martial law during the sixteenth and early seventeenth centuries, created 'the ideal conditions for a rebellion'.[152] It is hard to believe that, in an era of state expansion, land appropriation and religious tensions those affected would submissively accept the stripping of their political, social and economic means and liberties.

Tensions between native and newcomer societies led to the outbreak of the 1641 rebellion. Assertions that both communities lived in peace beforehand were indicative of the central component to 'civility' – that the restrained exercise of justice by English colonisers promoted non-violent behaviour.

---

[146] Philip Robinson, The plantation of Ulster, Dublin 1994.

[147] Armstrong, Protestant war, 15.

[148] Canny, Making Ireland British, 451–5; Ford, 'Living together, living apart', 5, 22.

[149] History of the Irish confederation and the war in Ireland, 1641–1649, ed. J. T. Gilbert, Dublin 1882, i. 2; John Temple, The Irish rebellion: or, An history of the beginnings and first progresse of the generall rebellion raised within the kingdom of Ireland, upon the three and twentieth day of October, in the year 1641: together with the barbarous cruelties and bloody massacres which ensued thereupon: by Sir John Temple knight, Master of the Rolles, and one of his majesties most honourable privie councell within the kingdom of Ireland, London 1646, 16; Perceval-Maxwell, The outbreak of the Irish rebellion, 28–9, 286.

[150] Rankin, Between Spenser and Swift, 85.

[151] Canny, Making Ireland British, 457–8.

[152] Micheál Ó Siochrú, God's executioner: Oliver Cromwell and the conquest of Ireland, Dublin 2008, 18–21; Edwards, 'The escalation of violence', 34–78.

Civility provided the rhetoric for colonial administrators and planters alike to portray their own actions in the best possible light and to construct negative views of the native Irish. In times of rebellion, natives could be suitably demonised to rally English authorities to support the colonial venture. Some contemporaries were aware of the vast chasm that existed between rhetoric and reality. As Michel de Montaigne noted: 'Every one gives the Title of Barbarity to every thing that is not in use in his own Country.'[153] In an Atlantic world context, colonial adventurers were keen to appeal to their audiences by portraying their government as fair and just, while at the same time underlining their own superiority. Barnaby Rich, admittedly a political outcast, did at least acknowledge the disastrous consequences of the continual implementation of martial law in Ireland: 'Natyves of Irelande surprised by conquest, wer[e] at that tyme brought to a constreyned obedience, yet not into that voluntary subiection but that they euer more sought to shake of the *Englyshe* gouernment.'[154] William Camden encouraged Elizabeth I not to use excessive force in Ireland 'lest the violent auarice of some particular men might kindle and inflame a new rebellion'.[155] In theory at least, the Stuart administration did not endorse the use of violence without just cause. They also had a lexicon to draw upon to deflect attention away from their frequent implementation of martial law.

The language of civility was manipulated to describe the native Irish as violent, barbaric and bestial. These depictions however, were shaped by the political realities witnessed in the sixteenth and seventeenth centuries and cultural constructions of barbaric people. In times of peace, Irishmen were described as almost civil, benefitting from just governance, education and religious instruction. In times of war, Irish natives fitted into the trope of incivility that evolved in the English imagination. By focusing on the violence of the natives and calling for revenge, English settlers distanced themselves from any possible incrimination, deflected potential criticisms from England and lobbied for wholesale military interventions in Ireland. The portrayal of Irish natives, therefore, reflected the cycles of violence that the country experienced throughout the early modern period. These accounts oscillated between calling for revenge or for reconciliation. The one constant factor was the representation of colonial government in Ireland as fair, using violence only when prompted to do so by native Irish and Old English aggression such as during the Nine Years' War and later in the 1641 rebellion. This justified English rule as a civilising influence and it legitimated all subsequent actions taken by colonial governments in response to

---

[153] Michel de Montaigne, *Essays of Michael, seigneur de Montaigne in three books, with marginal notes and quotations of the cited authors, and an account of the author's life*, London 1685, 366.

[154] Edward Hinton, 'Rych's anothomy of Ireland, with an account of the author', *PMLA* lv (Mar. 1940), 73–101; Flanagan, 'The anatomy of Jacobean Ireland', 158–80.

[155] Camden, *Annales*, bk II, 51.

violence. When natives rebelled, outraged colonists, keen to avoid admitting culpability, blamed the native hierarchy and called for revenge. While this may reflect the sense of colonial insecurity that any indigenous rebellion prompts, the desire for revenge also had a biblical precedent, a point discussed in chapters 4 and 5. Above all, 'civility' provided cultural frameworks and political validation for the expansion of English control across Ireland. The inability, however, to understand the effect of this social, religious, cultural and political encroachment upon native Irish society had drastic consequences.

2

Imagined Violence? The Outbreak of the 1641 Rebellion in Ireland

Accounts written after the 1641 rebellion expressed surprise that the native Irish took arms against the colonial order. Under the happy stewardship of King Charles I, they argued, the three kingdoms enjoyed relative peace and tranquillity in comparison to the 'distempers' of Europe. This might explain why modern-day historians have emphasised the peaceful condition of Ireland in the 1630s. Such sentiments, however, were a deliberate reconstruction of the past in order to paint life in Stuart Ireland and Britain in the best possible light. In truth, the end of Charles's reign was fraught with tension. Matters were not helped by the personality of the monarch; Charles lacked the sort of traits that would have been conducive to dealing with, or mitigating, opposition caused by his various fiscal, social and religious policies. In Ireland rumours that trouble was afoot in the three kingdoms circulated from the mid-1630s, which drastically unsettled local communities, particularly when the Bishops' Wars broke out in Scotland. The actions of those who adhered to the Scottish National Covenant would reverberate across the three kingdoms for the following two decades.

The background to the 1641 rebellion

The presence of a new Protestant and English social order greatly exacerbated tensions in Ireland throughout the early seventeenth century. The frequent use of martial law, the expansion of the Stuart state and the plantation of Ulster could prompt violent unrest, as was attempted during the O'Catháin conspiracy of 1615.[1] In 1641, on one level, personal scores were being settled and popular justice sought as memories of previous injustices surfaced. Some degree of accommodation did occur between the two communities. Native Irish sheriffs were appointed, such as Myles O'Reilly in County Cavan, and plantation towns became convenient venues for the exchange of news, gossip and material goods for sale. Yet, the relative success of the Ulster plantations meant that the spectre of future colonisation along similar lines always hung over Ireland. To make matters worse, Thomas Wentworth, the lord lieutenant and later earl of Strafford, challenged Catholic and Protestant

[1] Gillespie, *Conspiracy*.

claims to own land in various parts of the country, in order to accrue revenues for the crown. The Old English, already aggrieved at his plans for further plantations in Connaught, sought to stop the rot and prevent the further deterioration of their status. They feared for their prospects at the hands of avaricious chief governors and New English adventurers.

The Old English had further cause for concern – Wentworth held the carrot of the Graces (a series of economic concessions offered to the Old English in the 1620s but never granted) before their eyes only to remove it once they had acquiesced in his demand for a subsidy.[2] Throughout his lord lieutenancy Wentworth simply played various factions against one another in Irish politics in order to serve his master, Charles I.[3] Ireland's aggrieved Catholic population watched events in Scotland closely after the eruption of the Bishops' Wars. The covenanters, through taking up arms against the king, managed to secure a series of concessions from Charles I which were of particular interest to Catholic nobles in Ireland: self-determination, free parliaments and their own religious settlement. The prospect of a similar arrangement in Ireland appealed in particular to the Old English who sought to re-establish their stranglehold on power and privileged position in Irish politics. In effect the covenanters had provided a guidebook for those who opposed the rule of Charles I, not just in Ireland, but also in England.

As early as February 1638, John Bramhall, the bishop of Derry, speaking of events in the wider three kingdoms, prophetically warned his ally William Laud, the archbishop of Canterbury, 'What a desperate example the contumacious Nonconformists in Scotland have given both to England and Ireland, who have hearts and hands as well as they.' Bramhall was concerned that the covenanters would set a dangerous precedent. He was also fearful of the ramifications of Wentworth's militant design to seize lands of dubious ownership in the name of the crown. He argued that the 'loyal Irish' would be further isolated from the political system should Wentworth proceed and introduce new settlers: 'This will cause terrible suffering both among the English and the Irish, who have a prophecy that they shall weep over the English graves.' Here, Bramhall quoted a common belief among the native Irish that would later spur on those who joined rebel forces in 1641.[4] None the less, Bramhall's letter revealed that some were considerably concerned about the consequences of Wentworth's policies and of the crisis in Scotland. As Bramhall warned, when rebellion broke out, the rebels followed

---

[2] Clarke, The Old English, 75–89.

[3] Armstrong, Protestant war, 7–9; Perceval-Maxwell, The outbreak of the Irish rebellion, 28–9.

[4] John Bramhall to Archbishop William Laud, 23 Feb. 1638, CSPI, 1634–47, 182. This was a proverb that was commonly mentioned in the depositions: declaration of Michael Doyne, TCD, MS 838, fos 108r–112v at fo. 109v; deposition of Suzanne Stockdale, MS 810, fos 92–5 at fo. 92.

closely the example set by the Scots; this fact was recognised in early intelligence of their movement.[5]

Wentworth responded to Bramhall's concerns by arguing that the covenanters were fighting not for a Church but for a Scottish crown.[6] Publicly, the native Irish agreed with Wentworth and later praised the king for asking them 'in a parliamentary way' to assist him against the Scots. They promised that 'they will be ready to lay down their lives and estates for correction of the disordered factions in Scotland'. Along with the Old English and New English MPs in the Irish parliament they granted four subsidies to the king to fund an army expedition against the Scots.[7] All sides used this crisis to curry favour with the king. To prove their loyalty to Charles I, Ireland's Catholic elites would provide more than just financial assistance. Frustrated by the English parliament's refusal to co-operate with the king against the covenanters, Wentworth turned to the earl of Antrim to raise an army of Irish Catholics, although news of this army was poorly received in England. It was the most controversial policy that Wentworth pursued in his career. Both parliament and the covenanters feared that popish agents or 'evil' councillors had infiltrated the king's court and sought to establish Catholicism across the three kingdoms. They took aim after Wentworth declared that the Irish army could be used to quell rebellion 'in this kingdom'. Although he was probably referring to Scotland, Westminster MPs argued that he meant England. This statement contributed to the events that finally led to his execution for treason on 12 May 1641.[8]

Meanwhile, John Pym, the unofficial leader of parliamentary opposition to the king, built his career on the use of anti-popish rhetoric (usually directed at Laud, who pioneered many of the 'popish' changes in the Anglican Church). Such language could not have eased the fears of Old English and native Irish Catholics, nor could the increasing militancy of the Ulster Scots. Matters had already been complicated by the appointment of John Borlase and William Parsons as lords justices. This marked the promotion of two men who spent the latter half of the 1630s trying to appropriate the land of the Old English in Connaught.[9] In May 1641, after Wentworth's removal and just months prior to the outbreak of rebellion, the native Irish, reminding the king of their loyalty during his Scottish crisis, petitioned Charles to remove 'national distinctions' from the plantations

---

5   Examination of Owen Connelly, 22 Oct. 1641, TCD, MS 809, fos 13r–14v.

6   Bramhall to Laud, 7 Aug. 1639, and Thomas Wentworth to Edward Conway, 13 Aug. 1639, CSPI, 1634–47, 220–1, 222.

7   Irish Council to Secretary Nichols, 23 Mar. 1640, ibid. 239.

8   See Eamon Darcy, 'The Three Kingdoms', in Laura Knoppers (ed.), The Oxford handbook of literature on the English rebellion, Oxford 2013, 44–64.

9   Perceval-Maxwell, The outbreak of the Irish rebellion; Jane Ohlmeyer, 'Strafford, "the Londonderry business" and the "new British histories"', in Julia Merritt (ed.), The political world of Thomas Wentworth, the earl of Strafford, 1621–1641, Cambridge 1996, 209–29.

and allow more native Irish tenants. The newly-appointed lords justices attached a note to their petition that stated: 'We cannot recommend the increasing of the Irish tenants.'[10] From the outbreak of trouble in Scotland, therefore, Catholics used this crisis to prove their loyalty and to lobby for greater religious, parliamentary and economic privileges. They hoped to take control of lands that had been made available in Ulster after many Scottish people had fled back to Scotland after the imposition of the Black Oath by Wentworth. Their New English colleagues, however, undermined native Irish and Old English Catholic attempts to communicate with the king and blocked their designs to shore up their landed interests after the removal of Wentworth, leaving them further disenchanted with the colonial order. The confederation of Kilkenny, the administrative and political organisation that emerged after the outbreak of rebellion, would later complain that Parsons did not serve the public interest and worked to increase his landholdings at the expense of Catholic nobles. The appointment of two lords justices who were unsympathetic to their grievances, coupled with the threat of more land confiscations caused further concern. Ireland's Catholic population, furthermore, was troubled about the anti-Catholic rhetoric emanating from London. They feared being encircled by a militant Protestant alliance across the three kingdoms.

Covenanting success in Scotland had a two-fold consequence in Ireland. First, natives feared that English or Scottish forces would attack Ireland's Catholic population. After the outbreak of the 1641 rebellion, rebels expressed concerns over the intentions of the 'Puritan faction' in Scotland and England. It was alleged that they: 'intended (as the said Sir Phelim averred) to enact such Lawes whereby the Inhabitants of Ireland should conforme in Religion to the Church of England, or otherwis[e] to bee deprived of life, libertie & Estates'.[11] When the O'Neills seized Monaghan town, they claimed that their actions were 'onelye to secure themselves agaynst an order made att the Counsell table of Ireland to hange all them that should refuse to Come to Churche on the All Saints daye after'.[12] Secondly, the Scots provided an example of how to express their grievances in a military fashion. Hugh Óg MacMahon, one of the leading conspirators, confessed to Owen Connelly, the prophet of the 1641 rebellion, that the Irish rebels hoped to 'imitat[e] Scotland' with their actions.[13] The replacement of Wentworth with New English politicians exacerbated tensions in Ireland that had been polarised along sectarian lines since the 1580s and involved sensitive issues

---

10 Note on the Irish petition to the king, 27 May 1641, CSPI, 1634–47, 292.

11 William Peisley to James Butler, twelfth earl of Ormond, 2 Apr. 1641, and George Rawdon to Conway, 5 Dec. 1639, ibid. 274–5, 228; deposition of William Fitzgerald, 4 June 1642, TCD, MS 836, fos 82–6 at fo. 82v.

12 Deposition of Nicholas Simpson, 6 Apr. 1643, TCD, MS 834, fo. 182.

13 Information of Owen Connelly, 22 Oct. 1641, TCD, MS 809, fos 13–14 at fo. 14; deposition of William Fitzgerald, 4 June 1642, MS 836, fos 82–6 at fo. 83.

such as land tenure, freedom of religious expression and social status. These simmering tensions, magnified by an economic downturn in the late 1630s, led to the outbreak of the Irish front in the Wars of the Three Kingdoms. Thus the 1641 rebellion was a response to a range of political, economic and social pressures exerted by the Stuart monarchy and state authorities across the three kingdoms. It aimed to preserve their social status by preventing the further implementation and enforcement of measures that threatened Ireland's Catholics both in terms of their faith and their livelihood.

The outbreak of the Irish rebellion of 1641

One serious issue has tainted the historiography of the 1641 rebellion. Within months of its outbreak Protestant commentators claimed that the rising was a premeditated plot to murder all members of the reformed faiths in Ireland, cloaked in fabricated political and economic grievances. These commentators could point to the 1641 depositions as evidence and provide suitably gory and graphic testimonies to support their arguments. In response, Catholic commentators stressed their coreligionists' hardships and denied that their actions were designed to exterminate the Protestant population in Ireland. They claimed that the outbreak of popular violence was spontaneous and indulged in by the lower social orders without sanction from their social superiors.

While it is difficult to capture the scale of the killings that occured, it is possible to understand why so many Irish natives engaged in the outbreak of popular violence. Three distinguished historians of the 1641 rebellion grappled with the reasons behind the alleged loss of discipline that led to the contested massacres of English Protestants in Ireland. Michael Perceval-Maxwell argued that 'even if the leaders never intended any general or systematic massacre of the settlers, some of their actions tended to encourage the latent tendencies towards violence at the popular level'.[14] Nicholas Canny, in his formidable analysis of Ireland during the sixteenth and seventeenth centuries, argued that 'once the natural leaders [of the rebellion] were seen to be challenging the political and social order in Ulster, their example was immediately followed by other dissatisfied elements within the Catholic community of the province [of Ulster] whose grounds for grievance were different from that of the proprietors and were sometimes opposed to their interests'.[15] Raymond Gillespie attempted to understand the social and economic grievances of these 'unnatural' leaders of the rebellion.[16] The concept of the rebellion as a

[14] Perceval-Maxwell, *The outbreak of the Irish rebellion*, 228.

[15] Canny, *Making Ireland British*, 472.

[16] Raymond Gillespie, 'The end of an era: Ulster and the outbreak of the 1641 rising', in Brady and Gillespie, *Natives and newcomers*, 191–213, and 'Harvest crises in early seventeenth-century Ireland', *Irish Economic and Social History* xi (1984), 5–18.

two-tier revolt (dubbed the 'Canny' model by John Walter, but first framed in the seventeenth century)[17] became the standard historical interpretation in the second half of the twentieth century. It allowed historians to discuss the violence that erupted after 23 October 1641 and to paint its outbreak as a legitimate political protest, rather than a massacre of Protestant settlers. In one sense the historiography of the Irish rebellion has always had to pay heed to the contested political climate of Northern Ireland.

Work influenced by anthropological studies of, and political theories on, violence have modified this traditional interpretation of the 1641 rebellion.[18] Scholars of violence have stressed how contemporary accounts of riots composed by the elites manipulate the identity of leaders and organisers to lay blame on the popular element. Historians of 1641 may also have followed contemporary descriptions of the rebellion that blamed much of the violence on members of the lower social orders.[19] In reality, episodes of popular violence did not operate independently of the rebellion organised by Sir Phelim O'Neill. It may not have reflected the original aims of the leading insurgents, but those who participated in the violence believed that they had (and sometimes did receive) the backing of their social superiors.[20] Furthermore, the violence that followed was neither disorganised nor lacking in reason – it was not, in the words of Robin Clifton and Walter Love, an 'indiscriminate blackness'.[21] Although some acts were passionate expressions of mob justice, their very actions were performative, revealing a set of complex beliefs that contained a patterned meaning. In the words of Donald Horowitz, 'The crowd has lessons to teach; the victims have lessons to learn.'[22] Rumours of Protestant persecution of Catholics, the production of a forged royal commission and the support of the nobility justified their violent actions. Local figures of authority encouraged the lower social orders to join the rebellion while others stood by as settlers were attacked. Perhaps some of the actions of the leaders may have been understood as legitimising violence, when their intention may have been the exact opposite. None the less, Irish rebels attacked their Protestant neighbours in a number of ways,

---

[17] John Walter, 'Performative violence: patterns of political violence in the 1641 depositions', in Jane Ohlmeyer and Micheál Ó Siochrú (eds), *Ireland 1641: contexts and reactions*, Manchester 2013, forthcoming.

[18] William Smyth, *Map-making, landscapes and memory: a geography of colonial and early modern Ireland, c. 1530–1750*, Cork 2006, 107, 113, 143, 146; Walter, 'Performative violence'.

[19] Stathis N. Kalyvas, *The logic of violence in civil war*, Cambridge 2005, 43.

[20] Donald Horowitz, *The deadly ethnic riot*, London 2001, 343–7.

[21] Robin Clifton, '"An indiscriminate blackness"? Massacre, counter-massacre, and ethnic cleansing in Ireland, 1640–1660', in Michael Levene and Penny Roberts (eds), *The massacre in history*, Oxford 1999, 107–26; Love, 'Civil war in Ireland', 57–72.

[22] Horowitz, *The deadly ethnic riot*, 369. For a more detailed discussion of these points see also Walter, 'Performative violence'.

from ritual stripping, to urinating on Bibles and defacing Protestant artefacts and corpses. Many innocent members of the Protestant community were targeted and murdered in cold blood. It is, however, impossible to tell how many died as a direct result of the outbreak of violence during the rebellion and no attempt will be made to do so here.[23]

The first question that needs to be asked is what evidence is there that the upper social orders encouraged their social inferiors to take part in their rebellion? One of the first murders committed during the outbreak of the rebellion in Ulster was that of Arthur Champion a justice of the peace and an unpopular figure in his locality.[24] Champion was apprehended by members of the Maguire clan who claimed 'that they were spetially comaunded & Directed by the lord Maguyre Now in the Castle of Dublyn that they should not spare the said Arthur Champion ... but Murder & kill him & all the Crosses that were his follo[w]ers & tenants'. Champion was not murdered by members of the lower social orders, but by 'Don Carrage Maguyre of the Countie of Ffermanagh gent, Edmond Carragh Maguyre of Annaharde in the said countie gent Redmond mc Owin Maguyre of in the said County gent And Pattricke oge mcRoss Maguyre of Borsalla in the said Countie gent, & others to the Number of 100 persons or thereabouts'.[25] These men were members of the gentry, and even though the ennoblement of Protestants throughout the first half of the seventeenth century had brought social relegation to many prominent Catholic families, the native Irish lower social orders none the less still viewed them as their social superiors and leaders.[26] Don Carrage Maguire later boasted that he had killed Arthur Champion and some of his tenants, although no reference was made to his having permission from Lord Maguire.[27] In this case a symbolic attack on the local justice of the peace illustrated how the rebels were targeting leading figures of settler society.[28]

Thomas Pallat, an English settler, told Arthur Culme, based in County Cavan, of the murder of Champion and that the O'Reillys (a rebel clan) were moving through Cavan under the command of the high sheriff, Mulmore McEdmond O'Reilly, seizing arms and plundering the local population.[29] Mulmore, in fact, led the charge on Culme's castle. It has been shown recently how the nobility played a key role in organising the rebel-

---

[23] Horowitz dubbed such exercises as inherently fraught with difficulty: *The deadly ethnic riot*, 10.

[24] Raymond Gillespie, 'The murder of Arthur Champion and the 1641 rising in Fermanagh', *Clogher Record: Journal of the Clogher Historical Society* xiv/3 (1993), 54–66.

[25] Deposition of Alice Champyn, 14 Apr 1642, TCD, MS 835, fo. 196v.

[26] Ohlmeyer, *Making Ireland English*, 64–83.

[27] Deposition of Patrick O'Brian, 29 Jan. 1642, TCD, MS 835, fo. 82v.

[28] Kalyvas, *The logic of violence*, 336.

[29] Deposition of Arthur Culme, 9 May 1642, TCD, MS 833, fo. 127.

lion in Cavan.[30] Within the rebel movement in Cavan, however, there were dissenting voices. Compare the attitudes of Philip MacMulmore O'Reilly with those of Donnell, Mulmore and Cahir O'Reilly who each controlled a portion of the rebel army in Cavan.[31] Philip MacMulmore advocated a more conciliatory approach towards English settlers. He negotiated with the townsfolk for the peaceful handing over of Belturbet to the Irish rebels.[32] Upon seeing John Whitman, a deponent, stripped of his clothes, Philip MacMulmore compensated him.[33] The attempts of more extreme elements among the Cavan rebels to attack the house of William Bedell, bishop of Kilmore, where hundreds of dispossessed settlers had taken refuge, were thwarted by Philip MacMulmore who became increasingly disenchanted with the movement.[34] He later apologised to settlers for what they had suffered and criticised his fellow insurgents openly at a crowded meeting held in his house: 'you told me you had the kings broad seal to rise in armes, that you would but disarme the English and putt a gard into Bellturbet, and so suffer them all to enioy their goods, but you have deciued me, and I will beleiue you no longer'. Philip MacMulmore admitted later that the rebellion struck at their lawful king, contradicting earlier claims made by Sir Phelim O'Neill; this led to his arrest by Philip McHugh McShane O'Reilly, commander of the Cavan rebels.[35] A more hard-line element subsequently emerged in Cavan that spoke of 'denying the kinge', and claimed that 'the English have enjoyed their lands wrongfully and for too long'; a possible testimony to the influence of the Maguires in Fermanagh.[36] By the middle of November, it was clear that leaders of Irish society were actively encouraging members of the lower social orders to join in by preying on popular dissatisfaction with the colonial order. Cahir O'Reilly lamented that 'it was a pity that all the English in England & Ireland were not hang[e]d drawne

---

[30] Ciska Neyts, 'Mapping the outbreak of the rebellion: robberies in County Cavan (October 1641)', in Eamon Darcy, Annaleigh Margey and Elaine Murphy (eds), *The 1641 depositions and the Irish rebellion*, London 2012, 35–50.

[31] For a more detailed examination of Philip MacMulmore's conduct during the outbreak of the rebellion see Cope, 'The experience of survival', 295–316.

[32] Deposition of Richard Lewis, 30 Dec. 1641, TCD, MS 833, fo. 34v; deposition of Thomas Smith, 8 Feb. 1644, fo. 265.

[33] Deposition of John Whitman, 14 July 1643, TCD, MS 832, fo. 58.

[34] 'A true relation of the life and death of the right reverend father in God William Bedell, lord bishop of Kilmore in Ireland', in Thomas Wharton Jones (ed.), *Camden Miscellany* civ, London 1872, 65, 78, 80–1; deposition of Thomas Crant, 13 Feb. 1642, TCD, MS 832, fo. 219.

[35] Deposition of Richard Castledine, 19 July 1642, TCD, MS 833, fo. 115; deposition of Elizabeth Woodhouse, 4 Jan. 1642, fo. 90; deposition of John Whitman, 14 July 1643, fo. 273v; examination of Arthur Culme, 11 May 1642, fo. 209.

[36] Deposition of Thomas Taylor, 3 Jan. 1642, ibid. fo. 68; deposition of Dorothy Moigne, 23 Apr. 1642, fo. 36; deposition of Richard Lewis, 30 Dec. 1641, fo. 34v.

and quartered before now'. Edmond O'Reilly cursed the lords justices with 'divers opprobrious words'.[37]

There are numerous instances of local Irish leaders granting their followers permission to execute Protestant settlers. Phelim O'Neill is alleged to have ordered his followers to murder Lieutenant James Maxwell.[38] After the battle of Kilrush, Walter Bagnel allegedly ordered the 'rude multitude' to execute John Stone and his wife.[39] Joseph Wheeler blamed Lord Mountgarret for encouraging others to join the rebellion and argued that he set 'an example to all the rest of the wicked Irish to rise also into Rebellion'.[40] John Walsh, a clerk from Kildare, claimed that the earl of Kildare organised the local gentry in October 1641 to defend the county. His subordinates, however, took this as a licence to seize goods and castles in the name of the rebellion.[41] Work by Nicholas Canny and William Smyth has shown how in certain regions members of the gentry and nobility organised the rebellion.[42] Scholars must be wary, however; quite often deponents may have deliberately sought to implicate prominent members of Irish society in an outbreak of popular violence, or they may have blamed them when they just refused to act in their defence.[43]

Aside from recruiting militias, local authorities organised community meetings. Here letters and texts were read aloud, and speeches were made encouraging popular participation.[44] Public readings of 'popular' texts informed a wider audience of the course of the rebellion and captured the hearts and minds of the native population. In one instance, Meredith Hanmer's 'Chronicle of Ireland', published in 1633, proved popular among Catholics in Dublin. John Kerdiff, a prisoner of Friar Malone, self-styled chaplain of the 'Catholic army', witnessed the reading of Hanmer's 'Chronicle', 'out of w[hi]ch they animated the Rebells with ye story of ye Danes discom-fiture of ye Irish tho[u]gh for the most p[ar]t unarmed and paraled the history of al[l] these tymes'.[45] In other cases small dramas or plays were enacted or read aloud among the Irish rebels. Consider 'a dialogue between Crosse and Gibbett' composed, most likely, in the first three months of

---

[37] Deposition of Elizabeth Gough, 8 Feb. 1642, ibid. fo. 2; deposition of Ambrose Bedell, 26 Oct. 1642, fo. 105v.

[38] Deposition of Robert Maxwell, 22 Aug. 1642, TCD, MS 809, fo. 9.

[39] Deposition of Thomas Clarke, 13 Aug. 1652, TCD, MS 812, fo. 127.

[40] Deposition of Joseph Wheeler and others, 5 July 1643, ibid. fo. 202.

[41] Deposition of John Walsh, 14 July 1645, TCD, MS 813, fo. 306.

[42] Smyth, *Map-making*, 146–7; Canny, *Making Ireland British*, 493.With the availability of the 1641 depositions online more work on the outbreak of the rebellion in various localities may illustrate how the rebellion was organised by members of the Catholic elites.

[43] Eamon Darcy, 'The social order of the 1641 rebellion', in Darcy, Margey and Murphy, *The 1641 depositions*, 97–112.

[44] Smyth, *Map-making*, 147.

[45] Deposition of John Kerdiff, 28 Feb. 1642, TCD, MS 839, fo. 15.

the rebellion. The 'dialogue' survived as it was transcribed by a deponent, Thomas Crant, who handed it over to Henry Jones, head of the deposition commission. From there the 'dialogue' was passed on to James Butler, the earl of Ormond, in March 1642. It is revealing that Crosse, one of the characters, represented an Irishman. He was aggrieved by the loss of religious, economic and political privileges. The plantations and the arrival of an unruly settler population from England angered Crosse the most. Gibbett was a member of the New English community; unconciliatory, negative, brash and largely unsympathetic to the plight of the Irish. The tone throughout the document reflected widespread discontent at the gradual loss of identity among the native Irish community.

The Irishman, Crosse, asked 'why feare yo[u] this, do not the Puritans sit/ In parliament theile take a course that fitt/ to suppress the Irish & out of hand/ Banish al popery fro[m] this land'. In Gibbett's reply Crosse stood condemned as one of the 'supersticious masse'. Gibbett admitted that 'though I am of Englands scum and com[e] in Raggs', Ireland offered ample opportunities for self advancement. 'Heare I may soone gro[w] great and fill my bags'. To add insult to injury, Gibbett claimed that he could manufacture a noble lineage to secure his claim to his Irish holdings at the expense of the natives. 'Then I may boudly p[ro]claime my self to be Come of some English antient family.' The dialogue ended with a rousing cry for the Irish natives to rise up against the plantations, and their lack of religious privileges:

> This winter all, will put in their Captanes pay
> Yet braue no men, but the[n] expect to see
> The right church soone stord to its liberty
> And I doe hope eare longe to see you backe
> Vnder a load of Puritans to crack
> And he fore tould this change that libertie lives since did chase
> The former divells and serpents fro[m] their place.[46]

Here Crosse echoed the concerns shared by both the Old English and native Irish communities as recorded in the 1641 depositions. Through preying on popular grievances, such as the dangers posed by militant Puritanism and rising religious tensions, rebel leaders sold the rebellion to the wider public. It is clear that members of the gentry and nobility were actively encouraging political engagement at a popular level through evoking the plight of the Catholic Church at the hands of a demonic Protestant enemy.

Other verses and songs adopted the themes explored in the 'dialogue'. Some embraced a more hard-line tone in support of the Irish rebellion. A song composed about Sir Phelim O'Neill celebrated his 'burnings & wastings

---

[46] 'A dialogue between Crosse and Gibbett', c. 1642, Bodleian Library, Oxford, MS Carte 2, fos 342–7.

of the Country' and how he had 'brought in Christmas before its time'.[47] The confederates at Kilkenny also composed verses to promote their movement. In a poem that circulated from 1642 and was printed in 1647, they voiced their allegiance to the king and justified their resort to arms: 'Most Gracious Soverainge, grant them we may have/Our ancient Land and Faith: tis all we crave./Your English, and your Scots, (not so content)/Claime all that's Yours, by Act of parliament.'[48] Through verse and ancient prophesies that predicted the triumph of the native Irish over the colonising forces, rebel leaders encouraged widespread popular support for the rebellion. Richard Bourke, a deponent from Fermanagh and prisoner among the rebels, witnessed the reading of 'an English booke printed in [the] Low Countries importing another prophecy of Sct Patrick (in ye handes of one of the Rebells)'. Bourke believed that 'all w[hi]ch prophecies the Rebells conceive to import the extirpation of the English, and the set[t]ling of the whole kindome in the Irish. And their prophecys are very com[m]only confidently & vehemently urged & iustified [by] their preists for vndoubted verities'.[49]

Predictions and ghostly apparitions helped to explain the course of the rebellion and incite support for it. The sight of bloody water near Loughgall in Armagh prompted one 'ould English papist' to instruct his neighbours to endorse the rebellion. Allegedly 'that [bloody] water presaged a great mischeefe & shedding of the English blowd: And therefore [he] incorraged the Irish to goe on against them saying that the Irish cawse was a good one, and that they needed not to feare'.[50] Strangers to Ireland noted how Irish natives attributed great weight to such apparitions. A colleague of the papal legate, Giovanni Rinuccini, observed how Irish people were 'given much to believe in these vain predictions'.[51] Deponents questioned whether such prophecies were sincerely believed or were merely tools to encourage others to join the rebellion. John Kerdiff testified how 'at Newry we found a prophesy much vndervaluing his Majestie whereby may be seen the loyalty of such as would entertaine such fopperies'.[52] Henry Jones later commented cynically that priests and friars 'animate[d] their disciples with some supposed extraordinary prophecies'. He also noted that bards

---

[47] Examination of Michael Harrison, 9 Feb. 1653, TCD, MS 836, fo. 132.

[48] Andrew Carpenter (ed.), *Verse in English from Tudor and Stuart Ireland*, Cork 2003, 227–8; George Wharton, *Bellum hybernicale or Irelands vvarre*, [Oxford] 1647.

[49] Deposition of Richard Bourke, 12 July 1643, TCD, MS 835, fos 238v–239r.

[50] Deposition of Katherine O'Kerry, 19 July 1643, TCD, MS 836, fo. 97.

[51] Giovanni Rinuccini to Cardinal Camillo Pamphili, 20 Nov. 1645, in *The embassy in Ireland of Monsignor G. B. Rinuccini, archbishop of Fermo, in the years 1645–1649 published from the original mss in the Rinuccini library* tr. by Annie Hutton, ed. Guiseppe Aiazza, Dublin 1873, 87.

[52] Deposition of John Kerdiff, 28 Feb. 1642, TCD, MS 839, fo. 15.

continually p[re]sent at the frequent riotous meetings ... dayly tickle their cares w[i]th songs and rithmes, setting forth the valiant acts of this or that notorious rebell in former tim[e]s, the defeats at such or such a places given to the English, prophesies of their future freedome from the Crowne of England, and reproaches upon our nation.[53]

The power of prophecies as a means of legitimising violence has oft been commented upon.[54] Canny has suggested that such rumours also facilitated the war effort and recruitment drive in Leinster.[55]

The readings of letters, texts, prophecies and verse raises an important question about audience during this period. Evidence suggests that during the 1640s public meetings were another valuable method of communication that facilitated political involvement at a popular level. So much so that in May 1659 Henry Cromwell banned such gatherings in an effort to prevent popular support for the restoration of the monarchy.[56] Here leaders could discuss the latest events, military strategies and matters of local governance with the wider community, and encourage support for the rebellion. From December 1641 until the end of 1642 native Irish and Old English elites organised meetings to discuss the course of the rebellion. For example, in Mullingar between four and five hundred people gathered before their leaders who read out a letter that recounted how the rebels needed men and arms to conclude the siege at Drogheda. The message returned by those in attendance was one of overwhelming support. One witness recalled how 'the whole assembly cryed out that they shold haue aide & that euerie one would goe in person rather then faile'.[57] In other areas these meetings also served as recruitment drives. In Wexford it was alleged that one James Bryan had a bag filled with 'two thousand billets and libells' that urged contemporaries to 'lay our heads together and march together'.[58] Meetings were not simply about enlistment, however. Local commanders could discuss the treatment of settlers, prisoners and the arrival of rival troops in the locality.[59]

The circulation of letters among rebel leaders served two purposes: first, they distributed news about their movements; second, if the letters conveyed

[53] 'A treatise giving a representation of the grand rebellion in Ireland', BL., MS Harleian 5999, fos 15, 24.

[54] Horowitz, The deadly ethnic riot, 74–5, 82, 155–8, 528–9; Walter, 'Performative violence'.

[55] Canny, Making Ireland British, 518. See also Smyth, Map-making, 121.

[56] By the lord lieutenant of Ireland, Henry Cromwell, Dublin 1659.

[57] Examination of John Smith, 29 June 1642, TCD, MS 817, fo. 70. See also Maurice Cuffe, 'A briefe narrative of the beginning and continuance of the commotion in the Co of Clare', BL, MS Add. 20,100, fo. 3.

[58] Examination of Peter Hooper, 27 Jan. 1654, TCD, MS 819, fo. 33.

[59] Deposition of John Shrawley, 23 Apr. 1644, TCD, MS 831, fo. 75v; Canny, Making Ireland British, 478; deposition of John Smith, 29 June 1642, TCD, MS 817, fo. 69.

good news, they could be read out to encourage support for the rebellion. Reports of the impending arrival in Ireland of troops from Spain and France offered one such opportunity. Francis Sachervall, a deponent held in the custody of Sir Phelim O'Neill, recorded how Catholic priests delighted in this news. Sachervall testified that priests with 'forged and feigned letters would reade and publishe at Masse and then dispers many Coppies of them vp and downe the Countrey'.[60] The reading of letters to large public gatherings was one of the most effective means of communication between rebel leaders and local civilians. In Cavan they regularly read out letters describing news from England and Dublin.[61]

At the heart of early modern communities lay the marketplace; it served as a platform for communication, offering a forum for informal information exchange, storytelling, gossiping as well as the presentation of official proclamations.[62] Most proclamations were ordered to be delivered 'in the marketplace of every market town, between ten and two o'clock'. Many deponents witnessed the reading of confederate (or rebel) proclamations in the marketplace.[63] Marketplaces were convenient venues for announcements to reach a wider audience as they were usually attended by large crowds from the locality. When the rebellion began to take hold across the country in the winter of 1641-2, marketplaces became convenient centres for the communication of news about the rebellion and confederate wars. Here, locals could learn of the coming of 'the English army' or other troop movements.[64] The logical place for any rebel movement to gather their forces upon taking the town was the marketplace. Jane Beare, a settler living in Armagh, recalled how Phelim O'Neill and his army convened at the town's marketplace before declaring that they would

> burne the towne And gather vp all the Englishmen And Carrie them downe to Charlemount And as the Irish themselfes did say thay Asked him what thay should doe with the women & Children he Replied that thay might make gunpowder of them if thay would And by *his power &* the said permission.[65]

As local Catholic figures of authority organised the rebellion another central issue emerged: it was widely believed that the rebellion was a pre-emptive

---

[60] Deposition of Francis Sachervall, 21 July 1642, TCD, MS 836, fos 109v–110r.

[61] Deposition of Richard Castledine, 19 July 1642, TCD, MS 833, fo. 116.

[62] James Masschaele, 'The public space of the marketplace in medieval England', *Speculum* lxxvii (2002), 383–421.

[63] Proclamation by the general assembly of the confederation of Kilkenny, 4 July 1645, *CSPI, 1633–47*, 404; examination of Robert Welsh, 30 Mar. 1643, TCD, MS 810, fos 216–17; examination of Faghny Mc Lisagh Farrell, 19 Jan. 1653, MS 817, fos 235–6; deposition of Nicholas Simpson, 6 Apr. 1643, MS 834, fo. 184.

[64] Examination of Henry Stokes, 25 July 1643, TCD, MS 812, fos 145–6.

[65] Examination of Jane Beare, 26 Feb. 1653, TCD, MS 836, fos 161–2.

strike against the intentions of Protestant authorities to root out Catholicism in Ireland. Donald Horowitz has convincingly shown that ethnic riots follow three phases: rumours, violence and killing. Rumours that precede ethnic violence often predict the outbreak of violence and the course that the violence would take.[66] Deponents and rebels alike recognised this. As Thomas Crant testified, Irish Catholics, upon hearing of the intentions of the Puritan parliament to extirpate them, 'they having Intelligence of that, Therefore they did begine first and would now continue and that all the whole kingdome did Rise'.[67] Prominent leaders of the rebellion passed these whispers on. In March 1642 Lord Mountgarret delivered a petition to Ormond declaring that 'the English and Scotts combyned and joined in a petition to his Majestie to bee lycenced … *to* come into Ireland with the Bible in one hand, the Sword in the other for to plant their Puritan Anarchicall Religion amongst vs, otherwise after to distroye vs'. Furthermore, this initiative, according to Mountgarret, had approval from Puritans across England, Scotland and Ireland.[68] Others reported that 'The parliament of England had *decreed* to force them to goe to Church or hange them.'[69] Many believed that Protestant forces intended to destroy Ireland's Catholics and so the violence that ensued 23 October 1641 was characterised by these rumours.

During the first hours of the rebellion Sir Phelim O'Neill summoned prominent members of the settler community in Armagh to explain his motivations and intentions to them. He offered assurances that he and his followers intended them no harm. He publicly blamed the anti-Catholic 'Puritan' parliament in London which forced him to seize arms held by English and Scottish settlers in the North.[70] In a proclamation of 24 October, O'Neill claimed that his actions amounted to a 'defence and liberty of ourselves and the natives of the Irish nation' as opposed to an attack upon the king or his colonial administration in Ireland. Manuscript copies of this proclamation circulated around the country, reaching as far as the lords justices in Dublin.[71] One of O'Neill's kinsmen, Turlogh O'Neill, informed his Armagh neighbours that the rebels would hand confiscated fortifications in Ulster

---

66 Horowitz, *The deadly ethnic riot*, 71–3.

67 Deposition of Thomas Crant, 13 Feb. 1642, TCD, MS 832, fo. 212v.

68 Richard Butler, Viscount Mountgarret, to Ormond, 25 Mar. 1642, TCD, MS 840, fos 25r–26v.

69 Quotation from deposition of William Raicye, 8 Jan. 1642, TCD, MS 834, fo. 137. There are numerous other examples, however: deposition of Donatus Conner, 28 Oct. 1642, MS 818, fo. 111v; deposition of Samuel Franck, 1 Feb. 1643, MS 815, fo. 326v; deposition of Robert Maxwell, 22 Aug. 1642, MS 809, fo. 6v.

70 Examination of Capt Thomas Chambers, undated, TCD, MS 836, fo. 37; deposition of Thomas Chambers, 2 June 1642, fo. 42; proclamation of Phelim O'Neill and Rory Maguire, 4 Nov 1641, fo. 18r–v. For an understanding of Phelim's actions at this moment see Canny, *Making Ireland British*, 471–2.

71 Copies of proclamation of Sir Phelim O'Neill and others, *CSPI, 1633–47*, 342.

over to armies fighting in the name of the king but not to the English parliament.[72] They later justified themselves by claiming that the king approved their actions.[73] In a testament to their political awareness, they explained that a commission would come from the king in Scotland, not England.[74] Claims of royal authority aided their attempts to control interpretations of their actions; in the words of the lords justices this 'seduced [volunteers] to their party'.[75] The belief that the English parliament intended to extirpate Irish Catholics provided a way for people to engage in violence and legitimised their actions as a means of defence in the face of an increasingly aggressive 'Puritan' parliament, and a tool to mobilise the wider population to join in the rebellion.

Rumours can be either false or true. False rumours can be disseminated either sincerely or in a deliberate attempt to eschew truth. Yet, a market had to exist for the rumour to take hold among the rioting population.[76] The rumours that precipitated the outbreak of violence exaggerated the strength of the settler community, accentuated the vulnerability of the native Irish and facilitated the engagement of the lower social orders in the assault on the Protestant population. It is easy to see how in the confusion of news, information, fact and rumour, deponents failed to see the ordering of violence that followed the outbreak of rebellion. Leaders of the rebellion tapped into popular discontent with the established order of Protestantism and English rule. They even provided the lower social orders with the necessary information to justify their actions (in the name of the king) or taunts to jeer their victims with. Dublin women were accused of shouting 'Siggy Sassinagh, Siggy Sassinagh, that is there comes English, which this deponent conceiveth was to sett on the people in armes'.[77] Confidence in the success of the rebel movement, as well as the profession of oaths and the exhortation of priests who claimed that the rebels had received an indemnity from the pope, and claims of royal support, added further legitimacy and encouraged others to suspend the normalities of peaceful society and engage in violent behaviour. Guilt was easily transferred to the settler population who

---

[72] Deposition of Charity Chappell, 20 July 1642, TCD, MS 836, fo. 44v.

[73] Deposition of Adam Glover, 4 Jan. 1642, TCD, MS 833, fo. 1; deposition of Elizabeth Woodhouse, 4 Jan. 1642, fo. 90.

[74] Deposition of Richard Jackson, 26 Jan. 1642, ibid. fo. 18; deposition of Thomas Taylor, 9 Jan. 1642, fo. 70v. At this time Charles I was in the process of negotiating with the Scottish parliament for greater recognition of their rights.

[75] Deposition of William Fitzgerald, 4 June 1642, TCD, MS 836, fo. 82v; deposition of Francis Sachervall, 21 July 1642, fo. 110; lords justices and council to Robert Sidney, second earl of Leicester and lord lieutenant of Ireland, 14 Dec. 1641, HMC, *Calendar of the manuscripts of the marquess of Ormonde, K.P. preserved at Kilkenny Castle* n.s. ii, London 1903, 42.

[76] Horowitz, *The deadly ethnic riot*, 75.

[77] Deposition of Edward Leech, 18 Mar. 1645, TCD, MS 810, fo. 245.

were blamed for the need for violence.[78] Yet, if one looks at the ordering of events, the targeting of victims and the geography of violence it is clear that the Irish rebels were attempting to show their settler neighbours who the new local authorities were and to portray their authority as absolute. These were violent acts of symbolic and strategic importance. Irish rebels resorted, therefore, to violent protest as they had done several times since the Reformation.[79]

Identifying the target group is difficult because in the early stages of the rising it was claimed that the Scottish commnunity would be left unscathed.[80] Historians have largely agreed that the rebels did this so as to divide the two communities and hence enhance the rebels' chances of success.[81] Rioters commonly blamed the 'Puritan parliament' in London and expressed fears that were shared among all the social orders. It was even claimed that the English parliament intended to force all English Catholics to attend Protestant services.[82] Ritualistic attacks on English and Scottish animals, however, suggest an added ethnic dimension. English cows had collops cut off whilst still alive and were slowly tortured to death.[83] Consider also the example of the trial of English cattle held allegedly by Irish rebels in Mayo in 1642. One witness, Walter Bourke, reported how they

> could not endure to see a beast of English breed to live amongst them, and not onely consent to destroy the Cattle, but w[i]th all derision and scoffing carriaged vsed to bring a booke before the cowe or sheepe of English straine they formerly tooke from the English and asked them whether they could reade and in case they were disposed at that tyme to spare the killing of them, one answered they could read and bidd their apparances should bee entred, and of otherwise disposed to kill them.[84]

Quite often, those who are targeted were figures of authority or of superior social status.[85] Thus, the rebellion was an attempt to wrest control away from English and Protestant authorities in Ireland.

The centrality of the marketplace to early modern life made it a convenient place to perform violent acts as a means of warning the settler population to accept their new authority. It was a very visible place to enact

---

[78] Horowitz, *The deadly ethnic riot*, 96; Kalyvas, *The logic of violence*, 142–4.

[79] Clodagh Tait, 'Riots, rescues and "Grene Bowes": Catholics and protest in Ireland', in Robert Armstrong and Tadg Ó hAnnracháin, *Insular Christianity: alternative models to the Church in Britain and Ireland*, c. 1570–c. 1700, 66–87. I am grateful to Dr Tait for providing me with an advance copy of this article.

[80] Horowitz, *The deadly ethnic riot*, 81–7.

[81] Canny, *Making Ireland British*, 480–4.

[82] Deposition of George Creichton, 15 Apr. 1643, TCD, MS 833, fo. 227v.

[83] Deposition of Robert Maxwell, 22 Aug. 1642, TCD, MS 809, fo. 9.

[84] Deposition of Walter Bourke, 11 Dec. 1642, TCD, MS 831, fo. 169.

[85] Horowitz, *The deadly ethnic riot*, 166.

THE IRISH REBELLION OF 1641

violence, so much so that Martha Lone's neighbours warned her not to attend the market, for if she did, she 'wo[u]ld be killed there'.[86] Before the Portadown massacre the prisoners were paraded at the marketplace and then cast into the river Bann.[87] After the outbreak of rebellion in Tralee, the local Protestant community fled to the castle there, where they were besieged by members of the Catholic elites, including Florence McCarthy and Donnell McCarthy. When the rebels successfully captured the castle some of the more prominent members of the settler community were executed on the spot. Special attention was given, however, to Lawrence Trisham, the gaoler of Tralee prison, who was hanged at the market cross in the town.[88] Many others reported the hanging of people at the market cross.[89] This act was no doubt intended as a very graphic warning to others in the vicinity of the new structures of power at play. Such symbolic acts of violence challenged the colonial order. In 1643 Charles Coote dispatched a messenger to Castle Coote in Athlone. The messenger was subsequently captured by the local rebel commander, Tibbott McAuley: 'the poore messinger aforesaid was publiquely, and before a great assembly hanged to death'.[90] The marketplace therefore offered a very public venue for the cleansing of the Protestant and settler populations.

A common survival strategy adopted by settlers was to convert to Catholicism in order to preserve their lives. This practice became so widespread that the deposition commission began to record the names of those who converted. Sometimes, however, conversion did not guarantee one's safety. George Atbee, an Englishman, converted to Catholicism, and joined the household of Sir Jasper Herbert. Upon attending a market at Phillipstown in King's County, William Owie, a rebel, apprehended Atbee. He then 'knocked out [his] brains with a clubb & hee lay dead in the streete vntill Euening'. The very next week, Owie repeated this performance with another apostate.[91] It is clear, therefore, that such public displays of killing served to remind the settler population, whose loyalty and collaboration was in doubt, that the native Irish held the reins of authority in their locality. Such violence, in short, was strategic and tactical.[92]

One characteristic of ethnic riots is the targeting of rival group members' bodies and property. Attacks on the property of the target population served as a precursor to attacks on settlers themselves.[93] In the 1641 rebel-

---

86 Examination of Martha Lone, 23 Feb. 1654, TCD, MS 830, fo. 242v.
87 Deposition of Elizabeth Price, 26 June 1642, TCD, MS 836, fo. 101v.
88 Deposition of Arthur Blenerhasset, 25 Feb. 1643, MS 828, fo. 199v.
89 Examination of Alice Williams, 13 Sept. 1652, TCD, MS 826, fo. 146v.
90 Deposition of Thomas Le Strange, 12 Jan. 1644, TCD, MS 814, fo. 231v.
91 Deposition of James Dowdall, 9 Mar. 1644, ibid. fo. 217v.
92 Kalyvas, The logic of violence, 27, 88–9.
93 Horowitz, The deadly ethnic riot, 72.

lion Protestant artefacts became targets for Catholic aggression. Rebels also attacked buildings where services of the reformed faith were celebrated, and prominent English-style houses – a violent rejection of the colonial order.[94] Those who owed money to members of the settler community immediately destroyed all evidence of their indebtedness, suggesting a meaning to the mayhem. As in the French wars of religion there was a religious ordering to the violence that also served as a protest against colonisation. At the marketplace in Belturbet, the O'Reilly rebels collected together Protestant books and Bibles and burned them. Other deponents also described the mass burnings of Protestant Bibles and books in prominent public places such as the town market square. In Mountrath, for example, some rebels tore two Bibles into pieces 'with most horrible indignation telling the English dogges as they called them should neuer come to howle there more'.[95] As Protestant artefacts were destroyed, Protestant churches were also attacked. One Bryan Lynch, a convert to Catholicism, entered the church in Power-scourt and burned the pews, pulpits, chests and Bibles there.[96] In Armagh the rebels entered the church and proceeded to burn the pews, pulpit and all the 'best' parts of the church. This was followed with the ritual defecation on Protestant Bibles there.[97] In Belturbet church, seats were targeted and burnt along with Protestant books and Bibles.[98] Christopher Parmenter, a Donegal gentleman, recorded how most of the Protestant churches were set alight in Tyrone, except those that served as arms stores.[99] Similarly in Carnew, County Wicklow, the pulpit was torn down while the seats were set on fire and the church destroyed.[100]

After the Reformation in Ireland, prominent Catholic churches were consecrated for Protestant services. In certain towns local rebels reclaimed these buildings for the practice of Catholicism. In New Ross, County Wexford, priests encouraged the locals to dig up Protestant corpses (dubbed 'heretiques') in order to consecrate the church.[101] Some practising Protestants were killed in the grounds of their churches, possibly in an attempt to purify the area of 'heretical' influences. Their bodies were prominently displayed for all to see.[102] Sometimes services were interrupted and the congregation

---

94 Smyth, *Map-making*, 142–3.
95 Deposition of Richard Parsons, 24 Feb. 1642, TCD, MS 833, fo. 279; deposition of Henry Bolton, 21 Feb. 1643, MS 814, fo. 161; deposition of Dennis O'Brennan, 12 Apr. 1642, MS 815, fo. 217.
96 Deposition of Henry Fisher, 25 Jan. 1642, TCD, MS 811, fo. 47r–v.
97 Deposition of John Montgomery, 26 Jan. 1642, TCD, MS 834, fos 131v–132r.
98 Deposition of John Anderson, 11 July 1642, TCD, MS 833, fo. 99.
99 Deposition of Christopher Parmenter, 28 July 1643, TCD, MS 839, fo. 136r–v.
100 Deposition of Calcott Chambre, 24 May 1645, TCD, MS 811, fo. 175.
101 Deposition of William Whalley, 5 Sept. 1642, TCD, MS 818, fo. 24v.
102 Deposition of Thomas Poe, 19 Sept. 1643, TCD, MS 839, fo. 138; deposition of Susanna Wyne, 4 Feb. 1642, MS 835, fo. 189.

was attacked. In the words of one deponent, the rebels claimed that 'they were at the divils service and it was a good deed to burne the house over their heads'.[103] Possession of churches and the purification of the church-yards meant that many bereaved Protestants could not bury their dead there. Margaret Caesar, from Carrickmacross in County Monaghan, appealed to the local town marshal for permission to inter her husband in the local churchyard, which he refused. Other deponents had similar complaints or noted that rebels wanted to remove Protestant corpses from such grave-yards.[104] In Meath, the altar, the central focus of the Catholic mass, was restored to its former position.[105] Such actions purged churches of all Protes-tant artefacts and any reminders that 'heretics' had populated them at some point in the past.[106]

Special mention must be given to events in Kildare and Kilkenny – for they captured the imaginations of English printers who reported this event with great interest. The Catholic bishop of Kildare, Ross McGeoghegan, ordered priests and friars in Kildare to reconsecrate the cathedral as Cath-olic. This involved the removal of 'heretic' corpses from the graveyard. Deponents described in horror how their deceased relatives were dug out of the ground, sometimes before their eyes.[107] The corpses were then left exposed to the elements and served as a graphic reminder to the Protes-tant population of the new authority in Kildare. No doubt it traumatised those who remained behind rebel lines. This whole event was preceded by a conference held by McGeoghegan and other local Catholic clerics who had removed the 'chapter chest' from the cathedral in an attempt to purge it of heretical writings. The decision to reconsecrate the cathedral reflected growing confidence in the rebel movement at the time. Many believed that a victory against the forces of Sir Charles Coote at Naas would provide the necessary breathing space to conduct a wholesale extirpation of the 'English' population there.[108]

Victories against state forces offered opportunities for local populations to celebrate their success. After the defeat of a force near Kilkenny town, around 29 September 1642, seven severed heads (of six soldiers and one minister who were part of the defeated army) were brought to the market

---

[103] Deposition of William Murdoghe, 12 Nov. 1642, TCD, MS 833, fo. 175.

[104] Deposition of Margaret Caesar, 26 Apr. 1642, TCD, MS 834, fo. 38v; deposition of Nicholas Simspon, 6 Apr. 1643, MS 834, fo. 184r–v; deposition of William Murdoghe, 12 Nov. 1642, MS 833, fo. 175; deposition of Dennis Kelly, 23 May 1642, MS 816, fo. 184v; deposition of William Metcalfe, 31 Oct. 1642, MS 816, fo. 178; deposition of Nicholas Walsh, 6 June 1642, MS 814, fo. 158; deposition of Mary Woods, 23 Feb. 1642, MS 813, fo. 385.

[105] Deposition of George Gonne, c. 1643?, TCD, MS 816, fo. 105.

[106] Deposition of Joseph Wheeler and others, 5 July 1643, TCD, MS 812, fo. 203v.

[107] Deposition of Thomas Huetson, 15 Feb. 1642, TCD, MS 813, fo. 260r–v.

[108] Deposition of Rebecca Collis, 23 Feb. 1642, ibid. fo. 385v.

square on market day. The rebels, members of the extended Butler clan and the sons of Lord Mountgarret, were accompanied by 'their pip[e]s for ioy playing before them on horse back'. The heads of the soldiers were treated in a slightly different manner from that of Mr Bingham, the minister, which was targeted by local women:

> Elize Butler a reputed mother of seuerall bastards yet the daughter of the said Lord Mountgarret stabbd cutt and slasht those heads: the said Alice Butler drawing her skeine slasht at the face of the said W[illia]m Alfrey & hitt him on the nose: & those that could but gott a blow stab at those heades seemed to account themselues happie. And the rebells then and there putt a gagg in the mowth of the said Mr Bingham the minister & laying the leafe of a bible before him bade him preach saying his mowth open wyde enowghe.[109]

The choice of the marketplace was symbolic for a number of reasons. Not only did it provide a visible arena for the local population to witness their recent triumph over an 'English' force, it was also the site where, according to some deponents, Catholics had been executed by the state. William Lucas witnessed the trial of Captain Chambers, a 'heretic' who was brought to be gibbeted at Kilkenny market cross but was moved away from there for he was 'not worthy to die where one of their religion was putt to death'.[110]

The violence that accompanied the outbreak of the 1641 rebellion, therefore, aimed to strike at English and Scottish manifestations of colonial power. There was an added religious dimension to this as Protestant corpses, bodies, artefacts and churches were targeted as a means of expressing popular discontent with the emerging colonial order in Ireland and to celebrate Catholic identity; this explains why ministers and local figures of authority were mainly targeted by the rebels. The demonisation of the enemy as Protestant, attacks on Protestant ministers and churches, suggests that many were mobilised to defend the Catholic faith. While they may not have attempted to cleanse the countryside of aberrant ethnic populations, deponents certainly believed that this was the case and as such the 1641 depositions also offer a keyhole through which historians can view the psychological trauma that many experienced during the 1640s.

The mythology of massacre in Ireland

The lack of centralised information regarding the rebellion meant that the oral relation of news was subject to change, interpretation, elaboration and exaggeration. Hence, much of the controversy about the 1641 depositions has focused on hearsay and eye-witness testimonies and has debated

---

[109] Deposition of Joseph Wheeler and others, 5 July 1643, TCD, MS 812, fo. 203; deposition of William Lucas, 16 Aug. 1643, fo. 220.

[110] Deposition of William Lucas, 16 Aug. 1643, ibid. fo. 220v.

whether they verify that a massacre of the Protestant population did occur. Local commanders were aware of the malleable nature of oral news reports and acted to influence the public's interpretation of their intentions. Such actions were a means of expressing authority, exerting control and ensuring collaboration from local populations. The failure of the original plan for the rising meant that some areas were under settler control and others under native Irish rebels. The success of their war effort hinged on popular support and civilian behaviour. This explains the organisation of meetings, the readings of letters and texts and expressions of summary justice against the settler community. They rallied Irish Catholics behind their banner. With the breakdown of authority, loyalties were dictated not by political preferences but by survival instincts.[111] Expressions of military control and performative violence could ensure the collaboration of civilian populations who were frequently threatened.[112] Therefore, the outbreak of violence served as a means of dissuading the settler population from taking military action against the rebels. It is possible to capture the success of this tactic through an investigation of deponents' comments on atrocities that they witnessed and heard about. Such hearsay evidence captures the trauma of the settler population and the effectiveness of these gruesome displays of violence.[113]

The best example of this was the drowning of 100 Protestants over the bridge of the River Bann in Portadown. Twenty-eight people deposed about the incident, one of the bloodiest in Ireland during the 1640s. Only one of the twenty-eight deponents witnessed the event. All the rest related what they had heard about it. According to William Clarke, sole survivor of the atrocity, around 100 prisoners were driven six miles 'like hogs', 'during which time manie of them were sore tortured by strongling and halfe hanging and many other crueltye[s]'. Upon their arrival at the river the prisoners were forced into the water with swords and pikes. Other prisoners who were ordered onto the bridge found that it had been 'cut doune in the midst' causing them to be 'thrust downe headlong into the said river'. Those who swam to save their lives were shot. Clarke secured his escape by bribing the rebels.[114] As the sole survivor of this massacre, it can be assumed that he, along with the Irish rebels who committed these actions, disseminated subsequent reports of what had happened. Thus, it is interesting to compare how the story of the Portadown massacre changed during its passage through the web of oral communication.

Elements of what happened were exaggerated, tweaked and fabricated. Clarke related how 100 Protestants had been killed having been driven from a prison camp at Loughgall. Initially others from Portadown began to assimi-

---

111 Kalyvas, The logic of violence, 91–3.

112 Ibid. 111, 117.

113 Smyth, Map-making, 103–66.

114 Deposition of William Clarke, 7 Jan. 1642, TCD, MS 836, fos 2r–3v.

late the information related by Clarke, and/or the rebels who committed the atrocity. Alice Greg, Richard Warren and George Pipes all testified how they had heard about the murder of 100 Protestants at Portadown.[115] Fellow prisoners based in Loughgall related how 100 people perished at the Bann who had earlier been held in captivity among them.[116] This figure was exaggerated almost immediately as the story passed from mouth to mouth. Ann Smith, from Kilmore parish in Armagh, heard how 150 Protestants had been killed there.[117] Joyce Kinde, Richard Newberry, Margaret Bromely, Christian Stanshawe, Francis Sachervall, Edward Saltenstall, 'Mrs Simpson', Thomas Green, Elizabeth Trewman, Ellenor Fullerton, Katherine Coke and Philip Taylor all testified to a range of numbers of people killed from 140 to 196.[118] The common link between these higher totals is that all the deponents gave their testimonies after Clarke, thus the story had time to circulate and change in accordance with the dynamics of oral culture.[119] The only aberration is provided by the deposition of John Wisedom who deposed on 8 February 1642, roughly four months after the atrocity. Wisedom heard from William Pitchfork, a neighbour, that eighty Protestants had perished. It is interesting to note that as the story passed through Monaghan a deponent, Roger Holland, testified that he had heard from the Irish rebels that only sixty-eight persons were drowned at the bridge.[120] At the same time, however, two rebels told Joane Constable that 156 Protestants were murdered there.[121] In some cases deponents recorded the discrepancies between the various accounts of the atrocity circulating by word of mouth. John Kerdiff related

---

115 Deposition of Alice Greg, 21 July 1643, ibid. fo. 95v; deposition of Richard Warren, 7 Jan. 1642, fo. 10; deposition of George Pipes, 24 July 1643, fo. 100.

116 Deposition of Nehemiah Richardson, 20 Apr. 1642, ibid. fo. 67.

117 Deposition of Ann Smith and Margaret Clark, 16 Mar. 1643, ibid. fo. 73v.

118 Deposition of Joyce Kinde, 10 Feb. 1653, ibid. fo. 143; deposition of Richard Newberry, 27 June 1642, fo. 60v (Hillary Simms is mistaken in her analysis of Newberry's deposition where she stated that Newberry testified to the murder of eighty Protestants: 'Violence in County Armagh, 1641', in Brian Mac Cuarta [ed.], *Ulster 1641: aspects of the rising*, Belfast, 1993, 123–38 at p. 126); deposition of Margaret Bromely, 21 Aug. 1642, fo. 40; deposition of Christian Stanshawe, 23 July 1642, fo. 75v; deposition of Francis Sachervall, 21 July 1642, fo. 109; deposition of Edward Saltenstall, 1 June 1642, fo. 70v; relation of Mr Simpson, n.d., fo. 21; deposition of Thomas Green, 10 Nov. 1643, fo. 94; deposition of Elizabeth Trewman, 14 May 1643, fo. 117; deposition of Ellenor Fullerton, 16 Sept. 1642, fo. 50v; deposition of Katherine Coke, 4 Feb. 1644, fo. 92; deposition of Philip Taylor, 7 Feb. 1642, fo. 7.

119 Clarke deposed on 7 Jan. 1642 along with Richard Warren (who was a fellow prisoner). Both deposed that 100 Protestants had perished there. All the deponents are mentioned in n. 118 above.

120 Deposition of Roger Holland, 4 Mar. 1642, TCD, MS 834, fo. 118. Others in Monaghan testified that they had heard about the loss of 140 at Portadown: deposition of John Montgomery, 26 Jan. 1642, fo. 131v.

121 Deposition of Joane Constable, 6 June 1643, TCD, MS 836, fo. 88.

how he had heard that 'about threescore 80 or an 100 of the inhabitants of Lough[g]all were cast into ye rever & there drowned'.[122]

Aside from the different numbers of people killed, details within the story told by Clarke changed also. He originally testified as to how the victims of the assault were tortured while being driven to the river. Others began to elaborate on this and malleable details within the story began to change. Philip Taylor had been 'credibly tould and beeleveth' that some of the victims of Portadown had their hands tied behind their backs while cast into the river.[123] In contrast, other details remained the same; Owen Frankland and Christian Stanshawe reported how they had heard that those who attempted to swim to shore were thwarted by 'the rebells [who] with their musketts knockt out their braynes'.[124] As the news of this atrocity spread through the northern counties providential details were added to the story, as settlers and rebels alike attributed godly significance to the event. Katherine Coke, from Clanbrassil in Armagh, returned to the scene of the atrocity nine days after it occurred. She saw 'a vision or spiritt in the shape of a man' in the river, 'in the place of drowneing bolt upright brest high'. The ghostly man stood 'with elevated and closed handes & stood in that posture there' until the arrival of the English army in the area. After this other ghosts appeared that she 'heard of but saw not' who made 'much scriching & strang[e] noises'.[125] Stories about ghostly visions and sightings spread rapidly through the northern counties. Thomas Green reported how he had heard that 'the carcasse of one of the men Protestants drowned there would be noe meanes be gotten to sinck nor to goe away with the streame'.[126] Joane Constable described how 'divers' of the rebels discussed the apparitions. The blood of those murdered on the bridge 'remained ... and would not be washed away'. More ghosts began to appear, 'somtymes of men & somtymes of women brest highe above the water'. Like Alice Greg, Constable noted how the visions 'did most extremely and fearfully skrich & cry out for vengeance and blowd against the Irish that hadd murthered their bodies there'. The effect on the native Irish was telling, 'their cryes & skritchings did soe terrify the Irish thereabouts'.[127]

The rumours of these ghostly sightings travelled along the oral grapevine through the north-east of Ireland. Irish rebels were also concerned about the appearances of the visions. Owen Roe O'Neill, a confederate commander who had served in the Spanish army, hearing of these apparitions on his return to Ireland in June 1642, travelled from Dundalk to the site of the

---

122 Deposition of John Kerdiff, 28 Feb. 1642, TCD, MS 839, fo. 13v.
123 Deposition of Philip Taylor, 7 Feb. 1642, TCD, MS 836, fo. 7.
124 Deposition of Owen Frankland and Christian Stanshawe, 23 July 1642, ibid. fo. 75v.
125 Deposition of Katherine Coke, 4 Feb. 1644, ibid. fo. 92.
126 Deposition of Thomas Green, 10 Nov. 1643, ibid. fo. 94v.
127 Deposition of Joane Constable, 6 June 1643, ibid. fo. 89r–v.

atrocity. According to Elizabeth Price, a former prisoner of the O'Neills, Owen Roe and his troops waited until the evening time for the ghost to appear. 'Then and there vpon a sudden their appeared vnto them a vision or spiritt assumeing the shape of a woman waist highe vpright in the water naked'. Price described the ghost's 'elevated & closed hands ... her haire disheivelled very white'. With an eerie flourish Price finished her description of the ghost: 'Her eyes seeming to twinckle in her head, and her skine as white as snowe which spiritt or vision seeming to stand straight vpright in the water divulged and often repeated the word Revenge Revenge Revenge.' O'Neill sent a priest and a friar to speak to the apparition, but to no avail. The ghost would only converse with a Protestant cleric from an English regiment stationed nearby. Afterwards the ghost remained for several weeks according to Price and 'cried all and every night beginning about twilight as aforesaid'.[128] The story of the drowning and massacres spread throughout Ireland during the 1640s. As late as 25 June 1646 Anthony Stephens in Roscommon told the deposition commission that he had heard how Protestants were thrown over the bridge at Portadown. Despite assertions by other deponents that the ghostly apparitions frightened the Irish rebels, Stephens maintained that the ghosts 'little animated or struck remorse into the hearts or consciences of the offenders'. None the less, it is interesting to note that the main parts of the story encapsulated by Price's testimony such as the cry for revenge, remained within Stephens's account: 'There have bin heard often the cryes of Revenge reveng & oth[e]r strang & formidable expressions by [these] spirits.'[129]

The immediate effect of this massacre upon the local population cannot be underestimated. Robert Maxwell lived within thirteen miles of Portadown and described how both rebels and settlers were 'daily affrighted' by reports of these ghosts. Unfortunately it is not clear whether the rebels Maxwell referred to were out in arms or members of the civilian population.[130] Either way, the massacre itself served to ensure some form of control over the local population. In the words of James Shawe:

> all those that lived about the bridge of Portadowne were soe affrighted with the cryes & noise made there of some spiritts or visions for Revenge, that they durst not stay but fledd away thence, and this deponent observed and sawe them to come thence soe (as they protested) affrighted to Markethill saying they durst neither stay there at Portadowne nor returne thither for feare of those cryes and spiritts.[131]

128 Deposition of Elizabeth Price, 26 June 1642, ibid. fos 102v–103v.
129 Deposition of Anthony Stephens, 25 June 1646, TCD, MS 830, fo. 43r–v.
130 Deposition of Robert Maxwell, 22 Aug. 1642, TCD, MS 810, fos 10–11.
131 Deposition of James Shawe, 14 Aug. 1643, TCD, MS 836, fo. 112v.

Moved by the stories of this supernatural sighting, members of the rebel forces such as Toole McCann expressed remorse at murdering so many people at the bridge, particularly after reports of the ghostly sightings became widespread. Others were just terrified.[132]

Another means of measuring the extent of trauma experienced by deponents is revealed by looking at certain types of violence that they witnessed or heard of second hand. Many deponents described how the corpses of their fallen brethren were denied Christian burial and left exposed to the elements and subsequently eaten by either dogs or 'fowls of the air'. Dorothy Rampaigne, a settler in Fermanagh, whose brother was Nehemiah Wallington, a London artisan, deposed that her husband, Zechariah, along with other Protestant members of her community was murdered by the Maguires. The soldiers afterwards allegedly 'left their bodies vnburied exposed to beasts & fowles to feed on'.[133] Deponents in Cavan described how Protestant corpses were left unburied 'till doggs spoyled their Corps'.[134] Thomas Le Strange, witnessed the consecration of a Protestant church into the Catholic faith and testified that the Irish rebels 'layd [corpses] naked vpon a hedg where they were left exposed to publique view and to be devowred of doggs, swyne or any thing els that would fasten on them'.[135] After the massacres in the north of Ireland some deponents described how many of the corpses of the victims were 'lay there till the doggs & Ravenous creatures devowred them'. A deponent from Armagh claimed that almost all Protestants who had perished during the rebellion were denied proper Christian burial:

> most of the protestants in all of the Cuntry thereabouts the Rebells distroyed and murthered by drowning burning hanging the sword starveing & by other deathes exposeing their slaughtered bodies to be devowred by doggs swyne & other Ravenous creatures.[136]

The exposure of corpses to birds and 'ravenous creatures' had a deeper significance to contemporaries. In 1 Kings, soldiers who fought for sinful rulers like Jeroboam, Ahab and Baasha, and members of sinful communities such as the Philistines would be killed by God and their carcasses eaten by dogs or 'fowls of the air'.[137] It was also a sign of the Apocalypse.[138] At a very basic

---

132 Deposition of Richard Newberrie, 27 June 1642, ibid. fo. 61; deposition of Joane Constable, 6 June 1643, fo. 89v.

133 Deposition of Dorothy Rampaigne, 4 Sept. 1643, TCD, MS 835, fo. 247.

134 Deposition of Thomas Crant, 13 Feb. 1642, TCD, MS 832, fo. 214; deposition of Adam Glouer, 4 Jan. 1642, MS 833, fo. 1; deposition of John Wheelwright, 18 Aug. 1643, MS 833, fo. 272.

135 Deposition of Thomas Le Strange, 12 Jan. 1644, TCD, MS 814, fo. 231v.

136 Deposition of William Holland, 13 Sept. 1642, TCD, MS 834, fo. 160.

137 1 Samuel xvii.46; 1 Kings xiv.11; xvi.4; xxi.24.

138 Revelation xix.18.

level, therefore, the denial of proper Christian burial during times of conflict could be interpreted within an Old Testament or Revelation framework. This helped contemporaries to rationalise the violence that they experienced and to understand their own role in such events.

Furthermore, it was widely believed among the settler population that Irish rebels cut unborn babies out of pregnant women's stomachs. Philip Taylor, from Armagh, related how the rebels 'aforesaid killd a dyers wife of Rosstrevor at Newry & ript vp her belly she being with chyld'.[139] Ann Dutton in Donegal alleged that 'James McIlbridy of Maughrilosky in the said County yeoman a notorious Rebell whoe killd one William McKenny & his mother in law and his wiffe and ript vp her belly shee being greate with child, & tooke & cutt the child out of her wambe'.[140] Elizabeth Price also heard Irish rebels boasting that 'they tooke an Englishwoman nere the bridge of Portadowne by name, the wife of Arnold Taylor; when she was great with child, And that they ripped vp her bellie soe that the child fell out of her wombe'.[141] In the most bizarre example of this particular type of atrocity, Thomas Clarke, a Dublin merchant who had been in Wexford during the rebellion, conversed with some of the rebels about a recent defeat that they had suffered at Ross:

> the Deponent being deliuerd out of [Kilkenny] prison in the yeare 1643 Came to Ros[s] aforesayd wheare one James Deuerex of Clonleah in the County of Waxford being in Discourse asked this Examinent wheather he thought that the Great Army that Came from Dublin did beatt the Irish Army att the battel of Ros: this Deponent Maiking Ansur that he thought the English army by the prouidence of God did beatt the Irish, but the aforesayd Deuerex replyd no: it was *by* John Stone and his wife and Chilldren which ware Murdred: two of the women being buryed neere to the place wheare the batle of Ros was fought one of the sayd women *was* big with Chilld and the other hauing a small Chilld which was hanged in a with by her and the woman that was big with Chilld some of the Roges haueing striped her hangd her and riped vp her bely letting the Chilld fall out and soe left them naked vntill Richard *FitzHarrys* of Colbacke in the County of waxford Caused them to be buried.[142]

Here, the local community took this biblical image and framed it in a providential narrative to claim that the defeat of the Irish was down to the expression of vengeance by the dead. William Timmes in Tipperary related how he had heard that Hugh O'Kennedy attacked Thomas Clarke's wife and their child: '(being yong) did the sd Hugh o Kenedy take by the heeles & dashed

---

139 Deposition of Philip Taylor, 7 Feb. 1642 , TCD, MS 836, fo. 7.
140 Deposition of Ann Dutton, 2 Nov. 1642, TCD, MS 839, fo. 129v.
141 Deposition of Elizabeth Price, 26 June 1642, TCD, MS 836, fo. 104v.
142 Deposition of Thomas Clarke, 13 Aug. 1652, TCD, MS 812, fo. 129v.

out his Branies against the stones'.[143] Elizabeth Croftes, from Cavan, deposed that 'Some of the children[']s braines [were] dashed out against the stones'. She also qualified this information; the source was 'some poore English, then present, and divers of the Rebells have confidently related it vnto her'. Likewise, many other deponents testified that they heard about the dashing of children's heads against stones.[144] Such stories were either memories of atrocities committed during the Nine Years' War, or were examples of how biblical images of violence shaped the deponents' descriptions of massacres that they had heard about.

In the entire corpus of the depositions, there is only one deponent who witnessed an attack on a pregnant woman. On 11 November 1641, members of the O'Byrne clan accosted Timothy Pate in Wicklow. Before his goods (largely cows and household stuff) were stolen the rebels 'had his bible first burned'. They attempted to decapitate Pate, but were prevented by the efforts of his pregnant wife. 'In revendg … the said Bolgar [the leading insurgent at Pate's house] struck her with the hatchett vpon the belly she being great with Child (which putt her into much paine & affrightes: & after shee was brought a bedd the Child djed).'[145] It is noteworthy that when deponents described such attacks as a product of hearsay they reverted to formulaic expressions of the phrase that were remarkably similar to those contained in the King James version of the Bible. Yet, in this instance Pate witnessed the atrocity and used different sentence construction and vocabulary. Instead, Pate focused on the pain of his wife and subsequent still-birth of his child. Perhaps this biblical tale had become internalised by Protestant settlers in Ireland and this dictated their perceptions of what sort of violence would occur if they felt God punished them, hence the language through which it was expressed had resonances of passages in the Bible. In this instance, however, the trauma of witnessing the attack meant that the deponent focused on the suffering that he and his wife experienced and the loss of their child.

While the depositions are rife with confusing, contradictory and conflicting testimonies of murder and mayhem, second-hand information captures the degree of fear that settlers experienced after the outbreak of violence in October 1641. Many of the stories within the depositions capture how deponents heard of the deaths of hundreds, possibly thousands, of seemingly innocent Protestants and atrocities that reminded them of biblical tales, which provided a ready interpretation that God was punishing them for their sins. Despite the transmission of stories through the oral grapevine it is possible to reconstruct the main elements of the tale. Certain specifics, and inconsequential details, were tweaked, exaggerated or dreamed up.

143 Deposition of William Timmes, 5 Mar. 1646, TCD, MS 821, fo. 194.
144 Deposition of Elizabeth Croftes, 8 Mar. 1643, TCD, MS 832, fo. 55.
145 Deposition of Timothy Pate, 6 June 1643, TCD, MS 811, fo. 170.

Sometimes, rumours were mixed together. 'Many strange crueltyes wer[e] committed by the Rebells ... as drowning of six & twelue women att one tyme in boghooles ... drowning of multitudes.'[146] John and Isabell Gowrly related how rebels had burned Armagh town and only left twenty people surviving.[147] However nebulous the details of individual atrocities are, the 1641 depositions accurately capture the fear of deponents and settlers, their immediate interpretation of the violence that followed 23 October 1641 and the trauma that they suffered at the hands of their neighbours.

Rumours of the intentions of the 'Puritan' parliament served a clear function for the rioting population. It provided those of the lower social orders with a motive to attack the settler population and justified the use of violence. Natives feared the 'Puritan' threat from England and Scotland.[148] Local elites harnessed these rumours as part of their recruitment drive across the country. This is evident in the knowledge possessed by the Irish rebels of events that occurred across the three kingdoms in the early months of the rising. Those of the 'common sort' of Irish or 'lower rabble' knew of the anti-popish lean-ings of the English parliament.[149] As this news travelled by word of mouth, details became skewed and the story took on a more sinister character. The arrest of the queen's confessor and the dissemination of this fact is a perfect example. By the time that the news arrived at Cavan it was alleged that parliament wanted to kill the queen and had already executed some of her friars.[150] Thus, news of 'high' politics trickled down to the lower social orders as they attempted to understand the reasons behind the rebellion. Such news served to mobilise the wider native population to take part in the rebellion. As will be shown in the next chapter, leaders of the rebellion would go to great lengths to downplay these religious grievances in their correspondence with colonial authorities and to deny that any atrocities had occurred.

High profile attacks on the settler population encouraged further support for the rebellion among members of local societies who disliked their colo-nial neighbours or the faith that they espoused. Executions of prominent members of settler society in public places warned those who thought about opposing the emerging Catholic authorities across Ireland. It is interesting that most of the eye-witness testimonies recorded the deaths of male family members, neighbours and prominent members of the settler community. Most of the hearsay evidence, however, described attacks on women and children, the vulnerable in society. When settlers fled these areas to Dublin

---

146 Deposition of Mary Twyford, 10 May 1642, TCD, MS 836, fos 77–8.
147 Deposition of John and Isabell Gourly, 7 Nov. 1642, ibid. fo. 57.
148 Horowitz, *The deadly ethnic riot*, 75, 85, 87.
149 Deposition of Thomas Crant, 13 Feb. 1642, TCD, MS 832, fo. 212v; deposition of Henry Reynolds, 4 Jan. 1642, MS 833, fo. 57.
150 Deposition of John Mc Kewne, 12 Nov. 1642, TCD, MS 833, fo. 165v.

they no doubt exchanged information with others and this is captured in the 1641 depositions. They are a product of the vivid processes of oral communication in early modern Ireland. To some extent the stories of atrocities that circulated around the countryside reveal how successful rebel tactics were at shocking the newcomer population. Settlers fled from their local communities and those who stayed behind rarely threatened their new overlords. A question remains, however. How did state authorities interpret this information and how did they present it to the wider world?

3

Manufacturing Massacre:
The 1641 Depositions and the Wars
of the Three Kingdoms

The 1641 depositions record how the rebellion spread from its epicentre in Ulster to the rest of the country. They reveal the grievances of those who took part, capture the trauma experienced by the victims and contain a wealth of information on the range of responses of the native Irish community. While collecting the testimonies, prominent members of the colonial administration consulted them. They then published some of the information through English printers and disseminated it to political figures across the three kingdoms. As a result, Catholic commentators claimed that the 1641 depositions were gathered for the purpose of composing anti-Irish and anti-Catholic propaganda. Prior to the establishment of the deposition commission, however, the lords justices gave up-to-date information from Ireland to various institutions and leading figures in British and Irish politics, expressing their concerns about their future in Ireland. Did their initial conclusions on the rebellion shape later interpretations? What influence did the news that they disseminated about the Irish rebellion have on Irish and English politics? The purpose of this chapter is to understand how the colonial administration and the deposition commission portrayed events in Ireland to the wider world.

Initial intelligence from Ireland on the 1641 rebellion

The outbreak of the rebellion occurred at a moment of considerable weakness for the lords justices in Ireland. In October 1641 the colonial authorities lacked a standing army of sufficient strength that could be mobilised quickly to suppress the rebellion.[1] Had the mission to seize Dublin castle succeeded it would be difficult to imagine how the Irish Protestant community could have restored the king's authority in Ireland. As a result, the first reports on the outbreak of the rebellion stressed the vulnerability of the settler community, highlighted how they had been overwhelmed by a demonic 'popish' population and how innocent Protestant nobles, gentry

---

1 Armstrong, *Protestant war*, 15–16, 19; Temple, *The Irish rebellion*, 26.

and poor were being attacked in their thousands. A key goal of this section, therefore, is to provide an analysis of how the Irish Protestant administration in Dublin castle portrayed and represented the beginning of the rebellion to authorities in the other two kingdoms.

The lords justices became aware of the outbreak of rebellion when an inebriated Owen Connelly, a native convert to Presbyterianism, arrived at the house of William Parsons in the early hours of 22 October 1641. He had been drinking with his foster brother Hugh Óg MacMahon who informed Connelly that 'great numbers' of the Catholic 'noblemen and gentlemen' were determined to seize Dublin castle and take the ammunitions within. Next:

> they intended first to batter the Chimnies of the said Towne, and if the Cittie would not yeeld, then to batter downe the howses, and soe to cutt off all the Protestants that would not joine with them, Hee saith further ... that the Irish had *prepared* men in all parts of the Kingdome to destroy all the English inhabiting there tomorrowe morning by ten of the clock, and that in all the seaports and other townes in the Kingdome, all the Protestants should bee killed this night, and that all the posts that could bee could not prevent it.

According to Connelly, MacMahon and his fellow conspirators pledged their 'due allegeance' to King Charles I, and criticised the 'tirannicall Governement' in Ireland.[2] Before the rebellion had even begun therefore, colonial authorities believed that a massacre of Irish Protestants would take place.

The king, then stationed in Scotland, learned of the plot from Arthur Chichester, nephew of former Lord Deputy Chichester. On 24 October Arthur informed the king that 'the septs which have risen are all of the Romish religion' and that 'only one man' had been murdered, presumably Arthur Champion. He believed that Champion's murder and the subsequent lighting of fires rallied the local population to the rebel cause.[3] The next day, building upon information given by Owen Connelly, the lords justices wrote to the lord lieutenant of Ireland, the earl of Leicester, revealing a 'damnable Papist plot' to seize Dublin castle and key fortifications across the country. Those Protestants who refused to join in would be 'cut off'. This would allow 'Papists [to] become possessed of the Government and the Kingdom at the same time'. Castle Blaney had been lost as had the house of the earl of Essex, while rebels 'plundered the town [of Carrickmacross], and burned divers houses, and it since appears that they burned divers other villages and robbed and spoiled many English, and none but Protestants, leaving

---

[2]   The examination of Owen Connelly, 22 Oct. 1641, TCD, MS 809, fos 13–14.
[3]   Viscount Arthur Chichester to the secretary attending the king, 24 Oct. 1641, *CSPI, 1633–47*, 342.

the English Papists untouched as well as the Irish'.[4] Despite informing the lord lieutenant that Catholics called for Protestants to join them in their defence of the king, the lords justices maintained that this was a Catholic conspiracy to extirpate Protestants. Not all was lost, however, as the lords justices confirmed that two of the leading insurgents had been arrested, Hugh Óg MacMahon and Lord Conor Maguire, along with other members of their party. As they had little intelligence from the north of Ireland, they could not confirm MacMahon's testimony that all Irish Catholics were involved in the plot. If this was the case 'then indeed we shall be in high extremity and the kingdom in the greatest danger that ever it underwent, considering of our great want of men, money and arms to enable us to encounter so great multitudes as they can make'. They also expressed the hope that the Old English 'will continue constant to the King in their fidelity' and promised to victual the Old English, if all of the native Irish community joined the rebellion, although Robert Armstrong has cast doubt on the sincerity of these sentiments.[5] They requested that the Irish parliament be prorogued to avoid further assemblies gathering in Dublin.[6] In a postscript, the lords justices informed Leicester that the sheriff of Monaghan and Dr Faithfull Teate, a minister, had arrived in Dublin and revealed the loss of Monaghan town and that the sheriff of County Cavan, Myles O'Reilly, had joined the rebels 'being a papist and a prime man of the Irish'.[7] Early intelligence about the rising interpreted the events as another example of Irish perfidy and Catholic subversion. In the weeks that followed the lords justices believed that the rebellion was solely inspired by religious grievances.

Over the next week, local leaders in the north-east of Ireland loyal to the colonial administration wrote increasingly desperate missives to Charles I. Chichester warned that 'the plot against us is deeper, and our danger greater' as 'all papists' had joined in the rebellion, while Archibald Stewart warned that most of Ulster had been lost to a force of 10,000 men.[8] Another observer in the north of Ireland, Sir George Rawdon wrote to his master, Lord Conway and informed him that Lisnagarvy, Belfast and Carrickfergus were still in Protestant hands, but contradicted the lords justices' claims to the earl of Leicester that they trusted militia forces organised by the Old English: 'The army is not trusted even in the Pale, though many of the soldiers resent this want of confidence.'[9] A letter to the earl of Leicester

---

[4] Lords justices and council to the lord lieutenant, the earl of Leicester, 25 Oct. 1641, ibid. 343; lords justices and council to Leicester, 25 Oct. 1641, HMC, *Ormond*, n.s. ii. 3.

[5] Lords justices and council to Leicester, 25 Oct. 1641, HMC, *Ormond*, n.s. ii. 4; Armstrong, *Protestant war*, 26.

[6] Lords justices and council to Leicester, 25 Oct. 1641, HMC, *Ormond*, n.s. ii. 5.

[7] Ibid. ii. 6.

[8] Chichester to the king, 27 Oct. 1641, and Archibald Stewart to the king, 28 Oct. 1641, *CSPI, 1633–47*, 344.

[9] Rawdon to Conway, 6 Nov. 1641, ibid. 345.

dated 25 October 1641 described how the lords justices ordered the arrest of conspirators based in Dublin and disseminated a proclamation providing information about the rebellion. What they failed to tell Leicester was that they blamed 'some evill-affected Irish papists' for the rising and accused them of 'wicked and damnable Plots'. This caused considerable controversy among both the Old English and native Irish communities as the proclamation circulated throughout the country.[10] Sir William St Leger, lord president of Munster, acted as one of the channels for the Dublin administration to distribute official proclamations around Cork.[11] Describing the reception of the text, he confessed that it 'was not so well advised to have settled the humours and disposition of the people, and this hath wrought the clean contrary effect, for they were bad before, and now they are ten times worse'. One person in particular caught St Leger's attention: 'I did read this proclamation to O'Sullivan. At the reading of the words "ill-affected Irish papists" I did never in my life observe more venomous rancour in any man's face than was in his.'[12] A later proclamation apologising for the sectarian tone employed by the lords justices failed to mitigate these tensions. Richard Bellings, future secretary to the confederation of Kilkenny later commented how 'it cannot be imagined how much the nation was amazed at this expression'.[13] The emphasis on the religious ordering of the rebellion by the lords justices encouraged Catholic communities in Ireland who had not yet risen in arms to take action.

By 5 November 1641 letters from the lords justices to the houses of parliament conveyed their considerable distress. They informed the secretary of state, Sir Henry Vane, that many of the king's forts and castles were lost and that the rebels had 'slain many of his good subjects, robbed and spoiled thousands of them, destroyed and wasted several counties, imprisoned many of honourable quality, and have and still do exercise such acts of barbarism and cruelty in all places where they come as could not be expected to come from Christians'.[14] Lest the lords of the council in Westminster were in any doubt about events in Ireland they also received another letter the same day that contained further details of the rebels' cruelties – some were 'hewed to pieces', while members of the nobility, such as Lord Blaney's family, were imprisoned. The lords justices used highly condemnatory language to describe the actions of the Irish rebels: 'their fury begins to threaten the English Plantations in the Queen's County and King's County'. Native Irish sheriffs and other local

10 Temple, *The Irish rebellion*, 22–3.

11 Sir William St Leger to Richard Boyle, first earl of Cork, 7 Nov. 1641, and St Leger to Cork, 10 Nov. 1641, and 26 Feb. 1642, in *The Lismore papers*, ed. Alexander Grosart, London 1886–8, iv. 217–18, 220; v. 5–6.

12 St Leger to Sir Philip Perceval, 5 Nov. 1641, HMC, *Report on the manuscripts of the earl of Egmont*, London 1905–9, i/1, 144.

13 *History of the Irish confederation*, i. 18.

14 Lords justices and council to Sir Henry Vane, 5 Nov. 1641, HMC, *Ormond*, n.s. ii. 7.

administrators had betrayed their positions of authority and joined the rebellion. Their intentions were portrayed by the lords justices in stark terms:

> They threaten all the English to be gone by a time or they will destroy them utterly, and indeed they give out publicly that their purpose is totally to extirpate the English and Protestants, and not to lay down arms until by an Act of Parliament here the Romish religion be established and that the Government be settled in the hands of natives.

The lords justices used such information to canvass English authorities for aid, mentioning their 'extreme want of money and armes' and how they could not trust the Catholic Old English.[15] Within a fortnight of the rebellion breaking out the lords justices therefore had effectively rendered the rising as a Catholic conspiracy and indicated that it was only a matter of time before the Old English would join it.

The lords justices' early characterisation of the rebellion as a religious war reveals their thoughts on communications between themselves and the rebels. In a proclamation dated 24 October 1641 and deliberately sent to the lords justices Sir Phelim O'Neill declared that their actions were 'for the defence and liberty of ourselves and the natives of the Irish nation'. O'Neill did not mention any religious grievances,[16] but the lower social orders rallied to an anti-colonial and anti-Protestant banner. On 10 November 1641 a letter addressed to Lord Dillon by unnamed rebels listed their main grievances as political: 'they cannot hold office, and that strangers rise over the heads of the Irish and Old English'. Admittedly, they lamented the implementation of recusancy laws – but their main grievances were due to the increasing political and economic isolation of that native Irish.[17] A petition sent from the gentry and commonalty of Cavan argued that their actions were in the name of the king, stressing their loyalty to the crown. In fact, all dispatches addressed to colonial authorities made similar claims. Toward the end of the petition the O'Reillys of Cavan stated that 'we must have freedom of conscience and honest government'.[18] The lords justices, however, dismissed this petition and ordered the O'Reillys to return to their houses and restore property that they had taken from settlers.[19] The rebel hierarchy were desperately trying to convince the colonial authorities that their actions were not religiously inspired. Despite attempts by both the Old English and the native Irish to negotiate with the lords justices their

---

[15] Lords justices and council to the lords of the council, ibid. ii. 7–8.

[16] Proclamation of Phelim O'Neill, 24 Oct. 1641, *CSPI, 1633–47*, 342.

[17] Extract of a letter from some of the rebels to Lord James Dillon, 10 Nov. 1641, ibid. 345.

[18] 'Copy of the remonstrance of the "Gentry and Commonality" (the insurgents) of Co. Cavan, of their grievances, common with other parts of Ireland', ibid. 348.

[19] Ibid.

grievances fell on deaf ears as Parsons and Borlase lobbied prominent figures across the other two kingdoms for men and supplies.

When news arrived on 12 November 1641 from Sir Henry Vane that supplies were to be sent to Ireland the lords justices and council expressed gratitude, but continued to describe their plight as increasingly desperate. On 13 November a letter to the earl of Leicester revealed how the lords justices blamed Jesuits and friars for turning the Old English against them and that Spain had supplied money and arms. They mentioned the petition of the Cavan rebels who made 'religion part of their pretences' and that 'some priests, friars and Jesuits have undoubtedly been very industrious to advance these mischiefs'.[20] On 22 November they regaled Vane with evidence of various cruelties committed by the Irish rebels such as how some men's hands were cut off and their eyes plucked out while others were stripped naked, which proved indicative of the 'inveterate and virulent hatred they bear to the English nation'. This was an attempt to coax Vane to mobilise English politicians to send over more troops and supplies to Ireland: 'We must still repeat our suit for hastening our supplies, hoping that God may be pleased to let us but live to vindicate the honour of the English nation on these bloody rebels, whose rage hath executed such inexampled inhumanity and cruelty on so many of the English.'[21] On the same day they informed the king's lord lieutenant that native Irish clans in Wicklow had 'taken up the rebellious example of their traitorous ancestors' and joined the rebellion along with Irish inhabitants in Leinster. These new recruits stripped English settlers and 'demolished and defaced the buildings and improvements of the English'. The lords justices stressed the ethnic and religious dimensions to the rebellion. Calling once again for supplies they warned of the malignant influence of Jesuits, friars and priests and claimed that religion had a powerful influence over the wider population through encouraging them to partake.[22] On 27 November the lords justices responded to a letter from Leicester that suggested that they had been castigated for interpreting the actions of the native Irish as being prompted by religious grievances. They assured Leicester that they did not want 'to make it a war of religion', and blamed rebel insurgents for advancing this version of events.[23]

Meanwhile, the lords justices repeatedly reminded their correspondents of the dire conditions faced by the 'English' of Ireland. They reported by late November that Ulster was effectively lost along with Wicklow and Wexford. Here 'English' people were 'stripped naked and banished thence by the fury and rage of the rebels'.[24] Evidence suggests that the lords justices feared that

---

[20] Lords justices and council to Leicester, 13 Nov. 1641, HMC, *Ormond*, ii. 15.

[21] Lords justices and council to Vane, 22 Nov. 1641, ibid. ii. 18.

[22] Lords justices and council to Leicester, 22 Nov. 1641, ibid. ii. 20.

[23] Lords justices and council to Leicester, 27 Nov. 1641, ibid. ii. 30–1.

[24] Lords justices and council to Leicester, 25 Nov. 1641, ibid. ii. 25.

nobody believed their tale: 'The dangers here are fully as bad as we represent. Let no one minimise them.'[25] Aware of events in the wider three kingdoms and of growing anti-Catholic sentiment in London, on 3 December they assured Leicester that this was in fact a war of religion:

> The rebels now boldly threaten that as soon as they have subdued us they will send thirty thousand men into England to spoil all the kingdom as they have done this and to force all men to become Papists, so you see they declare it a war for religion and in despite of us, and by that means gain strength to their party daily and weaken us.[26]

The lords justices may have believed that by placing an emphasis on the Catholic dimension to the rising, supplies would be be more readily forthcoming from England.[27]

In contrast to the desperate missives sent by the lords justices in late November 1641, northern figures of authority such as Sir Arthur Teringham were increasingly confident of the response of colonial forces. Teringham informed the king and Lord Conway that Scottish nobles and gentry such as the lord of the Ards, Sir William Stewart and Sir James Montgomery were successfully crushing the revolt and even recommended them for the king's consideration for their loyal actions.[28] Ormond, in a private letter to the king, could offer no concrete details as to the aims and intentions of the native Irish rebels and believed that 'our counsels are divided' on what the rebellion was and how it should be suppressed.[29] The situation rapidly deteriorated, however, when the Old English, or the 'Lords of the Pale', joined in the rebellion as reported to the king on 12 December 1641. Ormond believed that this would now place religious and political grievances on an equal footing whereas the native Irish stressed their political and economic grievances.[30] In truth, the lords justices had already endorsed the theory that the rebellion was a religious war against Irish Protestants. On the same day a more hardline anti-Catholic element within the colonial administration

---

[25] Lords justices and council to Leicester, 26 Nov. 1641, *CSPI, 1633–47,* 351. See also lords justices and council to Leicester, 30 Nov. 1641, HMC, *Ormond,* n.s. ii. 31–2.

[26] Lords justices to Leicester, 3 Dec. 1641, HMC, *Ormond,* n.s. ii. 33–4.

[27] Ulick Bourke, earl of Clanricard, would later blame parliament for portraying the rebellion as a war of religion: Clanricard to the king, 22 Jan. 1642, in Thomas Carte, *A collection of letters, written by the Kings Charles I and II the duke of Ormonde, the secretaries of state, the marques of Clanricarde, and toerh great men, during the troubles of Great Britain and Ireland serving to verify and clear up matters related in the history of the life and times of James the first duke of Ormonde, and published by way of appendix to that history, whereof it makes,* London 1735, iii. 56.

[28] Arthur Teringham to Conway, 30 Nov. 1641, and Teringham to the king, 30 Nov. 1641, *CSPI, 1633–47,* 351.

[29] Ormond to the king, 1 Dec. 1641, ibid. 351–2.

[30] Ormond to the king, 12 Dec. 1641, ibid. 353.

informed the king that the kingdom of Ireland lay 'desperately bleeding', rather than adopting the more pragmatic tones of others. Sir John Temple, the master of the rolls, sought to ensure that the king was under no illusions as to the intentions of the rebels and the extent of their treachery: the rebels claimed a royal commission for their actions. The native Irish were spurred on by Catholic clergy and as a result: 'They march on furiously destroying all the English, sparing neither sex nor age throughout the kingdom; most barbarously murthering them, and that with greater cruelty than ever was yet used among Turks and infidels.'[31] Temple's letter to the king continued the lords justices' policy of portraying the rebellion in the worst possible light and was noteworthy in being the first direct communication to Charles that informed him that the rebels claimed his authority for their actions.

Up until mid-December 1641, correspondence between the political bureaucracies in Ireland and England portrayed the rebellion as both a religious assault and colonial revolt with little mention of the rebels' desire to align themselves with the king.[32] For example, in November 1641, the lords justices reported that 'the preservation of his Majesty's honour' proved part of the rebellious design but stressed that religion 'works most powerfully on the minds of men, and that some priests, friers, and Jesuits have undoubtedly been very industrious to advance these mischiefs'.[33] On 14 December the lords justices wrote to the earl of Leicester with a report on the rebellion for the king. They noted that the rebels' 'main end and drift' was to protect Charles's 'royal crown and sovereignty of this his kingdom'. Accordingly, twenty proclamations with the king's signature were sent back to Ireland to disprove these claims, although the lords justices would later lament that this was too little too late.[34] In truth, the refusal of the lords justices to parley with leading Catholic nobles and their excessive application of martial law forced the Old English officially to take up arms against the colonial order. A petition dated 14 December 1641 informed the king of their decision to take part in the rebellion and blamed the belligerence of the lords justices.[35]

As a result of Sir Phelim O'Neill's production of a forged commission from Charles I, rumours of royal complicity in the rebellion circulated widely in Ireland, though not in England, from its inception. When London printers and parliamentarians learned of this, they were unsure of how best to deal with this propaganda coup. In December 1641 Joseph Hunscott, a printer

---

[31] John Temple to the king, 12 Dec. 1641, ibid. 354.

[32] See for example, Temple to Charles I, 12 Dec. 1641, ibid; lords justices and council to Leicester, 4 Dec. 1641, HMC, *Ormond*, n.s. ii. 35–6.

[33] 'Remonstrance of the gentry and commonality of Co Cavan', 6 Nov. 1641, *CSPI, 1633–47*, 347–8; lords justices and council to Leicester, 13 Nov. 1641, HMC, *Ormond*, n.s. ii. 13–17.

[34] Lords justices and council to Leicester, 14 Dec. 1641, HMC, *Ormond*, n.s. ii. 42–5, 81; proclamation printed in Carte, *Ormond*, iii. 53.

[35] Carte, *Ormond*, iii. 48–50.

sponsored by parliament, printed *The general remonstrance or declaration of the Catholics of Ireland*, and John Thomas printed *The coppy of a letter sent by the rebells in Ireland to the Lord Dillon*. These constituted parliament's first public airing of Charles I's alleged involvement in the Irish rebellion. The *General remonstrance* claimed that the Irish rebels fought for the king, but readers in London 'considered [this] little better than a libel'.[36] The circulation of these two pamphlets was part of a larger design to encourage popular dissatisfaction with the king. Subsequently, Charles responded by ordering the arrest of five MPs, including John Pym, and appointed his own official printer.[37]

Information despatched from the lords justices, therefore, clearly portrayed the rebellion through a religious prism and stressed the popish nature of the plot. News sent to Westminster and the king (or his lord lieutenant) would blame all Catholics in Ireland and argued that they had been surprised and overwhelmed by the insurgency. Their missives had little effect on English politics until they began to reveal how the rebels claimed that their actions were in defence of the king. It was this platform that launched the 1641 deposition commission into the mud-slinging match that led to the opening of the English front in the Wars of the Three Kingdoms.

Henry Jones, A *remonstrance of divers remarkeable passages*, and the outbreak of the English civil wars

The 1641 depositions became a highly contested source for the massacres of Irish Protestant settlers due to the fact that the colonial authorities in Ireland printed edited abstracts from the collection to lobby for greater financial support and military aid. The Dublin authorities were aware that the rebels stole settlers' property. Contemporaries therefore desired a record of financial and personal losses brought about by the rebellion. Two commissions, dated 23 December 1641 and 18 January 1642, established the agenda for the eight clergymen who constituted the deposition commission. They first covered 'what robberies and spoiles have beene committed'. Their remit then expanded to record 'traiterous or disloyall words, speeches, or actions ... numbers of persons have been murthered by the Rebels, or perished afterwards ... [and] what person, persons, Clergimen, or other Protestants have

---

[36] Robert Slingsby to John Pennington, 30 Dec. 1641, in D. F. McKenzie and Maureen Bell (eds), *A chronology and calendar of documents relating to the London book trade, 1641–1700*, Oxford 2005, i. 32; *A general remonstrance or declaration of the Catholickes of Ireland*, received of George Wentworth, London 1641; *The coppy of a letter sent by the rebells in Ireland to the Lord Dillon, to declare to his maiestie the cause of their taking up armes*, London 1641; *CSPI, 1633–47*, 355; *CSPD, 1641–3*, 218.

[37] McKenzie and Bell, *A chronology and calendar of documents*, i. 33.

become Papists'.[38] The depositions were to serve a two-fold purpose in the eyes of the lords justices. First, they desired that those dispossessed by the Irish rebels should be compensated. Secondly, they hoped that the depositions would serve 'posterity' and illustrate the 'great cruelties' perpetratrated on the Irish Protestant community. This would allow future generations to take note so that they 'be not used in the same manner, but that they be watchful to prevent it'.[39]

As soon as they began to be collected the 1641 depositions were also a form of intelligence on the nature of the rising, its participants and their intended military targets and activities. As a result, high-profile political players across the three kingdoms received information from the depositions even before they were first published, in April 1642. For example, by February 1642 the Old English had allied with their co-religionists having hosted a meeting in Crufty near Drogheda in December 1641. Accordingly on 4 March the lords justices informed the earl of Leicester that the Old English nobility were actively recruiting supporters for the siege of Drogheda. As evidence, the lords justices provided a copy of the deposition of Hubert Pettitt taken on 19 February 1642. They also expressed concern that the authorities in England had failed to clamp down on seditious printing that sullied Ormond's reputation. They urged that 'a course may be taken there to prevent the too great liberty taken in kind by the printers', suggesting an awareness among the lords justices and council of the printing pandemonium occurring in London at the time. They stressed that unity between the two kingdoms was a vital necessity as the rebels intended to travel to England if they succeeded in their rebellious designs.[40] This became a central premise of the first official report on the 1641 rebellion, written by Henry Jones and presented to the lords justices on 7 March 1642. It was later published as A remonstrance of divers remarkeable passages concerning the Church and kingdome of Ireland.

While the lords justices were digesting Jones's Remonstrance, John Pym, the spokesperson for parliamentary opposition, outlined his 'fears and jealousies' concerning the English monarch. At some moment during the composition of his speech Pym became aware of key information from Ireland, namely a copy of Thomas Crant's deposition and a pamphlet written by

---

[38] Lords justices and council to William Lenthall, 5 Nov. 1641, HMC, Ormond, n.s. ii. 12–13; Henry Jones, A remonstrance of divers remarkeable passages concerning the Church and kingdome of Ireland recommended by letters from the right honourable the lords justices and counsell of Ireland, and presented by Henry Jones doctor in divinity, and agent for the ministers of the Gospel in that kingdom, to the honourable House of Commons in England, London 1642, 13–15.

[39] Lords justices and council to Leicester, 11 Feb. 1642, HMC, Ormond, n.s. ii. 67; Clarke, 'The Commission for the Despoiled Subject', 241–60.

[40] Lords justices and council to Leicester, 4 Mar. 1642, HMC, Ormond, n.s. ii. 83; examination of Hubert Pettitt, 19 Feb. 1642, TCD, MS 840, fo. 12.

Tristam Whetcombe, mayor of Kinsale, entitled *The rebels Turkish tyranny*. Pym used this intelligence from Ireland to argue that the king's reforms of the performative aspects of Protestant services were master-minded by the queen's Catholic agents in London, that the war in Scotland was caused by Catholics and that the rebellion in Ireland was contrived by English Catholics. Using Crant's deposition as evidence Pym argued that the rebels intended to restore the king's royal prerogative and wrest his authority back from the 'Puritan' faction in parliament.[41] Traces of this exchange between the deposition commissioners or the lords justices and John Pym have not survived, but this suggests that some degree of collaboration had occurred.

Around the same time, Ormond received a copy of Thomas Crant's deposition from Henry Jones. Crant's examination implicated Ormond in the rebellion and revealed how one of the O'Reillys in Cavan reported that Ormond, along with Lords Antrim, Howth and Enniskillen had attempted to seize Dublin castle.[42] In the *Remonstrance* Jones appended edited versions of the depositions, including Crant's testimony. He omitted to mention that members of the native Irish community believed that Ormond was involved in the plot and took time in his own deposition (which ran to five pages in print) to exonerate Ormond from such accusations and to defend his reputation. Jones argued that such rumours were designed to encourage others to join in the rebellion and assured the wider world that the native Irish despised Ormond just as much as they did Charles Coote, a notorious commander of colonial forces in Ireland: '[They] place him in the rank of their mortal enemies.'[43] Jones, therefore, had political scores to settle and reputations to protect in the *Remonstrance*.

The *Remonstrance* was presented to the English parliament at some point after 7 March (probably on 14 March) and ordered to be printed on 16 March 1642.[44] It consisted of a short commentary on events in Ireland supported by an appendix of edited depositions to substantiate Jones's arguments. Like the lords justices and council, Jones portrayed the rebellion as a religious war and similar to the lords justices' earlier dispatches to the earl of Leicester, William Lenthall and the king, Jones stressed the victimhood, innocence and vulnerability of Protestant settlers. Jones's portrayal of the rebellion was shaped by a number of fundamental points. First, that the rebellion was a popish conspiracy that would spread from Ireland to the other two kingdoms. To make matters worse, the leaders of the rebellion – 'popish priests, friars and jesuits and other firebrands and incendiaries of the state' – along with

---

[41] 'Declaration of both Houses about fears and jealousies', 7 Mar. 1642: www.british–history.ac.uk/report.asp?compid=35796&strquery="Irish%20Rebellion"#p14, accessed 16 Dec. 2011.

[42] Deposition of Thomas Crant, 13 Feb. 1642, TCD, MS 832, fo. 213v.

[43] Jones, *Remonstrance*, 31.

[44] Rebellion in Ireland: www.british–history.ac.uk/report.aspx?compid=5554#sec–a9, accessed 20 June 2007.

'all the popish nobilitie and men of quality', expected aid from European Catholic powers such as France and Spain to achieve this goal.[45] Secondly, that the rebellion aimed to destroy English rule, English settlements and the established Church in Ireland: 'Their general expression is for a general extirpation, even to the last and least drop of English blood.' This project would be pursued by Irish Catholics with the same gusto as the Spanish inquisition.[46] Finally, that women and children were the most vulnerable in the conflict. Throughout his commentary on the rebellion Jones referred to attacks against women and children as the most common.[47]

As Jones believed (or wished to imply) that Irish nobles organised the rebellion and planned to massacre Protestant settlers in Ireland, he edited some of the depositions in the appendix to the *Remonstrance* to illustrate how the rebellion had broken out nationwide on 23 October 1641. Jones deliberately misconstrued the dating of the outbreak of the Irish rebellion through selective editing. This contradicted initial intelligence sent to England and the first pamphlets that described the rebellion, which detailed its gradual development from its epicentre in the north into other parts of the country. As Jones intended to portray the rebellion as an instantaneous and national outbreak, the timing of the event was central to his argument. Despite his contention that it 'appeareth to have been a long-laid conspiracy' the author glossed over the disparate elements that comprised the rebellious army and insisted that the rebels 'pretend as if the occasion moving them thereunto were new, unexpected and pressing'.[48] He reasoned that their inconsistent actions were indicative of the barbaric and primitive nature of the native Irish. The depositions consulted by Jones for the *Remonstrance* illustrated how the rebellion began in the north and spread through the rest of the country. However, he preferred to refer only to a date which became synonymous with massacre and cruelty, 23 October 1641. To support his argument Jones included only those parts of testimonies that identified the beginning of the rebellion as being between 23 and 26 October. The first mention of this ominous date occurred in Jones's deposition: 'As for the present rebellion, howsoever the first breaking out of this fire into a flame began first on the 23 of October 1641.'[49] Three more depositions mentioned 23 October as the beginning of the rebellion. Two more referred to 24 October 1641, with two deponents testifying that they encountered the rebels on 25 and 26 October respectively.[50] The main emphasis throughout was none the less

45 Jones, *Remonstrance*, 1, 3–4.

46 Ibid. 7.

47 Ibid. 8–10.

48 Ibid. 4.

49 Ibid. 23; deposition of Henry Jones, 2 Mar. 1642, TCD, MS 809, fo. 1. See also 'Relation by Henry Jones, D.D., of proceedings in Cavan, 1641–2', in *A contemporary history of affairs in Ireland from 1641–1652*, ed. J. T. Gilbert, Dublin 1879, i/2, 476–9.

50 For 23 October 1641 see the depositions of Henry Jones, John Kerdiff, Margaret

that 23 October was the planned starting point for their woe. Had Jones provided full transcripts of the diverse mix of depositions that he consulted, seventeenth-century readers would have become more aware of how the rebellion spread from the north and did not reach Wexford until the end of November.[51] That he did not do so added credence to Jones's description of the rebellion as a premeditated plot to extirpate Ireland's Protestant community.[52]

Jones wished to portray the rebellion as a Catholic attempt to rid Ireland of Protestantism. As a result he preferred to focus on religiously-inspired violence. A key aspect of English colonial identity was Protestantism and Jones argued that ministers were the main targets of rebel agression. He claimed that the Irish rebels 'with the deadliest venome spit against the persons of us the Ministers of the Gospel, towards whom their rage is without bounds'.[53] George Cottingham, a minister from Clogher, was placed in a 'miserable' condition despite being 'a painful labourer in the Lords vineyard'.[54] His colleague Roger Blyth, a vicar in County Armagh, died at the hands of the rebels while clutching Sir Phelim O'Neill's safe pass.[55] Jones suggested that these murders, as well as those of other clerics like William Fullerton, Thomas Strafford and James Sharpe, were indicative of a nation-wide trend, 'that among a multitude, we may content ourselves with a few ... all of which, the following examinations [in the appendix] shall speak more fully'.[56] Such generalisations were a common feature of news reports of the era: much was left to the reader's imagination.

In the appendix of edited depositions Jones's omissions were strategic. In order to portray the plight of Protestant Ireland as dire Jones omitted the fact that some of his deponents escaped from the north by obtaining a safe pass from the rebels.[57] Jones discovered in his trawl through the depositions

Farmeny and Elizabeth Bairsee: Jones, *Remonstrance*, 23, 39, 58, 67 respectively. For the depositions that mention 24 October 1641 see those of Edward Slack and Philip Taylor, ibid. 61, 62 respectively. The deposition of Grace Lovett related that she was ejected from her land on 25 October: ibid. 33. Finally, Thomas Middlebrook reported that on 26 October he heard a rebel say that 'within one forthnight they should have a new king of Ireland': ibid. 50.

[51] See, for example, the depositions of Occar Butts, 25 Jan. 1642, and Richard Cleybrook, 8 Jan. 1642, TCD, MS 818, fos 55–6, 62; Canny, *Making Ireland British*, 461–550.

[52] Jones, *Remonstrance*, 3.

[53] Ibid.

[54] *Fasti Ecclesiae Hibernicae: the succession of the prelates and members of the cathedral bodies of Ireland*, ed. Henry Cotton, Dublin 1878, iii. 103; Jones, *Remonstrance*, 10.

[55] James Leslie, *Armagh clergy and parishes: being an account of the clergy of the Church of Ireland in the diocese of Armagh, from the earliest period, with historical notices of the severall parishes, churches &c*, Dundalk 1911, 423; Jones, *Remonstrance*, 10–11.

[56] Jones, *Remonstrance*, 11.

[57] Deposition of George Cook, 22 Jan. 1642, TCD, 832, fo. 104; Jones, *Remonstrance*, 43.

that some of his ministerial colleagues had also converted to Catholicism. George Fercher, according to Jones, deposed that the rebels had confessed that the rebellion struck at English rule in Ireland and Scotland and that some members of the Scottish nobility had joined with them.[58] Fercher went on to say that 'Edmund Wilkinson Curate of the parrish of Clownesse [Clones] in the County Of Monaghan did revolt from the faith and went to masse shortly After the beginning of the rebellion And there after haveing Liberty to repaire unto Dublin, was killed by the Rebells on the Waie', a detail omitted from the *Remonstrance*.[59] Two more of Jones's deponents, Edmund Welsh and John Perkins, also testified that ministers in their locality converted to Catholicism. Perkins related how Thomas Brady, a vicar in Cavan, 'turned papist and went with the rebells'. Among other things the Irish rebels confiscated about £161 of his goods and chattels. Brady 'killed eight of [my] cattle' and forced Perkins to flee for safety.[60]

Jones played up to parliamentary criticisms of Henrietta Maria by including testimonies that spoke of the Irish rebels referring to themselves as the queen's army or the queen's soldiers. To emphasise religious links between Irish Catholics and the queen, Jones included instances where rebels expressed anger at the hanging of her confessor.[61] Accusations against the king and queen appeared frequently throughout the *Remonstrance*. Many of the deponents reported how the rebels alleged royal complicity in, or toleration of, the rebellion. It is for this reason that Jones's *Remonstrance* took on added significance in the spring of 1642. The *Remonstrance* contained seventy-eight edited depositions in the appendix that provided explanations of, and proof for, arguments made by Jones in his commentary. Of these, twenty-five asserted that the king supported the Irish rebels. The role of the king varied from tacit approval – 'the king [k]new of this rebellion' – to full complicity – 'they had authority from the king'.[62] Many deponents claimed that the rebels obtained a commission from the king, while others were offered a glimpse of the royal seal.[63] Admittedly, Jones did note in the *Remonstrance* that Irish rebels were divided in their loyalties between Charles I and a native king, such as Sir Phelim O'Neill. None the less, the damage had been done. The *Remonstrance*, along with other documents that came into Pym's possession in March 1642, provided parliament with sworn testimonies that placed Charles I at the heart of the violence and at the head of the rebel leadership.

---

58 Jones, *Remonstrance*, 18.

59 Deposition of George Fercher, 4 Jan. 1642, TCD, MS 835, fo. 30.

60 Deposition of Edmund Welsh, 22 Jan. 1642, TCD, MS 814, fo. 118v; deposition of John Perkins, 8 Jan. 1642, MS 833, fo. 47; Jones, *Remonstrance*, 49.

61 Deposition of Elizabeth Gough, 8 Feb. 1642, TCD, MS 832, fo. 119v; Jones, *Remonstrance*, 45, 49, 68.

62 Jones, *Remonstrance*, 23, 33, respectively.

63 Ibid. 32, 33, 37, 48, 56, 57, 58, 68, 71, 77, respectively.

Just prior to the presentation of the *Remonstrance*, Charles offered to lead an army into Ireland to suppress the rebellion. Having read the *Remonstrance*, Pym believed that the king would subsequently deploy this army against parliament. MPs relied upon the latest news from Ireland to lobby against the king's policies. Pym's 'feares and jealousies' speech cited information from Ireland, which confirmed suspicions that Irish rebels sought to establish Catholicism across the three kingdoms, and that the king supported them in this endeavour.[64] The Commons later invited the House of Lords into their chamber to hear a speech from Pym that argued against the king's intention to travel to Ireland.[65] After consulting Jones's *Remonstrance*, Pym requested a messenger to copy more of the examinations taken by Jones and his colleagues 'concerning [the] abettors of the rebellion, and what encouragement they have received from England'.[66] Unknown to Pym, Charles also lobbied Ormond for copies of the depositions, after the lords justices 'neglected to giue his Ma[jes]ties an account of that business'.[67] The whole affair underlined the centrality of the 1641 depositions to the events that led to the Wars of the Three Kingdoms.

Charles responded publicly with a rousing defence of his character and ability to rule.[68] Aware that the basis of parliament's 'feares and jealousies' rested on printed propaganda, he demanded stricter controls over the licensing of the press as censorship had by this stage largely broken down. He complained that 'so many seditious pamphlets or sermons are looked upon, and so great tumults are remembered, unpunished, uninquired into'. He modestly claimed that the Protestant religion and the laws of the kingdom were under the greatest threat when compared to his 'own rights or safety'. This justified his desire to lead an army against the Irish rebels.[69] Parliament retorted that they considered it 'most dangerous and unsafe' for the king to go to Ireland and campaigned repeatedly against it. Undertaking such a journey would, Pym argued, 'exceedingly increase the jealousies and fears of your people, and render their doubts more probable, of some force intended

---

[64] 'Declaration of both Houses about fears and jealousies', 7 Mar. 1642: www.british–history.ac.uk/report.asp?compid=35796&strquery="Irish%20Rebellion"#p14, accessed 20 June 2007.

[65] *The private journals of the Long Parliament 7 March to 1 June 1642*, ed. Vernon Snow and Anne Steele, New Haven 1987, 3. I am grateful to Sears McGee for sharing his wisdom on Sir Simmonds D'Ewes with me.

[66] Sir John Coke the Younger to Sir John Coke, 27 Mar. 1642, in HMC, *The manuscripts of the Earl Cowper, K.G., preserved at Melbourne Hall, Derbyshire*, London 1888–9, ii. 310.

[67] [Secretary Nicholas?] to Ormond, 1 Apr. 1642, MS Carte 3, fo. 80.

[68] Peacey, *Politicians and pamphleteers*, 56.

[69] 'The king's speech to the committee on their presenting the last Declaration to him', 12 Mar. 1642, in *Cobbett's parliamentary history of England: from the Norman Conquest in 1066 to the year 1803: from which last-mentioned epoch is continued downwards in the work entitled, 'Cobbett's parliamentary debates'*, London 1807, ii, cols 1125–6.

by those evil counsels near your majesty, in opposition to the parliament'.[70] Pym's speech contained arguments that had been previously aired in parliament but it also incorporated new information gleaned from the *Remonstrance*. An irritated Charles I defended himself by asking 'what greater comfort, or security, can the Protestants of Christendom receive, than by seeing a Protestant king venture and engage his person for the defence of that profession, and the suppression of Popery, to which we solemnly protested'. Turning his attention to Ireland, he warned of 'the growth and increase of the strength of those barbarous rebels, and the evident probability of foreign supplies, if they are not speedily suppressed'. In his reply Charles recognised that Jones's *Remonstrance* had provided parliament with the necessary evidence to block his expedition into Ireland. The king denigrated the findings of the *Remonstrance* as 'impossible' and wondered whether it 'may make an impression in the minds of many of our weak subjects'. Acknowledging the concern of the Commons, Charles I withdrew his proposal to go to Ireland, but warned that 'if we find the miserable condition of the poor subjects of that kingdom be not speedily relieved, we will, with God's assistance, visit them with succours, as our particular interest can supply us with, if you refuse to join with us'. This call for unity ended with a reiteration of his demand for 'the suppression of seditious Sermons and Pamphlets'.[71]

The controversy entered the wider domain through the tit-for-tat publication of speeches on the issue.[72] In the end, sensing Charles's political fragility, parliament launched a further attack on the king by announcing the Nineteen Propositions. These, along with the Remonstrance on Hull and the Militia Ordnance, sought to limit the king's powers. They also voiced parliament's claim to be the state's sole judicial power. In effect, parliament had thrown down the gauntlet to the king.[73] In response, Charles adopted a two-fold strategy. First, in an attempt to rally support, he sought to reposition the monarchy as an agent that could work with parliament but not be subordinated to it.[74] Secondly, he pressurised the deposition commissioners to compose another account of the rebellion that refuted implicit criticisms

[70] Ibid. ii, cols 1170, 1172, 1173–5.

[71] 'The king's answer to his petition against his going into Ireland', ibid. ii, cols 1180–3. In response to this on 28 March 1642, Pym called for greater activity in the suppression of seditious pamphlets but confessed the probability that 'we shall never suppress them'. *Private journals of the Long Parliament*, 98.

[72] *The hvmble petition of the Lords and Commons assembled in parliament, unto his majesty (with the reasons moving them, to advise his majesty) to decline his intended journey into Ireland*, London 1642; *His maiesties answer to a petition presented to him at Yorke, Aprill 18 1642*, London 1642; *The petition of both houses of parliament to his majestie, concerning his intended going to Ireland*, London 1642.

[73] Allan Macinnes, *The British revolution, 1629–1660*, Houndsmills 2005, 146–7; Ian Gentles, *The English revolution and the Wars in the Three Kingdoms, 1638–1652*, London 2007, 93.

[74] Macinnes, *The British revolution*, 147–8; Peacey, *Politicians and pamphleteers*, 241.

levelled against him in the *Remonstrance*. This led to the publication of *An abstract of certain depositions* in the summer of 1642.[75]

The *Abstract*, attributed to Roger Puttocke, one of the deposition commissioners, discredited many of the charges made against the king in the *Remonstrance*, and aimed at a much wider audience than Jones's work as it circulated as a cheap eight-page pamphlet. The king's seal adorned the title page to signify the legitimacy of Puttocke's endeavour. Most of the vitriol in the pamphlet was reserved for the Catholic clergy who wanted to 'have their church lands back and kingdom back from the English'. The nationalistic sentiments of the rebels found voice in their assertions that 'they would have none to govern them, but a born Irish man'. Irish ambivalence towards the king did not appear in Puttocke's *Abstract*. Instead the rebels were united in their desire to 'deny the king', and regarded 'not King Charles, the king of England'. To prove this Puttocke included depositions that chronicled the extent of popular support for Sir Phelim O'Neill to become king of Ireland. According to Puttocke, the pope was sponsoring the Irish rebellion and sought to expel English people from Ireland, establish Catholicism there and separate Ireland from the crown.[76]

The claims of Jones and Puttocke flatly contradicted the public announcements made by Sir Phelim O'Neill and his fellow insurgents and directed at the lords justices. As the *Remonstrance* galvanised the royalist effort in England, it also prompted the confederates to enter into the printed debate of the 1640s. Confederates used their propaganda to argue that Jones and his colleagues among the lords justices and council had exaggerated the scale of violence that had occurred in the early days of the rebellion. They alleged that the colonial administration was just as violent and had acted belligerently toward Irish Catholics. Furthermore, they sought to distance themselves from allegations of atrocity in order to stress their loyalty to the king, and to emphasise their religious and political grievances. The point to note is that as the conflict between king and parliament turned into a civil war, all three kingdoms were drawn into a protracted, bloody and bitter conflict.

Contesting the cessation of arms and lobbying London

The butchery that characterised the first phase of the rebellion abated due to the influence of commanders newly-arrived from Europe to fight in Ireland such as Robert Monro, Owen Roe O'Neill and Thomas Preston. The formation of the confederation of Kilkenny added credibility to the rebel movement and facilitated negotiations with the king. Charles hoped to secure

---

[75] Deposition commission to Henry Jones, 20 July 1642, TCD, MS 840, fo. 49r–v; [Roger Puttocke], *An abstract of certain depositions*, London 1642.

[76] Puttocke, *An abstract*, passim.

support from Ireland against his opponents in England. His decision to negotiate with the confederates exacerbated tensions within the Protestant community in Ireland. In March 1643 the king publicly announced his plans to consult with a delegation from the confederation at Trim.

Here, the confederates outlined the full extent of their grievances *vis-à-vis* the Protestant-controlled English administration in Ireland. These were later published under the title *A remonstrance of grievances presented to his most excellent majestie, in the behalf of the Catholicks of Ireland*.[77] Proposals to negotiate a ceasefire between the king and the confederates in mid-1643 upset the delicate political equilibrium among the Protestant community in Ireland. An explosive meeting occurred in June between those who favoured the king's plans and those who did not: an irate Sir John Temple captured the extent of opposition to the motion when he roundly criticised Ormond and his followers for pursuing this 'dishonourable' policy.[78] Ireland's Protestant community was effectively split along royalist/parliamentarian lines.

Some members of the colonial administration were also particularly aggrieved at the very public criticism directed against them by the confederates. The *Remonstrance of grievances* laid the blame for the rebellion on the actions of the English administration in Ireland, of which Temple and his colleagues were prominent members, and argued that they had blocked Catholic access to political and religious privileges. The confederates singled out Sir William Parsons, one of the lords justices, in their critique of the English administration in Ireland. They noted his 'immortall hatred' of Catholics and stressed that this threatened the 'welfare and happinesse of this Nation'. Parsons and his allies were accused of trying 'to make themselves stil greater and richer, by the totall ruine and extirpation of this people'.[79] As a result of their actions, the Catholics of Ireland, according to the author of the *Remonstrance of grievances*, had been forced to take up arms as their concerns were 'slighted by the said Lords-Iustices'. As proof they pointed to the prorogation of the Irish parliament by Parsons upon the outbreak of rebellion.[80] This contrasted sharply with rival accounts of the Irish rebellion that portrayed 'rebel' behaviour as an orgy of massacres committed against Protestant settlers. Through blaming the sabre-rattling towards the Old English community of Sir William St Leger, Sir Charles Coote and Sir William Parsons, the *Remonstrance of grievances* defended their taking up arms as wholly legitimate. In short, 'every man saw that the estates of Catholicks were first aymed at, and their lives next'.[81]

---

[77] *A remonstrance of grievances presented to his most excellent majestie, in the behalfe of the Catholicks of Ireland*, Waterford 1643.

[78] Philip Sidney to Dorothy Percy Sidney, countess of Leicester, 18 June 1643, MS Carte 5, fo. 482.

[79] *Remonstrance of grievances*, 7–8.

[80] Ibid. 18–19.

[81] Ibid. 22. See also p. 163 below.

A report sent to the king on 16 March 1643 demonstrated the extent of opposition to Charles's decision. William Parsons and John Temple lobbied for the suppression of the rebellion. They argued strongly that the insurgency could only end when 'the sword abated these rebels'. They reminded the king that many had died at the hands of the Catholic rebels and cited the deposition of Robert Maxwell who alleged that 154,000 Protestants had been killed in the north of Ireland.[82] However, Charles I imprisoned those who stood in the way of his intention to parley with the confederates and rewarded those deemed 'reliable'.[83] Parsons, in particular, had been identified by the *Remonstrance of grievances* as a supporter of the king's enemies in England. It noted Parson's allegiance to the 'malignant party' and claimed that he indulged them in their desire 'to extinguish [the Irish] Nation and Religion'.[84] In response, the king replaced Parsons with Sir Henry Tichborne, commander at Drogheda. This was followed by the arrest of Sir John Temple and Sir Robert Meredith in August 1643. Temple had earlier lamented privately that 'I expect nothing but ruine'. Predicting 'much mischiefe', he regretted the decision to negotiate a military settlement with the confederates: 'I hold a peace with the rebells here, which is the maine dessigne, as ruinous as our warr.'[85] Parsons's political allies were calling for a full-scale military conquest of Ireland, not a ceasefire.

During this time the deposition commission published another pamphlet in an attempt to discredit the king's alliance with the confederates. They identified with the policies of Parsons and Temple and provided the necessary propaganda to support them. Their publication was presented from the viewpoint of a deponent, Thomas Morley, and portrayed all Catholics of Ireland as violent, barbaric and unaccustomed to the rules of war. Morley's *Remonstrance of the barbarous cruelties and bloody murders committed by the Irish rebels against the Protestants in Ireland both before and since the cessation* followed the same style as Puttocke's *Abstract* and was aimed at a popular audience. The title page recounted Morley's experience of the rebellion and the extent of his financial losses. Like Henry Jones in his *Remonstrance* Morley focused on cruelties committed against Protestant and English women and children. Chronicling cruelties in the text with the names of the deponents

---

[82] William Parsons and others to Charles I, 16 Mar. 1643, HMC, *Ormond*, n.s. ii. 244–53; the deposition of Robert Maxwell, TCD, MS 809, fos 5r–12v. See also Armstrong, *Protestant war*, 82–3. Temple had argued something similar to the king in December 1642 as well. See *A true declaration of the last affaires in Ireland, shewing the late overthrowes given to the Irish rebels*, London 1642.

[83] Armstrong, *Protestant war*, 85.

[84] *Remonstrance of grievances*, 17–8.

[85] Temple to William Hawkins, 23 Apr. 1643, in *Report on the manuscripts of the right honorable Viscount De L'Isle, V.C. preserved at Penshurst Place Kent*, London 1966, 429; Temple to Dr Temple, 20 June 1643, MS Carte 5, fo. 498v; Temple to Leicester, 20 June 1643, MS Carte 5, fos 500r–501v.

in the margins, Morley's *Remonstrance of barbarous cruelties* noted that the victims of the rebels' outrage were 'loyal subjects'.[86] These loyal subjects were portrayed in stark contrast to the 'popish rebels' whose society represented what would have appeared to seventeenth-century readers as an inversion of the social order: 'One Philip O'Reilly then and yet shierffe of the county, relenting at their continued cruelties, his own son told him that if he did revolt from that action and authority; he ought to die and should surely be hanged.'[87] Their mission was to destroy Protestant Bibles and houses, and to conduct an indiscriminate slaughter of the settler population in Ireland.

Morley's *Remonstrance of barbarous cruelties* was heavily based on the deposition of Robert Maxwell. Four pages rely entirely on Maxwell's testimony, describing attacks on English animals, and atrocities committed across Armagh. This section was perhaps the most gruesome in the pamphlet. Morley described how women's corpses were violated sexually and how some corpses were left exposed to the elements and others left face down so as they could only see hell.[88] A postscript reminded readers that ministers were the main targets of rebel aggression, as had been argued by Jones, and was aimed, no doubt, at shocked Protestant audiences in England who opposed the cessation of arms: 'The Generall cruelty to Ministers against Protestants and that religion duly exercised by the Papist-rebells scornfull malicious and contemptuous words and blasphemies, are so many and frequently used, and by too wofull experience found and proved by a multitude of witnesses.'[89] Morley's pamphlet appeared in June 1644 when the most vocal criticism of the king's actions was being prepared by an imprisoned John Temple. It was to be a vitriolic condemnation of the confederates and a staunch defence of the political faction of which he was a prominent member.[90]

Temple's experience of both politics and print during this period shaped his grand vision for the future of the English colony in Ireland. John Adamson has argued that Temple's manifesto, published as *The Irish rebellion* along with Adam Meredith's *Ormond's cvrtain drawn* in 1646, formed part of the propaganda campaign waged by Parsons and Temple (the Independent party) to oust from the Irish administration proponents of the cessation of

---

[86] Thomas Morley, *A remonstrance of the barbarous cruelties and bloody murders committed by the Irish rebels against the Protestants in Ireland both before and since the cessation*, London 1644, 1.

[87] Ibid. 2. Morley was presumably referring to Myles O'Reilly here.

[88] Ibid. 6–10.

[89] Ibid. 13.

[90] Raymond Gillespie, 'Temple's fate: reading *The Irish rebellion* in late seventeenth-century Ireland', in Ciaran Brady and Jane Ohlmeyer (eds), *British interventions in early modern Ireland*, Cambridge 2005, 315–33 at p. 325; deposition of Jane Stewart, 23 Apr. 1644, TCD, MS 831, fos 73r–77v.

arms (or the Ormond party).[91] To a certain extent this may have been the case, yet, on closer analysis, it is clear that these two publications served another purpose. Primarily, both responded to confederate accusations contained in the *Remonstrance of grievances* and defended the record of the Borlase and Parsons administration. Their printing signalled a change in the tide of power with the appointment of Philip Sidney, Viscount Lisle, in 1646 as parliamentary lord lieutenant.[92] If Temple had prepared his text in 1644, why did it take him such a long time to publish *The Irish rebellion*?

Prior to his imprisonment, Temple had become involved in a series of spats with Sir Philip Perceval who accused him of corruption and revelled in his subsequent imprisonment. The appointment of Lisle as lord lieutenant, however, signalled a change in Perceval's political fortunes. In 1647 Perceval and Temple competed with one another to secure a favourable candidate as baker for the army in Ireland. The appointment of Thomas Hill, Temple's choice, underlined the ascendancy of Lisle's supporters.[93] Temple's campaign to remove Perceval culminated in the latter's impeachment in 1647. Perceval died before official proceedings against him commenced,[94] but before his death he had hired one of the deposition commissioners, John Watson, to publish an account of the rebellion based on the depositions, which may have pushed Temple to print *The Irish rebellion*. Watson urged Perceval to allow him to proceed with his book, and guaranteed that

> Having p[er]used Sr John Temple's Relation of the Irish rebellion and looked over myne owne rough draught, I fynd his doth here and there touch upon those heads whereon I have ditaled, and even in the point of Cruelties (when he is largest) presume myne may adde something.[95]

Furthermore, Watson suggested that Temple had limited access to the originals, 'besides myne hath much w[hi]ch he never saw'.[96] Temple, no doubt aware of the possibility of a rival publication, published *The Irish rebellion* and made alterations to Meredith's *Ormonds cvrtain drawn* in order to criticise

---

[91] John Adamson, 'Strafford's ghost: the British context of Viscount Lisle's lieutenancy of Ireland', in Ohlmeyer, *Ireland from independence to occupation*, 128–59, 139–40.

[92] Ibid. 141. It must be pointed out that Lisle only spent three months in Ireland as lord lieutenant – he returned to England after a failed expedition to relieve Munster in April 1647, without ever visiting Dublin: C. H. Firth, 'Sidney, Philip, third earl of Leicester (1619–1698)', rev. Sean Kelsey, *ODNB*: www.oxforddnb.com/view/article/25523, accessed 26 Nov. 2009.

[93] Thomas Piggott to Perceval, 19 Feb. 1647, HMC, *Egmont*, i/2, 362; Val Savage to Perceval, 21 July 1647, ibid. i/2, 433; Armstrong, *Protestant war*, 213–14.

[94] Patrick Little, 'Perceval, Sir Philip (1605–1647)', *ODNB*: www.oxforddnb.com/view/article/21913, accessed 17 Dec. 2008.

[95] John Watson to Perceval, 22 May 1646, BL, MS Egerton 46,929, fo. 151.

[96] Ibid.

Sir Philip Perceval. This prompted Perceval to accost Samuel Gellibrand, Temple's printer, in order to have his name omitted from the tract.[97]

Temple's *Irish rebellion* defended his political bedfellows and praised the deposition commission (despite Watson's criticisms of *The Irish rebellion*) as a necessary component of the Borlase and Parsons administration. The depositions 'were in great wisdom designed by them for no other ends then to have some general account of the losses suffered by the British, and the Cruelties by the Irish exercised upon them'. Taken with all 'care and circumspection' Temple noted that they had been 'commonly decried, and held by the Irish as very injurious to their countrey men'. He claimed that deponents 'were of severall conditions, most of them British, some of Irish birth and extraction, very many of good quality, and such as were of inferiour rank were not rejected if they were known sufferers'. Addressing confederate criticisms over the veracity of the statements taken, Temple argued that 'what is given in by them upon hearsay, they for the most part depose, that they received it out of the Rebels own Mouthes while they were in restraint amongst them'. In a dramatic twist, Temple claimed that most of those who left a deposition were so wounded or worn out from their sufferings that they perished soon afterwards. Allegedly the depositions were 'bequeathed unto us, with their [the deponents'] last breath'.[98] In short, Temple argued that the depositions were valid evidence for the massacres of Protestant settlers in Ireland.

In *The Irish rebellion*, Temple blamed Catholic gentry and clergy for starting the rebellion and for plotting the seizure of Protestant goods. The initial murders that had occurred on 23 October 1641 were personal vendettas, but what followed was an indiscriminate bloodbath that aimed to impose an 'Irish' order at the top of the social hierarchy. In order to portray this, Temple only included bloodier atrocities mentioned in the depositions and removed deponents' descriptions of their own individual suffering. Edward Banks, Elizabeth Baskerville, Charity Chappell, Mary Corne, Henry Fisher, Thomas Fleetwood, Eleanor Fullerton, James Geare, John Gormley, Jane Grace, John Grissell, Julian Johnson, Katherine Madison, Nathaniell Mawe,[99] Mary Parkin and James Stevenson all testified to the death of a relative, or to how they were stripped or tortured by the rebels, yet none of these incidents appeared in the deposition section of *The Irish rebellion*. Others made up for this omission. Mary Barlow, Joane Constable, Margaret Farmeny, Thomas and Elizabeth Green, Anne Hill, Elizabeth Price, Ann Read and Magdalen Redman all mentioned cruelties which they or their families had suffered at the hands of the rebels, including imprisonment, stripping, or the death of family members. This may reflect, however, the author's economical use of space. None the less, Temple maintained a grim

---

[97] HMC, *Egmont*, ii. 356, 425, 430–1. See also Adamson, 'Strafford's ghost', 139.

[98] Temple, *The Irish rebellion*, [1–11], 'Preface to the reader'.

[99] Incorrectly called 'Samuel Man' by Temple.

fascination with massacre stories. As part of this he included descriptions of alleged mass graves for Protestants dug by Irish rebels. Here the rebels 'laid the carcasses of those dead persons in great ranks into vast and great holes, laying them so close and thick, as if they had packed up herrings together'.[100] Similarly, he claimed that many thousands were drowned, with 'one thousand men out at severall times in severall troops at Portadown'.[101]

Instances of kindness towards Irish Protestants by the native Irish contradicted the picture that Temple intended to paint of the rebels. Like Jones, Temple depicted the Irish rebels as a disorganised rabble confused in their motivations and callous in their actions and claimed that Catholic lawyers and clergy had duped them into taking up arms. Temple's use of the depositions emphasised the barbarity and cruelty of their actions towards Irish Protestants. Temple neglected to include how Owen Roe O'Neill chastised Phelim O'Neill for killing Protestant prisoners in his custody. Elizabeth Price, a deponent cited frequently by Temple, fleshed out the details of this event. Owen Roe allegedly punished some of his subordinates 'in p[ar]t of revenge & destestacon of their odious actions, burned some of the Rebells howses at Kinard and sayd he would Joyne w[i]th the English army to burne the rest'.[102] Much as in early intelligence on the rebellion Temple portrayed the plight of the English colony as desperate and Ireland's Catholics as vehemently anti-Protestant. In effect, Temple lobbied for the political and legal exclusion of those guilty of rebellion.

Temple's appeal to Lord Lisle underlined the perilous condition of the colonial project in Ireland. Lord Conor Maguire tried to destroy the records of plantation towns in Fermanagh, an indication of how the Irish rebels allegedly wanted to destroy all remnants of English rule in Ireland.[103] Throughout the text Temple used the terms 'British', 'English', 'Protestant' and 'Christian' almost interchangeably in order to speak to as wide an audience as possible. To avoid alienating the king, he made no criticism of him. Similarly, he described victims as suffering regardless of their social status. Women and children were particularly vulnerable. The rebels were described in formulaic terms and compared to the Spanish as they tried to expel the Moors in the fifteenth century.[104] Despite this comparison with the prototype cruel Catholic, however, Temple maintained that this was a separatist movement cloaked in a language of religious grievances: 'We must beleeve that their designe clearly was to destroy and root out all the British and Protestant planted within this kingdom, to cut off the Soveraignity of the Crowne

---

[100] Temple, *The Irish rebellion*, 89.
[101] Ibid. 92.
[102] Deposition of Elizabeth Price, 26 June 1642, TCD, MS 836, fo. 102v; Temple, *The Irish rebellion*, 134–5.
[103] Temple, *The Irish rebellion*, 91–2.
[104] Ibid. 83.

of *England*, and so to deliver themselves from their long continued subjection to the English nation.'[105] Temple, therefore, aimed to make his text as inclusive as possible by evoking as much sympathy as possible for the victims of the Irish rebellion in order to revive English interest in Ireland. Aware that the Long Parliament was divided along political and religious lines as both Independent and Presbyterian factions took hold in 1646, perhaps Temple hoped that by reminding the factions in parliament of England's longstanding interest in Ireland some form of consensus would emerge for a military reconquest of Ireland.

Temple's *Irish rebellion* may have become foundational to Protestant historiography on the 1641 rebellion, yet its publication marks the centrality of print and the London print trade to Irish statecraft. Politicians from across the political and religious spectrum lobbied for support through the medium of print. In Temple's case, *The Irish rebellion* (like all the other deposition publications during this period) used the plight of widowed settlers and their children to evoke responses from the political hierarchy in England. Like Jones's *Remonstrance* Temple produced largely hearsay evidence on this point. Regardless, events were portrayed as an indiscriminate massacre conducted by a barbaric native Irish population with the support of Old English gentry which should (in his opinion) have known better. In effect, Temple lobbied for the full-scale military conquest of Ireland and the segregation of native and newcomer populations with 'a wall of separation' between them. Within a year an expeditionary force, to be led by General Philip Skippon and General Edward Massey, was to arrive in Ireland, but nothing came of this force.[106] Temple would have to wait until 1649 and the arrival of Oliver Cromwell to see his wishes granted.

The intelligence gathered by the lords justices in the early stages of the rebellion, and presented to the wider world, immediately presented the rebellion as a Catholic plot. Their promises to include the traditionally loyal Old English in an army to suppress the rebellion were insincere and the harsh implementation of martial law by leading commanders such as Charles Coote and William St Leger hastened their involvement in the rebellion. Over the spring of 1642 the deposition commission gathered a significant amount of information about the course of the rebellion that reflected its regional variations, the pattern of violence, the negotiations of order between settler and native populations, and the multitude of motivations that prompted people to take up arms. Despite this, the lords justices and the deposition commission disseminated details about the rebellion that characterised the actions of the native Irish and the Old English as

[105] Ibid.
[106] Andrew Warmington, 'Massey, Sir Edward (1604x9–1674)', and Ian Gentles, 'Skippon, Philip (d. 1660)', *ODNB*: www.oxforddnb.com/view/article/18297, accessed 23 Apr. 2009; Armstrong, *Protestant war*, 213–16; Woolrych, *Britain in revolution*, 371–2.

religiously motivated and not as a result of improper colonial governance. Accordingly, through using contemporary constructs of civility, the lords justices and the deposition commission exonerated their regime as a cause for the rebellion. Confederate criticisms were met with strenuous denials and detailed accounts of how Ireland's barbaric Catholics were behaving toward their Protestant neighbours.

Oft decried as propaganda, the 1641 depositions when they appeared in print certainly served a polemical purpose. Yet, the significance of what they contained is not readily apparent without looking at the wider context of English politics and the English front in the Wars of the Three Kingdoms. When this is considered, it is clear that the authorities in Ireland deliberately portrayed the rebellion to suit English political audiences. The 23 October 1641 did not mark the beginning of an indiscriminate massacre of the Protestant population in Ireland nor was it solely inspired by religious affairs. The Catholic gentry and nobility of Ireland had clear political, social and economic grievances that were consistently ignored and their attempts to parley with colonial authorities were rejected. Professions of loyalty to the king exacerbated tensions between Charles I and his parliament and paved the way towards agreements to the cessations of arms of 1643, 1644 and 1646, which all met with staunch opposition from Protestant Ireland. They lobbied against these ceasefires through the medium of print. The publication of Temple's *Irish rebellion* marks the apex of their achievements. Within a year plans fully to conquer Ireland were well in hand, although due to political divisions in Westminster they failed to materialise.

The appearance of the 1641 depositions in print also illustrates a crucial aspect of the early modern worldview: attitudes toward violence. Why did the deposition commission pay so much attention to attacks on women and children? Were their reports on the 1641 rebellion unique in this respect? The purpose of the next chapter is to contextualise reports on the 1641 rebellion by comparing them with pamphlets that described other 'bloody' events during the Thirty Years' War (1618–48) and in the Americas during the early modern period. This will reveal how contemporaries portrayed violent events and show how depictions of the 1641 rebellion were sourced from Englishmen's cultural constructions of violence and their views on the wider sectarian and religious conflict across the Atlantic world and Europe.

4

The 1641 Rebellion and Violence in the New and Old Worlds

The seventeenth century, in the eyes of numerous scholars, was an exceptionally violent time to be alive.[1] War and rebellions in Ireland and the Atlantic world were followed by violent conquests by colonial armies. Accounts by *conquistadores*, English colonists and detached observers all recounted the brutality of these armed conflicts. The highly charged confessional character of European political and social relations precipitated violent events such as the St Bartholomew's Day massacre, the Piedmont massacre and facilitated the interpretation of the Thirty Years' War through a sectarian prism. The purpose of this chapter, therefore, is to investigate whether there were similarities between how the Irish rebellion was presented in English newsbooks and pamphlets and the portrayal of atrocities that occurred across the New and Old Worlds. It focuses entirely on reports of violent events published in the seventeenth century and provides a vital snapshot as to how such incidents were portrayed by English printers. Were pamphlets that described events in Ireland exceptional in their brutal and bloody content? What factors shaped the construction of these accounts?

Atrocities during the Thirty Years' War

The proliferation of news reports on the Thirty Years' War indicates a high level of interest in events in Europe among Englishmen and women. These pamphlets have come under much scrutiny. Barbara Donagan believed that news from Germany provided English people with a prime example of a bloody conflict that warned them 'of the poverty, depopulation and barbarism war could bring to a once prosperous country'. Donagan's analysis, however, focused on particularly gory accounts from Germany. Joseph Cope has traced similarities between representations of the war in Germany and the 1641 rebellion.[2] Their studies focused on a small number of publications,

---

[1] Geoffrey Parker and Lesley Smith (eds), *The general crisis of the seventeenth century*, London 1997; Clarke, 'Ireland and the general crisis', 79–99; Julius Ruff, *Violence in early modern Europe*, Cambridge 2001.

[2] Cope, *England and the 1641 rebellion*, 89–103; Donagan, 'Codes and conduct', 65–96 at p. 70.

and did not include a detailed analysis of all the pamphlets that reported the course of the Thirty Years' War. Furthermore, John Theibault argued that historians have overlooked key cultural aspects of these publications. Composed replete with a rhetoric of death and destruction, these works emphasised the suffering of German Protestants in order to elicit funding from England.[3] Much of the work on the representation on the Thirty Years' War relies upon a small sample that is unrepresentative of how the conflict was portrayed. Similarly, 'bloody' news from Ireland was only one aspect of pamphlet reports on the 1641 rebellion. Readers learned about troop movements, state proclamations and other official correspondence between leading political figures, a fact that has been overlooked by many historians.

As shown in the previous chapter, politicians could use news stories to lobby for various political policies throughout the 1640s. This was not a new phenomenon in English, Irish or British politics, however. Key political figures of the time spoke with great sympathy of their afflicted Protestant brethren in Germany. Speeches by Sir Simonds D'Ewes reflected his concerns over Spain's motivations and Jesuit intentions in the conflict.[4] Some pamphlets simply offered news of various military encounters and lacked the dramatic descriptions contained in many of the publications discussed by other historians.[5] Many of these works described troop movements, military engagements and the *realpolitick* of the Thirty Years' War and of European diplomacy. Some reports referred to the confessional tensions of the time, with praise being lavished upon Protestant commanders such as Gustavus Adolphus.[6] Their content, rooted in the rhetoric of death and destruction, furthermore, served a didactic purpose when preachers and politicians began to outline moral lessons from events on the continent that England had to learn. For example, Benjamin Rudyerd warned that Europe was in the midst of a confessional crisis and expressed hopes that parliament would not follow

[3] John Theibault, 'The rhetoric of death and destruction in the Thirty Years War', *Journal of Social History* xxvii (Winter 1993), 271–90.

[4] Simonds D'Ewes, *A speech delivered In the House of Commons, July 7th 1641*, London 1641; *More nevves from the Palatinate; and more comfort to every true Christian, that either favoureth the cause of religion, or wisheth well to the king of Bohemia's proceedings*, London 1622; *The Spaniards perpetvall designes to an vniversall monarchie: translated according to the French*, London 1624; *Camilton's discoverie of the devilish designes and killing projects of the Society of Jesuites*, London 1641.

[5] *The great and famovs battel of Lvtzen, fought betweene the renowned kng of Sweeden, and Walstein*, London 1633; *Good newes from Alsasia and the Palatinate, the fift of Iune*, London 1622; *The exact and true relation of that bloody battell fought betweene his royall majestie of Swethland, and the imperiall army the 5 and 6 of November 1632*, Edinburgh 1633.

[6] *The new starr of the north, shining vpon the victorious king of Sweden*, London 1631; *A relation of the king of Svveden, his happie and incomparable successe and victories, against the forces of the emperour*, London 1631; *An elegie upon the death of the most illustrious and victorious Prince Gustavus Adolphus king of Swethland*, London 1633; *The tvvo famous pitcht battels of Lypsich, and Lutzen wherein the ever-renowned Prince Gustavus the Great lived and died a conqueror*, London 1634.

in Germany's footsteps and would solve the religious crisis that England faced.[7] Pamphleteers followed Rudyerd's lead and provided accounts of the war replete with moral lessons.

Publications highlighted the moral failings of Germany and noted the decay of German society. Particular examples were Philip Vincent's *Lamentations of Germany* (1638), *Warnings of Germany* (1638), *Lacrymae Germaniae: or, The tears of Germany* (1638) and *The invasions of Germanie* (1638). There is one major connection between these pamphlets: all came from the press of John Rothwell. Vincent, the author of *Lamentations of Germany*, was a theologian and skilled propagandist. He shaped his account, as did the authors of Rothwell's other publications, to warn readers of the folly of their sins and to cajole them into leading a more moral and pious life. The religious lessons were clear for all to see: 'I commend you to the protection of the Lord Almighty, desiring you to joyne your prayers to Him to divert the judgements inflicted; and in His goodness and wisedome to make up the breaches of the distressed and distracted Germany.'[8] Divine providence shone on the elect and great weight was attributed to the signs and wonders from God that German Protestants ignored, much to their detriment.[9] These works were written in formulaic prose that reflected the trope of atrocity publications of the era.

Descriptions of the conflict were suitably dramatic and infused with hyperbolic, symbolic portrayals of the conflict. *Lacrymae Germaniae* hailed Germany as formerly 'the glory and delight of princes' but now sat as a 'defloured virgin', because German Protestants had sinned.[10] This tract portrayed the conflict as a total war that encompassed the entire Catholic population of Europe which attacked Protestant churches, ministers and people. Such interpretations were not unique to Rothwell's publications. *A trve relation of the proceedings of the Bauarian and Spanish forces before the City Heydelburgh* (1622) claimed that Catholics had received a papal indulgence exonerating them of cruelties committed against Protestants and described Jesuits as 'hatefull' to Protestants.[11] *Two very lamentable relations* (1620)

---

[7] *Two speeches by Sir Beniamin Rudyard concerning the Palatinate*, London 1641, 2. For an excellent discussion on Rudyerd's career in the 1620s and 1630s see David Smith, 'Sir Benjamin Rudyerd and England's "wars of religion"', in Michael Braddick and David Smith (eds), *The experience of revolution in Stuart Britain and Ireland: essays for John Morrill*, Cambridge 2011, 52–73, esp. pp. 60–6.

[8] *Lacrymae Germaniae*, London 1638, 'To the reader'.

[9] *Warnings of Germany*, London 1638, 'The preface'; Philip Vincent, *Lamentations of Germany*, London 1638, 2. This was not unique to Rothwell's publications, however. *A lamentable list, of certaine hidious, frightfull, and prodifious signes, which have bin seene in the aire, earth and waters, at severall times*, London 1638; Gillespie, *Devoted people*, 40–6; Walsham, *Providence*.

[10] *Lacrymae Germaniae*, 'To the reader'.

[11] *A trve relation of the proceedings of the Bauarian and Spanish forces before the City Heydelburgh*, London 1622, 5, 7.

reported that churches were consecrated into the Catholic faith, purged of Protestant artefacts, cleansed of Protestant corpses and religious books destroyed.[12] In a similar manner Catholics targeted Protestant women and children and 'fearfully violated and ravished' them.[13] At this point, European military figures were beginning to adhere to an emerging military etiquette, which moderated the conduct of sieges and battles that were prone to butchery. All leaders of Europe agreed that it was against the laws of war to kill the weak and unprotected, particularly women and children.[14] Reportage of the deaths of civilians reflected wider concerns that combatants adhere to established laws of war. Those who refused to exercise such moderation (according to London printers) were usually Catholics and accordingly demonised in contemporary print.

One of Rothwell's publications, Vincent's *Lamentations of Germany* requires more detailed scrutiny. Like Rothwell's other publications, the *Lamentations of Germany* contained numerous biblical references that established cues for readers to follow and to interpret their content through a providential lens. Within the first two sentences of this pamphlet Vincent outlined the correct interpretation of his text: 'Behold here, as in a Glasse, the mournefull face of a sister Nation, now drunke with misery; according to what God threatned by the Prophet *Ieremy*.'[15] Contemporary readers would have understood that Vincent referred to the anonymous voice that lamented the loss of Rachel's children, 'there was a voice heard, lamentation, and weeping, and great mourning'.[16] In this manner, Vincent sought to create a sense of grief that would allow his readers to relate to their German brethren. It also reinforced the notion that readers would 'learne righteousnesse by the judgements of God which are made manifest'.[17] Vincent's depictions of the violence that occurred in Germany closely resembled those contained in the Book of Revelation: corpses left on the street, exposed to 'Fowles of the ayre [who] may therein eate ... the flesh of all men both free and bond, both small and great' are images derived from the description of the Apocalypse in the Bible.[18] Like Rachel who mourned for her dead children in the book of Nehemiah, readers of the *Lamentations of Germany* were reminded of a passage from Romans xii.15: 'in respect of them, first let us sympathize: grieve with them that grieve'. This prompted the reader to fast and pray for

[12] *Two very lamentable relations*, London 1620, [2].

[13] Ibid. [13]; Vincent, *Lamentations*, 19–21.

[14] Donagan, 'Codes and conduct', 78; Parker, 'Etiquette of atrocity', 143–68 at p. 152.

[15] Vincent, *Lamentations*, sig. A3.

[16] Matthew ii.17–21.

[17] Vincent, *Lamentations*, sig. A4

[18] Ibid; Revelation xix.17–18.

the victims as dictated by Nehemiah.[19] Readers would no doubt have been aware that Vincent also encouraged them to think about their own sins.[20]

The most important framework within which to interpret the *Lamentations of Germany* was the Book of Lamentations. Vincent adorned the title page of the *Lamentations* with the quotation: 'Is it nothing to you, all ye that passe by? Behold and see, if there be any sorrow like unto my sorrow, which is done unto me, wherewith the Lord hath afflicted me, in the day of his fierce anger.'[21] Knowledge of the original biblical text, the sort of knowledge that would have been typical of a seventeenth-century Puritan, would indicate how this piece was to be interpreted. Here, Vincent reminded his readers of the graphic description of God's decision to punish the Israelites by sacking Jersulaem. The first chapter of Lamentations opens with a widow weeping for her fallen brethen after the sack of the city: 'The Lord hath trodden under foot all my mighty men in the midst of me: he hath called an assembly against me to crush my young men: the Lord hath trodden the virgin, the daughter of Judah, as in a winepress.' Subsequently this widow, having been punished by God, duly began to think of her own sins and was struck in awe of God's power: 'The Lord is righteous; for I have rebelled against his commandment.' Now aware of the consequences of her sins, the widow then warns other people: 'hear, I pray you, all people, and behold my sorrow: my virgins and my young men are gone into captivity' – the cry of a sinner.[22] The widow then accepts God's punishments and repents for her sins. Finally, she cries out for revenge: 'Do unto them, as thou hast done unto me for all my transgressions.'[23] Like many of Rothwell's publications the *Lamentations of Germany* encouraged readers to reflect upon their own faith and to seek vengeance for the victims of Catholic atrocities.

Vincent's work is a product of the early modern cultural construction of atrocity publications. Vincent demonised the barbaric Catholic enemy – 'nor Turkes nor infidels have so behaved themselves' forcing their victims to eat their own excrement and various forms of torture being inflicted upon them, including slow burning.[24] He condemned those who refused to grant quarter and singled out the Croat forces for particular criticism on this point.[25] The illustrations that accompanied the text focused predominantly on the plight of women and children, who were forced to commit a range of intolerable actions. Women ate their own children and their friends, some poisoned themselves to 'hasten death', others were raped by soldiers and

---

19 Vincent, *Lamentations*, [6, 9], 'Preface to the reader'; Nehemiah i.1–4.

20 Nehemiah i.7.

21 Vincent, *Lamentations*, title page.

22 Lamentations, i.

23 Lamentations i.22.

24 Vincent, *Lamentations*, 11–15.

25 Ibid. 31.

cast into rivers.[26] The denial of the standard rules of war, the demonisation of the enemy and the emphasis on the helplessness of the victims were key attributes of atrocity publications of the era.

Rothwell's press was also responsible for other works that encouraged popular piety among the lower social orders, such as the first edition of Samuel Clarke's *Generall martyrologie*.[27] Under Rothwell's imprint too was James Cranford's *The teares of Ireland* (1642). Cranford, a Puritan minister and warden for the Stationers Company, blended Jones's *Remonstrance* and other massacre pamphlets that depicted events of the Irish rebellion with quotations from the Bible designed to shape certain reader responses. Surveying events across Europe, Cranford remarked upon the tense religious divide and appealed for Protestant unity. Repeating Jones's assertions that the rebels intended to go into England Cranford argued 'Is not Ireland our sister Nation? Doe not our flesh and our bloud suffer there? Doe we not heare of their threatenings breathed against us?'[28] Such religious overtones dominated the text. Cranford supported his description of Ireland and England as sister nations through his unacknowledged reference to Judges ix.2, describing the two as 'I am your bone and your flesh'.[29] In a reference to the Book of Lamentations, Ireland called out to her sister nation, 'was there ever sorrow like my sorrow'?[30] Cranford reassured readers of God's love for his followers. Describing the Irish rebels as 'bloudy men', he warned, evoking the book of Psalms, that 'the bloudy men shall not live out halfe their days'. Implicitly Cranford reminded the reader of God's promise: 'Cast thy burden upon the lord and he shall sustain thee: he shall never suffer the righteous to be moved.'[31] *The teares of Ireland*, by personifying the voices of the victims of

---

[26] Ibid. 18, 23, 27, 49, 57.

[27] Kathleen Noonan, '"Martyrs in flames": Sir John Temple and the conception of the Irish in English martyrologies', *Albion* xxxvi (Summer 2004), 223–55 at p. 234.

[28] James Cranford, *The teares of Ireland wherein is lively presented as a map, a list of the unheard off cruelties and perfidious treacheries of bloud-thirsty Jesuits and the popish faction: as a warning piece to her sister nations to prevent the like miseries, as are now acted on the stage of this fresh bleeding nation: reported by gentlemen of good credit living there, but forced to flie for their lives, as Iobs messengers, to tell us what they have heard and seene with their eyes, illustrated by pictures: fit to be reserved by all true Protestants as a monument of their perpetuall reproach and ignominy, and to animate the spiris of Protestants against such bloudy villains*, London 1642, 'Preface to the reader'. See also Acts ix.1–5.

[29] Cranford, *Teares of Ireland*, 'Irelands warning to England'.

[30] '[is it] nothing to you, all ye that that pass by? Behold, and see if there be any sorrow like unto my sorrow, which is done unto me, wherewith the Lord hath afflicted [me] in the day of is fierce anger': Lamentations i.12.

[31] 'Cast thy burden upon the Lord, and he shall sustain thee: he shall never suffer the righteous to be moved. But thou, O God, shalt bring them down into the pit of destruction: bloody and deceitful men shall not live out half their days; but I will trust in thee': Psalm lv.20–1.

the Irish rebels, called for revenge cloaked in biblical imagery and reinforced the Protestant identities of the two kingdoms.

Cranford, like Vincent, demonised the enemy, in this case the Irish Catholic rebels, 'whose principles are steppt in bloud, tolerating Rebellion against King and Kingdome, murdering of princes, blowing up of parliament, sowing seeds of division betweene confederate Kingdomes'.[32] They enacted tortures 'exceeding all parallel, unheard off among Pagans, Turks, or Barbarians, except you would enter into the confines of hell it self'.[33] The war engulfed the entire countryside, with innocent Protestant settlers being attacked and 'no way or meanes for man, woman, or child to escape their fury'.[34] Cranford criticised the Irish rebels for granting quarter to Belturbet town and then the 'rabble' attacked the inhabitants, 'stript them all naked, and turn'd them out of their houses into the open fields in bitter cold weather, in a most vile and shameful manner, not affording them one of their lowzy rags to hide those parts which should be covered'.[35] The main targets for rebel agression were Protestant ministers,[36] while Protestant women were the victims of a nationwide campaign of rape,[37] and their children were seen as legitimate targets by the 'savage' and 'bloud-sucking' rebels.[38] As such *The teares of Ireland* both reflected the general output of Rothwell's presses and drew upon cultural constructions of war and violence that were written to mobilise readers to support various war efforts.

The Thirty Years' War in Germany provided printers with opportunities to sell material that described news of events there to an interested audience. The climacteric destruction in Germany, moreover, encouraged John Rothwell to print works that encouraged popular piety and donations to various collections for beleagured German Protestants. Not all news from Germany, however, focused on bloody events. Many attempted to record military movements, battles and political intrigues. These accounts were considerably less polemical and bloody than the works issued by Rothwell. English responses to the crisis in Germany were similar to printed reactions to the 1641 rebellion in Ireland. Particular attention was paid to moments when the codes of warfare were ignored, exposing women and children to a range of cruelties. These factors would also emerge in the representation of the Irish rebellion in London's print trade.

---

[32] Cranford, *Tears of Ireland*, 2.

[33] Ibid. 3.

[34] Ibid. 17.

[35] Ibid. 24–5.

[36] Ibid. 29–31, 54.

[37] Ibid. 32.

[38] Ibid. 28, 42, 61.

Printing the 1641 rebellion

Like printed news about the Thirty Years' War, the 1641 rebellion was reported in a range of ways, from diverse perspectives. Not all were sensationalised news accounts. There were two main types of publications on the rebellion. First, pamphlets that described news from Ireland, such as troop movements, encounters between enemy forces and the progress of the war. Secondly, pamphlets that described the massacre of Protestant settlers in order to lobby for the support of various political initiatives. The purpose of this section is to survey pamphlets published in London throughout the 1640s.

The first news accounts relied on the information provided by the authorities in Ireland and attempted to provide a taxonomy of the rising. Pamphleteers, such as the author of *That great expedition for Ireland*, offered their own views: 'This warre is not merely as they would make the world believe, a warre of Religion, but mixt with other considerations.'[39] John Thomas, the most prominent of all the printers of news on the Irish rebellion during its early stages, relayed information conveyed by the lords justices. Thomas's first publication, *The last nevves from Ireland*, circulated sometime after 5 November 1641. It contained a letter read out to the House of Commons on that date and information gathered from Owen Connelly's testimony, contextualised alongside other treasonable plots against the English state such as the Gunpowder Plot. The text assured readers that the Irish 'massacre the *English* in those parts [the north of Ireland], men women and children'. The murders of Arthur Champion, Thomas Ironmonger and Thomas Hayward fleshed out Thomas's generalisation. Towards the pamphlet's conclusion Thomas included a list of rebel aims such as the desire to shake off English rule, establish the Catholic Church and to murder the lords justices and all English and Protestants in Ireland.[40] Here 1641 fitted in with other Catholic plots that had been hatched against England.

The first reports from Ireland emphasised the largely localised aspect of the rising. By mid-November 1641 another publication from Thomas's press stated that 'wee as yet heare of nothing amisse in Munster or Le[in]ster'.[41] In time, however, the rebellion came to be depicted as 'universall throughout

---

[39] *That great expedition for Ireland by way of underwriting proposed, by both houses of parliament, and graciously assented vnto by his majesty is heere vindicated as pious charitable, lust, politice, profitable and obiections to the contrary clearely answered, by one who heartily wisheth the speedy promotion of this proposition of underwriting, as almost the onely remedy*, London 1642, 6.

[40] *The last nevves from Ireland being a relation of the hostile and bloody proceedings of the rebellious papists there at this present*, London 1641.

[41] *More newes from Ireland: or The bloody practices and proceedings of the papists in that kingdome at this present*, London 1641, no pagination.

the kingdom' and accounts were printed describing how rebels attempted to seize Dublin castle and possessed 'other Fortifications of the Kingdome'.[42]

Most publications expressed the belief that the rebellion formed part of an international conspiracy against the Protestant Church: 'We shall be utterly destroyed and rooted out of the kingdome, for they surpasse in strength and number being ten to one besides many supplyes from divers Papists in England, Spaine and France to the vtter subversion and overthrow of the Protestants here.'[43] Soldiers *en route* to Ireland were encouraged to go forth with 'courageous hearts, mixt with a religious fear' in order to fight 'for the defence of the good and religious warre'.[44] The publication of supposedly secret correspondence illustrated links with continental networks that reminded readers of the international popish threat that they faced.[45] As a result many of the early reports on the rising focused on the victims' religion and reported how Protestants had been cut down with swords, 'without any distinction of Sexe with Cruell Tyranny'.[46] Many were vague generalisations: 'They spare not the Protestants, whersoever they come, taking away their lives, and estates, utterly extirpating whole families.'[47] Thus, the first reports in English print claimed that victims were targeted for their religious beliefs.

Those who attacked Protestant settlers were described within the literary scaffolding erected by generations of colonial writings on Ireland. Polemicists explained Irish behaviour as part of their natural and genetic disposition. References to Ireland's long-standing troubled relationship with England complemented the clear sectarian threat outlined in other pamphlets. Former foolhardiness towards the 'true' disposition of Irish people would now cease to exist in the popular imagination; previous 'dotage' towards Ireland meant that many 'were blinded with the vaile of ignorance'.[48] Remembering the last major revolt in Ireland – the Nine Years' War – and the main protagonist – the earl of Tyrone – some alleged that Phelim O'Neill desired to avenge his death.[49] The disposition of the Irish meant that in some cases people were killed regardless of their religion. James Salmon's *Bloody nevves from Ireland* alleged that the 'Rebels doe scatter themselves up and downe the Country,

---

[42] *A great conspiracy by the papists in the kingdome of Ireland discovered by the lords, juistices, and counsell at Dvblin, and proclamed there October 23 1641*, London [1641], 2.

[43] *More newes from Ireland*, sigs A2–A3v.

[44] *Irelands complaint, and Englands pitie*, London 1641, 2.

[45] *The distressed estate of the city of Dvblin in Ireland at this present*, London 1641.

[46] *The last and best newes from Ireland: declaring first the warlike and cruell proceeding of the rebels who are all papists and Jesuits of that kingdome burnt up*, London 1641, sig. A3.

[47] *Late and lamentable news from Ireland, wherein are truly related, the rebellious, and cruell proceedings of the papists there, at this present, extracted out of the last letters from Dublin*, London 1641, 3.

[48] *More newes from Ireland*, sigs A2–A3v.

[49] *Still worse newes from Ireland, shewing in what a miserable estate the cittie of Dublin is, at this present time*, London 1641, sig. A2v.

murdering the English in great cruelty, not onely the *Protestants*, but even the very papists also in many places'.[50] Most, however, agreed that the rebellion was sectarian in nature. An alleged protestation of archbishops and bishops in Ireland alluded to this 'perdition of seduced people, which perish in the deluge of their Catholique Apostasie'.[51] This extended to the 'long … tyrannicall insolence' exercised by the rebels over 'the liberties, lives and consciences of the Protestants'.[52] As well as religious grievances pamphleteers did recognise the colonial dimension to the rebellion.

Due to a lack of information about the progress of the rebellion, accounts relied upon readers' imaginations, folk memories and anti-Irish/Catholic prejudices. More knowledgeable sources also appeared and competed with these sensationalist accounts. Some news reports contained information about the plundering of settlers' estates. A *late and trve relation* informed the London audience that the archbishop of Armagh's house had been raided and £4,000 taken in plate and money.[53] Written from the point of view of a dispossesed Irish Protestant from Kells in Meath who subsequently fled to Dublin, A *copy of a letter concerning the traiterovs conspiracy of the rebelliovs papists in Ireland* provided a unique account of the Irish rebellion. George Thomason, the English book collector, identified the author as 'Mr Alexander' on his copy of the work, but there is no mention of any such person in the Meath depositions.[54] None the less the pamphlet provided some details that can be verified tentatively in the depositions. Alexander's account described how members of his own community formed the main contingent of rebels in Kells. Others within his locality described how the natives of Meath joined in and celebrated the arrival of the rebels from Cavan and other northern counties.[55] Alexander made no mention of any alleged atrocities but like other publications of the period noted the suspected gun powder plot at Christ Church, Dublin.[56] It is interesting that Alexander spoke more about

---

[50] *Bloody nevves from Ireland, or the barbarous crueltie by the papists used in that kingdome*, London 1641, [5]. See also A *true and credible relation of the barbarous crueltie and bloudy massacres of the English Protestants that lived in the kingdome of Ireland, anno dom 1641*, London 1642, sig. A2v.

[51] *The protestation of the archbishops and bishops of Ireland against the toleration of popery agreed upon, and subscribed by them at Dublin, the 26 of November*, London 1641, sig. A2.

[52] *The truest, most happy and joyfull newes that ever came from Ireland*, London 1641, sig. A2.

[53] A *late and trve relation from Ireland: of the vvarlike and bloody proceedings of the rebellious papists in that kingdome, from Novemb 1 to this present, 1641*, London 1641, [last page].

[54] A *copy of a letter concerning the traiterovs conspiracy of the rebelliovs papists in Ireland*, London 1641 (Wing A911–A931).

[55] Ibid. 2; deposition of Katherine Graunt, TCD, MS 816, fo. 106.

[56] A *copy of a letter concerning the traiterovs conspiracy*, 4; *Joyfull news from Ireland, being a relation of a battell which was fought between the Protestants, and the rebels of Ireland*, London 1641.

his financial losses than of the massacre of Protestant settlers, unlike other publications of the time.

Other pamphlets contained intelligence of the rebellion which can be verified by the 1641 depositions. For example, A briefe declaration by 'G. S.' mentions events that are described in the depositions, although it is unclear whether G. S. had access to the originals. G. S. correctly identified Lord Conor Maguire as the main leader behind the plot to seize Dublin castle, and provided an account of the initial outbreak of the rebellion as reflected in the depositions from the region. G. S. catalogued the murders of Arthur Champion, Thomas Champion, Thomas Ironmonger, Henry Crosse, James Whitewood, John Maynes, Thomas Smith, William Ogden, Maximilian Tibbs, Richard Butler and Steven Wrixon from Cavan and Fermanagh as well as numerous others from Monaghan.[57] The Irish natives were suitably demonised and the victims of the conflict were helpless women and children. A briefe declaration spoke to Protestants across the three kingdoms. He reminded readers that 'As popery and treachery goe hand in hand, while Popery is kept under; so Popery and Tyranny are inseperable companions, when popery gets the upper hand.'[58] Irish Protestants' reports on the rising preferred to focus on the barbarity of the Irish Catholics and described the rebellion as part of an international popish conspiracy.

Sporadically throughout the 1640s other details were printed in contemporary pamphlets that did not relate to massacres which can be verified by the depositions. One particularly curious incident occurred in the deposition of John Cliffe from Wexford. Cliffe, while attempting to flee to Dublin through Arklow in Wicklow, heard 'by diuers psons that he giues credytt vnto' that numerous Catholic clerics attempted to destroy the library of George Andrews, the Protestant bishop of Fernes and Leighlin. Allegedly, 'whilest the books were burninge a swarme of bees came in at the window of the Rome where they [chased] the Preests & ffryers out of the [room]'.[59] Cliffe deposed in June 1642 and dated this incident to 5 March of the same year. In a pamphlet published on 9 September 1642, written in the format of a letter, the author informed his brother that Irish rebels attempted to burn their father's books. Suddenly, 'there came a swarme of Bees out of the garden into the house were the Rogues where & did sting them so bitterly, as that they were forced to flee away, and for that time left their mischiefe undone'.[60] Such incidents may reflect the complicated processes

---

[57] G. S., A briefe declaration of the barbarous and inhumane dealings of the northerne Irish rebels, and many others in severall counties uprising against the English, that dwelt both lovingly and securely among them, London 1641, 4–5.

[58] Ibid. 11; deposition of George Creighton, TCD, MS 832, fos 145r–160v.

[59] Deposition of John Cliffe, TCD, MS 818, fo. 109.

[60] Exceeding happy newvs from Ireland: declaring the proceedings of the Protestants army in Kildare, against the castle of Ithlone, the castle of Knock and Mores Castle Ogle, London 1642, 5.

through which information travels by word of mouth, or indeed, it may be a complete coincidence. None the less it illustrates the symbolic support of God for the efforts of Protestant forces to end the rebellion. As contemporaries constructed their worlds through an understanding that divine providence impacted on daily events these accounts offer revealing insights into the construction of news on the rebellion.[61]

The sectarian interpretation of the Irish rebellion was given further support in the spring of 1642 when it became clear that the Old English had decided to join their co-religionists. Prior to this, a reprint of a proclamation exonerating them from any blame in the outbreak circulated in London in late December 1641.[62] By Janurary 1642, however, news filtered through that 'our ancient English ... are now turned Irish'. The defection of the Pale in December 1641 meant that members of the Old English community assumed the behavioural patterns of the native Irish. They too 'refused to help their poore English neighbours, who are betrayed by their owne servants, and destroyed by their next neighbours, who strip them, not leaving them one shred to cover their nakedness, be they of what quality'.[63] Their treachery was further compounded by the fact that they had accepted arms from the lords justices only to turn against them.[64] While pamphleteers noted their involvement the rebellion was already interpreted as a popish plot: the union of the Old English and the native Irish did not change English portrayals of the rebellion to any great extent.

The existence of an Irish community based in London with extensive connections to prominent members of the Irish political, economic and social elite, ensured that more 'reliable' (as advertised by English printers) information could be found and subsequently printed. Reports that originated from Ireland tended to oscillate between fantastical accounts and more moderate reports about affairs in Ireland. For example, William Bladen (the main printer in Dublin) published *Irelands trve divrnall*, which offered two letters, one from Bladen to his son, the other from Nicholas Bernard (a dean living in Drogheda) to 'a friend of his in Dublin' dated January 1642. Bernard focused on events near Drogheda and concentrated on the repulsion of the rebel siege of the town. Bernard optimistically wrote that 'all we feare is a famine that we be not relieved from *Dublin* in time: yet we have victuals for a Moneth longer'. Similarly Bladen steered clear of fantastical descriptions of the Irish countryside and preferred to note the progress of 'our Army'. Accordingly 'they have done good service in burning fifteene or sixteene Rebellious Townes

---

[61] Gillespie, *Devoted people*, 40–6; Walsham, *Providence*. For a more specific example of this see Paul Seaver, *Wallington's world: a Puritan artisan in seventeenth-century London*, Stanford 1985.

[62] *The last and best newes from Ireland.*

[63] *The last nevves from Ireland; or a trve relation of the sad estate and feares of Dublin, and of the siege of Tredavgh by the rebels*, London 1641, 2.

[64] Ibid. sig. A2.

and Castles which harboured the enemie and brought with them Cattell and other pillage, but the Rebells themselves fled before our Army came to them'.[65] A letter from Bladen three days later, printed under the title of *A true and exact relation of the chiefe passages in Ireland*, sensationalised the conflict as exceptionally bloody. Having murdered Arthur Champion, the rebels now 'spare none, Ministers nor people, of what sort soever'.[66] Bladen related how 'one hundred and twenty they stript stark naked, and drave them upon a bridge, and forced them into the water, drowned those which could swimme they knocked in the head when they came to land', the first reference to the drownings over the bridge of the river Bann.[67] Bladen may have been calling desperately for aid from parliament, or trying to make a profit in an already cluttered print market in London.

Not all pamphlets that described the rebellion could be classified as 'factual' accounts; some were deliberately concocted solely for the purposes of turning a profit. Like John Rothwell, John Greensmith, grasped the potential presented by the Irish rebellion and accordingly published pamphlets that described allegedly up-to-date news from Ireland from mid-November 1641. However, it emerged by January 1642 that three of Greensmith's publications were complete fabrications. *Bloody newes from Norwich, Joyfull newes from Ireland* and *The apprentices of Londons petition* originated from the pens of Martin Eldred and Thomas Herbert, two Cambridge students.[68] Their compositions warned readers of the Catholic menace that English Protestants faced. *Bloody newes from Norwich* claimed that a Catholic uprising erupted in Norwich on 27 October 1641, inspired by events in Ireland. It continued by relating news from Ireland and claimed that 'Thus doe these bloody minded Rebels, dayly act their villany, by persecuting and murthering the poor Protestants.' Eldred and Greensmith were committed to prison although by February Greensmith could print again and orders for Eldred's release had been issued by parliament.[69]

With the exception of a handful of publications most of the works containing atrocity stories from Ireland lacked any coherent form of detail,

---

[65] *Irelands true divrnall, or A continved relation of the cheife passages that have happened there since the 11th of January unto this present*, London 1642, 3–8.

[66] *A true and exact relation of the chiefe passages in Ireland, since the first rising of the rebels*, London 1642, sig. A2v.

[67] Ibid. sig. A3.

[68] *Bloody newes from Norwich: or, A true relation of a bloody attempt of the papists in Norwich, to consume the whole city by fire*, London 1641; *Joyfull news from Ireland*; *The apprentices of Londons petition presented to the honourable court of parliament: humbly shewing unto them the manifold abuses of their apprentiship, how the Frenchmen, Dutch, and Walloones, doe deprive them of their ancient customes, and former liberties in their trade*, London 1641; CJ ii. 396 (25 Jan. 1642).

[69] CJ ii. 415 (7 Feb. 1642); *Londons teares, vpon the never too much to be lamented death of our late worthie member of the House of Commons, Sr Richard Wiseman knight and baronet*, London 1642; *Bloody newes from Norwich*, sig. A3v.

but were couched in generalisations and vague language. Take the description of the fictional rebel Vaul who terrorised the Irish countryside 'sparing neither man, woman, nor child … forcing of Matrons, and ravishing of tender virgins'.[70] A report from Galway offered similar generalisations, 'where they spare no cruelty to any Sex, estate, or degree whatsoever, and that even upon the Lords day: on which day of they are not shedding of bloud'.[71] Most elaborations provided details of particular incidents of cruelty but rarely identified the victims. *Worse and worse nevves from Ireland* related how Irish rebels on a murderous rampage conducted themselves:

> Cutting off their privie members, eares, fingers, and hands, plucking out their eyes, boyling the heads of little Children before their Mothers faces, and then ripping up their Mothers Bowels, stripping women naked, and standing by them being naked, whilest they are in Travell killing the Children as soone as they are borne, and ripping up their Mothers bellies, as soone as they are delivered; driving men, women and children, by hundred together upon Bridges, and from thence cast them downe into Rivers, such as drowned not, they knocke their braines out with Poles … ravishing wives before their husbands faces, and Virgins before their Parents faces.[72]

Similarly, on a rebel march towards Kilmouth, they murdered 'all the Protestants that they could meet with … some having their quarter torne in pieces, deflouring the women, and hanging their quarters upon the walls, and hanging some up by the heeles, whipping them to death, & others tare the flesh from their bones with pincers, and hanging little children upon hookes by the throats'.[73] Many of the publications relied on innuendo to stoke their readers' imaginations. Versed in the rhetoric of death, desctruction and anti-popery, 1641 fitted neatly in with sensationalist accounts of atrocity and violence from across the globe.

Snippets of bloody stories continued the process of demonising Irish Catholics with little evidence provided to support the veracity of their sources. *The victorious proceedings of the Protestants in Ireland* reported how seventeen rebels entered Duncannon and attacked a Protestant minister's house: 'they stript him and his wife naked, bound them backe to backe, cut off his privy members, then one after another another did ravish her upon her husband's backe, then cut both their throats'.[74] Other cruelties echoed

---

[70] *More happy newes from Ireland of a battell fought betwixt the Scottish volunteers against the Irish rebels*, London 1641, sig. A2v.

[71] *A treacherous plot of a confederacie in Ireland, with the rebels at Calway, with the furniture of guns and ammunition for warre*, London 1641, sig. A2.

[72] *Worse and worse nevves from Ireland being the coppy of a letter read in the house of parliament, the 14 of this instant moneth of December, 1641*, London 1642, 2.

[73] *The happiest newes from Ireland that ever came to England*, London 1641, sig. A2v.

[74] *The victorious proceedings of the Protestants in Ireland; from the beginning of March to this present, being the 22 of the same month*, London 1642, 15.

such callousness. Tristam Whetcombe alleged that the rebels in Cork raped a mother then roasted two of her children alive on 'a red hot spit' in front of their parents.[75] *A treacherous plot of a confederacie in Ireland* reported the hanging of Sir Thomas Sevell 'upon a tree in his own grounds, and cut his flesh in pieces, carrying pieces thereof up and downe in their hands, saying, this is the flesh of one of the Rulers against our holy Father the pope'. As with most publications of the period, descriptions of specific events were then utilised as evidence for subsequent generalisations of graphic violence. *A treacherous plot* continued by arguing 'these, and such like, are the miseries of that Kingdome of Ireland at this time'.[76]

Pamphlet titles, in particular, were equally prone to sweeping statements on the nature of the cruelties committed in Ireland. In December 1641, for example, a Greensmith publication appeared, offering 'a true Relation of all those cruell Rapes and Murders which have lately beene committed by the Papists in Ireland'. The stories within, however, were scant on detail and equally vague.[77] Historians have in fact found little evidence for sexual violence during the 1640s in Ireland. Mary O'Dowd suggested that this was due to seventeenth-century prudishness and described how she found very little evidence for 'rape and other violent attacks on women' in the depositions, although many were treated as legitimate targets by both rebel and colonial forces.[78] Nicholas Canny found more evidence for rape in the depositions but concluded that 'rape was not as widespread [as contemporaries] would expect'.[79] Most incidents of rape as reported in the depositions appear to be either based on conjecture or hearsay. For example, Gilbert Pemberton, an Armagh deponent, feared for the safety of his niece who 'being a pretty woman they tooke to themselves to keepe and to vse or rather abuse her as a whore'.[80] Certain actions were taken by the Irish rebels, however, to protect the settler population. Upon the outbreak of hostilities in 1641, a proclamation from the confederates, reprinted at London, outlined the terms of their engagement: 'No man upon peril of life shall commit rape or ravishment upon any wife, widow or maid, or any other woman within the said countie, nor strip any Catholicke or Protestant, man, woman, or any other whatso-

---

[75] Tristam Whetcombe, *The rebels Turkish tyranny, in their march Decem. 24. 1641*, London 1641, 2.

[76] *A treacherous plot of a confederacie in Ireland* [last page].

[77] *The kings maiesties speech on the 2 day of December, 1641 to the honourable house of parliament*, London 1641.

[78] Mary O'Dowd, 'Women and war in Ireland in the 1640s', in Mary Mac Curtain and Mary O'Dowd (eds), *Women in early modern Ireland*, Edinburgh 1991, 91–111 at pp. 101, 100.

[79] Canny, *Making Ireland British*, 544–5.

[80] Deposition of Gilbert Pemberton, 2 Mar. 1642, TCD, MS 836, fo. 8.

ever, of the cloaths of their body.'[81] Indeed, Job Ward, a prisoner among the rebels at Waterford noted that strict punishments were threatened against those who 'shall force or ravish any woman or mayde'.[82]

Regardless of the military codes of conduct and the paucity of evidence, Henry Jones, in a private report, maintained that 'wickednesse of that nature have comonly not witnesses';[83] pamphlets also accused native Irish rebels of indulging in indiscriminate rapes of the settler population in Ireland but with little evidence to substantiate the claims.[84] *Doefull news from Ireland*, alleged to be a letter from an Irish Protestant to his brother in England, detailed how the Irish rebels 'spared neither man, woman nor child Protestant and Papists, but after they had ravisht their wives and daughters, put them all to the sword'. The author claimed that settler women had three choices: 'First, whether they would renounce their Religion and marry such Irish men as they should tender unto them: Secondly, whether they would freely and willingly prostitute their bodies to so many seuerall men as would desire it. Thirdly, whether they would be kild and put to the sword.'[85] Those who wondered at the extent of suffering that Protestant women experienced at the hands of Irish rebels were left in no doubt by *Irelands tragical tyrannie*. In this, 'two letters' detailed events in Ireland, one, authored by the father of 'a Speehlesse Damzell' related how his daughter's 'hair was torn from her head, because she would not yield to their lust; there may you also perceive how her tongue was cut out of her mouth, because she would not blaspheme against her Maker'.[86]

While John Temple claimed that the native Irish lived in a society predisposed to the 'most notorious murthers, rapes, robberies, and all other acts of inhumanity and barbarisme', his ally, Chidley Coote, developed this to state that 'I am perswaded murthering and massacres without mercy, rapes, and rapines, burnings, devastations, and all manner of spoyles will be the greatest mercy received from them.'[87] Like Pemberton, Jones cautioned that the depositions contain

---

[81] *A true coppie of the lawes and rules of government, agreed upon and established by the nobles of the severall counties of Ireland*, London 1641, 3.

[82] Deposition of Job Ward, 23 July 1642, TCD, MS 815, fo. 285v. See also 'Instructions to be observed by the lord general of Leinster (from the confederates)', 14 Dec. 1642, CSPI, *1633–47*, 374. Canny argued that crimes of a sexual nature were deemed less horrific than the desecration of places of worship: *Making Ireland British*, 545.

[83] 'A treatise giving a representation of the grand rebellion in Ireland', MS Harleian 5999, fo. 32.

[84] *Bloody nevves from Ireland*, London 1641; *The happiest newes from Ireland; The truest intelligence from the province of Munster*, London 1642; *An alarvm to warre*, London 1642.

[85] *Dolefull nevves from Ireland sent in a letter*, London 1642, sig. A2v, [3].

[86] *Irelands tragical tyrannie*, London 1643, sig. A2.

[87] Temple, *The Irish rebellion*, 5; Coote, *Irelands lamentation*, 8.

frequent reports of the rebells violent attempts to carry away some and their carrieying away of other well educated & modest maidens & defraying them perforce, at best oftentimes constraining them through feare of death or viola-tion to marry against their will not onely farre inferior but even sometimes sordid & base wretches.[88]

Indeed, many pamphlets warned that 'daughters of the Nobilite and Gentrie of best account (and some Wives too) forced to be married to them'.[89] Both Canny and O'Dowd rightly focused on the fact that Irish rebels stripped Prot-estants of both genders as a means of degrading the colonial order. Forced marriages, however, also had a profound effect on those who described the Irish rebellion in print. Pamphleteer preoccupation with the perpetration of wholesale rapes and forced marriages against the settler population suggests a concern with the tainting of English and Protestant blood with 'barbaric' Irish and/or Catholic lineage. None the less, the extent of contemporary reportage of rape in contrast with what actually occurred suggests that deeply symbolic conceptions of the Irish rebels were at play in contemporary news reports.

The belief that much of the news from Ireland had been fabricated found voice in a small number pamphlets during the 1640s. An anonymous letter-writer complained that 'many idle rumours [are] divulged among you, concerning the present condition of Ireland, some of which are improb-able, other are so doubtfull, that men have just cause of suspition not to believe'.[90] This related to wider concerns over the disruptive influence of print in London during the early 1640s. *The poets knavery discouered* argued that such fantastical works were a product of 'roving fancies' and suggested their affect on attitudes in London: 'The whole City is embroydred with nothing but incredible lyes, that jars so much in the wearied eares of the World.'[91] According to the author of the *Poets knavery* thirty-seven publica-tions relating to Ireland were 'lyes'. The author of *No pamphlet* echoed the concerns expressed in *Poets knavery* and argued that very few atrocities were committed in Ireland. Only one person, according to *No pamphlet*, perished in Ireland and only 20,000 Irish rebels stood in open rebellion, most of whom were not armed. *No pamphlet*, like *Poets knavery*, noted how many would 'for a small gaine endeavour with opprobrious lines to abuse God and

---

[88] 'A treatise giving a representation of the grand rebellion in Ireland', MS Harleian 5999, fo. 32v. See, for example, the deposition of Raph Walmsley, 11 Mar. 1646, TCD, MS 814, fo. 267.

[89] *Irelands advocate: or, A sermon preched at a publicke fast held by authoritie, July the 27 in behalfe of bleeding Ireland*, London 1642, 18; Cranford, *The teares of Ireland*, 1.

[90] *The most blessed and truest newes from Ireland, shewing the fortunate successe of the Protestants, and Gods just vengance on the rebels*, London 1642, 3.

[91] *The poets knavery discouered, in all their lying pamphlets*, London [1642?], sig. A2.

Man'.[92] It is likely, however, that *Poets knavery* may have been criticising a rival printer of Irish news as all the works mentioned in the text relating to the 1641 rebellion were printed by John Greensmith.

Reports on the Irish rebellion, printed from November 1641 to February 1642, argued that the conflict was motivated by sectarianism, that Irish rebels indiscriminately massacred Protestants, with women and children being their main targets, and that the 1641 rebellion was a war that engulfed the entire population of Ireland. *The blovdy persecution of the Protestants in Ireland* described how Protestants 'have bin put to unheard of torments, women have bin slain in their husbands armes, and husbands embracing of the wives, the braines of children they daily dash out, and in a most damnable manner trample them under their feet'.[93] *The coppy of a letter sent by the rebells in Ireland* informed London readers that 'every man most treacherously revolted' and that the rebels 'were hungry for their prey'.[94] Some publications argued that the rebellion was an attempt to expel English rule and to engage in an indiscriminate massacre:

> [the] Rebels doe scatter themselves up and downe the Country, murdering the English in great cruelty, not onely the *Protestants*, but even the very papists also in many places. In which rage and cruelty of theirs, when they have most bloodily slain divers good Protestants of worth, they have hanged them up upon the Gates in great disdaine, and driving others out of their estates, which is the least injury.[95]

After the passing of the Adventurers' Act, the arrival of colonial reinforcements and the successes of the lords justices' forces in repelling the rebellion in the spring and summer of 1642, pamphlets reported more positive news.

The effect of these fabricated news reports about events in Ireland is reflected in the fact that after the passing of the Adventurers' Act, which aimed to raise funds for an army to suppress the rebellion, many pamphlets stressed how the situation in Ireland was under control and that Irish land was profitable. For investors to reap their dividend, English armies had to suppress the rebellion successfully. For those concerned about its legality, a ream of publications explained the legislative basis for the Adventurers' Act.[96] On 9 April 1642 a one-page proclamation circulated around London

---

[92] *No pamphlet, bvt a detestation against all such pamphlets as are printed, concerning the Irish rebellion*, London 1642, sig. A2.

[93] *The blovdy persecution of the Protestants in Ireland*, London 1641, sig. A2v.

[94] *The coppy of a letter sent by the rebells in Ireland to the Lord Dillon, to declare to his maiestie the cause of their taking up armes*, London 1641, 5–6.

[95] *Bloody nevves from Ireland* [final page, no pagination].

[96] *An act for the speedie and effectuall reducing of the rebells in his majesties kingdom of Ireland to their due obedience to his majestie and the crown of England*, London 1642; *A brief of an act of parliament, humbly desired for the relief of the distressed Protestants of Ireland, who have left their estates by the present rebellion there, and to enlarge and explain these former acts already*

to inform the public about the extent of investment poured into the Adventurers' Act by prominent members of parliament since its inception and to inspire confidence.[97] For those in any doubt as to how the act actually worked, other pamphlets circulated that described in laymen's terms the conditions of the Adventurers' Act. *Certaine propositions* informed readers that 'the papists of Ireland' had now forfeited their ownership of 'half of the lands of that Kingdom'. Calling for a sense of unity between Irish and English Protestants the *Propositions* offered 'charity ... [as] these distressed Protestants should receive some satisfaction'. Interestingly, the author made little distinction between Irish Protestant and English Protestant. Instead, implicit reassurances were offered stating that their ethnicity did not bar them from civility. 'The distressed Protestants, all of them such, as from their infancies have been bred, and lived Protestants, well affected in the religion, and very many of them having served in places and Offices of eminence and trust in that Kingdom, and done good service of the Common Wealth.' The Adventurers' Act would, according to *Certaine propositions*, provide an opportunity to rid Ireland of Catholicism and impose a Protestant state there 'as the Laws of the land required'. An act of godly significance, 'It will draw from Heaven a better blessing upon the proceedings, as so many prayers will be more daily added, for its prosperous and good successe'.[98]

Other voices, mostly from Ireland, also contributed to these discussions about the Adventurers' Act. As noted in *Certaine propositions* Irish Protestants needed 'encouragement ... with all possible diligence'.[99] In Drogheda, Nicholas Bernard, a colleague of Henry Jones, criticised the 'multitude of lying pamphlets you [London printers] have printed of our daily proceedings' and assured his readers that he knew 'well' of the progress of the 'Dublin Army' against the Irish rebels. Bernard, having heard about the Adventurers' Act, argued 'it will be too great'. He encouraged his readers to invest: 'the

passed, for the more speedy and effectuall reducing of the rebells of Ireland to their due obedience to his majesty, and the crown of England, London 1642; Propositions made to the Lords and Commons in parliament, for the speedie and effectuall reducing of the kingdom of Ireland: and the votes thereupon, by both houses presented unto the kings majestie. with his majesties gracious answer and royal assent thereunto, London 1642; A copy of a letter vvhich Master Speaker is ordered by the Commons house of parliament, to send to the members of that house, that are now residing in their severall counties, to further the advancement of the adventure for Ireland, London 1642.

97 *The names of such members of the Commons house of parliament, as have already subscribed in pursuance of the act of parliament, for the speedy reducing of the rebels, and the future peace and safety of this kingdome (a worke tending much to the glory of Almighty God, and the succour and reliefe of our distressed brethren in Ireland) together with the summes they have severally underwritten*, London 1642.

98 *Certaine propositions, whereby the distressed Protestants of Ireland, who have lost their goods, and peronall estates there, by means of the present rebellion, may be relieved, if his majesty and both houses of parliament shall so think fit*, London 1642, 5–8.

99 Ibid. 7.

land is as good as in England, and the seats as excellent, if you have a 100 or 200 of pounds, to under writ in this cause, and that you can be sure of land, as it is here declared, it would be much profit'. Bernard even suggested that 'the lords of the Pale, some of them offer themselves to come in now', providing hope that the rebellion could be brought to a swift end.[100] Other publications from March to May 1642 also went to great lengths to emphasise the success of 'English', 'Scottish' or 'Protestant' forces in Ireland at the time, to promote the Adventurers' Act. A letter from Stephen Johnson, published under the title *Exceeding good newes from the Neweries in Ireland* in April 1642, promised that 'we make no question but that we shall soone tame these Rebels, and bring them to obedance unto our Royall Soveraigne'. This premise, based on the success of English armies against the Irish rebels, dictated much of Johnson's account of events in Ireland. Reportedly 5,000 rebels met their doom at Waterford and a further 'one thousand as we might guesse by the dead bodies which they left behind to intombe the ground, which should have beene their graves'.[101] By the summer of 1642, therefore, it became necessary for English printers to emphasise the success of English forces in Ireland.

While English forces may have been more successful in Ireland from the summer of 1642 onward, printers were eager to maintain their demonic portrayal of Ireland's Catholic population. Many publications noted how Irish Catholic nobles encouraged the slaughter of Irish Protestants. A fictional speech from the (deceased) earl of Tyrone urged his followers to

Svvim svvim, vnto your desires, through Seas of blood, and let the Hereticks be the sole object of your hate: as yet you have done bravely, the God of Battell crovving you with vnparaller'd victory ... I ... daily delight my sence of seeing with bloody spectacles beare vpon your swords a bloody Ensigne, each point covered with the heart of an Hereticke.[102]

News from Ireland also celebrated the butchery committed by English, Scottish and Protestant commanders. *A speech made in the House of Peeres* complimented Sir Simon Harcourt's successes in Ireland and praised his soldiers for destroying mass-houses in Dublin and for threatening to hang priests.[103] *Confident news from Ireland* and *Exceeding joyfull newes from Ireland* lauded the

100 A true and perfect relation of all the severall skirmishes, brave exploits, and glorious victories obtained by the English Protestants, over the Irish rebels, when they raised the siege of Tredagh, London 1641, 1, 6–7.

101 Exceeding good newes from the Neweries in Ireland being, the true copie of a letter sent from Dublin the 20 of April 1642 to Sir William Adderton, now resident in London, from Mr Stephen Johnson merchant, London 1642, sig A2v [last page].

102 The rebels of Irelands wicked conspiracie against Kingsaile in the province of Munstearre, and County of Corke, London 1641, sig. A3.

103 A speech made in the House of Peeres: by the right honorable the earle of Monmouth, on Thursday the thirteenth of Ianuary 1641, London 1642, 8.

efforts of the lords justices: 'our gallowes are well adorned with priests, jesuits and friars, the complotters and broachers of all our present calamities'.[104] After the announcement of the Adventurers' Act numerous publications rejoiced in the killings of Irish civilians and soldiers.[105] Thus, contemporary accounts of the Irish front in the Wars of the Three Kingdoms viewed the conflict there as operating under particularly vicious military codes.[106]

Some pamphlets offered more optimistic advice about the Irish rebellion but were also painfully aware of the effect of previous fantastical accounts of the rebellion. They warned that 'our army hath not any pay these three weeks ... God turne the wind, that we may have some ease and comfort and Treasure'. Despite this, however, numerous successes were achieved against the rebels, one thousand slain at Drogheda and the victory of forty armed Protestants over five hundred without any losses recorded.[107] Others recounted the arrest of prominent popish plotters and the deaths of 2,000 rebels near Newry.[108] The extent of rebel failure lay in graphic descriptions of their demise: 'here is nothing expected but fire and sword, wee kill them and lay them in heaps'.[109] These works did not assuage niggling doubts that remained about the viability and profitabilty of the Adventurers' Act. It appeared that previous fantastical accounts damaged the potential for investment. Authors feared the end of the 'Commonwealth' and warned that those who refused to invest stood accused of leaving 'in miseable incertainty the safety of the Common-wealth, and I feare, the salvation of their owne soules'. The problem lay in the inability of parliament to raise the £1,000,000 required to support the Adventurer's army. Improved investment from Londoners would 'prevent a great disturbance and clamour at home'. *Timely advice* presented a list of questions and answers about the act that

---

[104] Quotation taken from *Confident newes from Ireland being a letter sent from Mr William Phillips, merchant, dwelling in Dublin, to Mr William Barbar, a worthy friend of his, and one of the gentlemen of the Inner Temple*, London 1642, 5; *Exceeding joyfull newes from Ireland or a true relation of a great and happy victorie, obtained by a Colonell David Douglasse and Sir James Carr, two Scottish commanders, with the helpe of the Scots planted in the north of Ireland, against the arch-rebels Philemy Oneale*, London 164[2].

[105] *Two famous and victorious bttells fovght in Ireland*, London 1642; *Exceeding good newes from the Neweries; Exceeding happy newes from Ireland: being a true relation of many passages of great consequence very joyfull and delectable to all true hearted Protestants*, London 1642.

[106] For a detailed discussion on the implementation of military codes in Ireland during the 1640s see Ó Siochrú, 'Atrocity', 55–86.

[107] *A faithfull remonstrance, of all the chiefe matters of note which have happened in and about Dublin, and other parts of Ireland, from the 26 of January, to this present, being the I of March, 1642*, London 1642, 3–5.

[108] *The prisoners of New Gates condemnation declaring every verdict of the whole bench at the Sessions House in the Old Bayly April 22 with the Jesuits and Freyers being censured by the parliament, five fryers being examined by a committee in the Court of Wards, with their confessions at the same time, also those 18 that were suspected to adjoin with the Irish rebels, with a pilgrim, and four more Irish souldiers*, London 1642, [6].

[109] *Two famous and victorious battells*, sig. A2v.

obviously hoped to quell any criticisms. Those who wondered about the nature of the postwar settlement with the rebels were assured that the colonial authorities would enact *lex talionis* against them.[110] English printers were clearly trying to mitigate fears that English forces would prove victorious in Ireland and to encourage investment in the act.

At various moments throughout the 1640s the clear polemical purpose of massacre pamphlets emerged. Take *A geographicall description of the kingdom of Ireland* for example. The preface to the reader noted how 'many have lately cast their treasure' and expected great 'advantage, knowledge, and delight thou mayst reap by it'. It allayed concerns about the rift between king and parliament caused by Jones's *Remonstrance*: 'Thou needst not fear to engage thy purse, in the survey of that Country, where so good a king was willing to engage his person.'[111] As a result the content of the pamphlet was dictated by two factors. First the profitability of Irish land that needed cultivation: 'A Countrey mountanous, woody and wild, loftily looking into the Ocean; in which are many fruitfull fields, and pleasant vallyes, beset thick with woods.'[112] Likewise Leinster offered 'fertile, healthfull, and beautifull place ... and exceeding plentifull in all provisions'.[113] The pamphlet served to provide the reader with an impression of how Ireland stood 'so fruitfull in soil, so rich in pasture ... profitable woods, inriched with many minerals'. In short, 'he will seeme short witted (whose wealth will bear it) that embraces not the present opportunity to inrich himself in a plantation of his posterity, in the middest of such wordly felicity'.[114] Secondly, afraid that previous reports from Ireland might discourage investment the tract downplayed potential concerns over risks involved.[115] Considerable damage had been caused by the outpouring of bloody news from Ireland, which discouraged potential investors. Matters were not helped by reports written by English settlers in Ireland which relayed how men, women and children had been 'most cruelly, and inhumanely hanged and murthered'.[116]

From the onset of the war rumours circulated that the rebellion would spread into England, although usually this related more to English fears of belligerent popish forces based in Europe. In time pamphlets emerged that instructed Londoners and Englishmen in how to identify an Irishman should one surface in England. 'Many of the Irish who come to England claim to be

---

[110] *Timely advice, or Motives to incite all men of ability to subscribe to the propositions for Ireland*, London 1642, sigs A2–A3v.

[111] *A geographicall description of the kingdom of Ireland*, London 1642, 'To the reader', sig. Ar–v.

[112] Ibid. sig. B2.

[113] Ibid. sig. Cv.

[114] Ibid. no pagination, last page of pt I.

[115] Ibid. sigs C2v, E.

[116] *The copy of a letter from Master Tristam Whitecomb, major of Kingsale in Ireland: dated the 21 of April 1642 to his brother Benjamin Whiecombe, merchant*, London 1642, sig. A2.

scots but there are ways of asking them to pronounce the letter 'h' 'which they cannot do'. Further instructions ordered them to 'vncover their bosomes, most of them weare Crucifixes, especially the women'.[117] On 25 January 1642 a proclamation issued at London ordered the arrest of suspected papists travelling to Ireland and ordered the expulsion of Irish 'papists' (no doubt some of whom could have been Irish Protestant refugees) for their behaviour: 'They have been, and are very disorderly, and much terrifie the Inhabitants where they come, and due care is not taken in all places for the suppressing and punishing of them.'[118] After the negotiation of the first cessation of arms in 1643 the use of Irish soliders by the king re-energised the debate and pamphlets circulated warning of the possibility of further massacres being committed against Protestants by the native Irish.[119] Parliamentary polemicists professed the fear that 'while the said popish army is advancing toward London, with hope that by this and other their divellish artifices they may find all in contributions here, whereby they may with lesse resistance pillage and sacke this City, cut the throats of all men of estates, and ravish their wives and daughters without difference'.[120] These related to fears of English Catholics as one report in September 1643 noted how Lancaster Catholics rose up in arms 'whereupon the Enemie [the Catholics] entred the Town and killed man woman and children with all barbarus crueltie, dragging poore people from their houses, and cutting their throats with Butchers knives: they set fire round the town and departed'.[121]

As the English civil war began to dominate news pages, some voices from Ireland cried for attention to remind audiences of the increasingly desperate plight that Ireland's Protestants faced. *Irelands lamentation since the late cessation*, written by Chidley Coote, commander of Protestant forces in Laois and Offaly during the 1640s, spoke negatively about Charles to encourage popular dissatisfaction with the royalist war effort. In *Irelands lamentation*

---

[117] Thomas Emitie, *A new remonstrance from Ireland*, London 1642, 5. See also Keith Lindley, *The English civil war and revolutions: a sourcebook*, London 1998, 83–5.

[118] *An order made by both houses of parliament, to prevent the going over of popish commanders into Ireland, and also to hinder the transportation of arms, ammunition, money, corne, victuals, and al other provision to the rebels, and for the sending back of the Irish papists lately come over,* London 1642.

[119] For a look on how this affected military ethics between the various sides in the Wars of the Three Kingdoms see Ó Síochrú, 'Atrocity', 55–86.

[120] *A declaration of the Lords and Commons assembled in parliament, concerning the pressing necessities of this kingdome, caused by the traitorous and bloody counsels and attempts of those pernicious and desperate councellors, still about the king, and protected by him, while they more and more manifest their implacable enmity to our religion, the parliament, and peace of all his majesties good subjects and dominions; endeavouring with fire and sword to root out our religion, and all that professe it here, as they still proceed to do in Ireland,* London 1643, [3].

[121] *Lancasters massacre or The new way of advancing the Protestant religion, and expressing loyaltie to the king and queene,* London 1643, 2; See also *Irelands misery since the late cessation,* London 1644.

Coote's hard-line, pro-militaristic stance is abundantly clear. Coote, like Temple, vehemently denounced the royalist administration in Dublin.[122] Thomas Crant's *Plott and progresse of the Irish rebellion* (1644), repeated this criticism, reminded readers of the follies of the royalist administration in Ireland and blamed Thomas Wentworth, the former lord lieutenant for the rebellion.[123] Crant and Coote preferred to focus on the religion of the Irish rebels, and 'evil councillors' who curried favour with the king such as the Ormond party. Crant, for example, reminded his audience of the extent of the Irish rebels' treasonable actions: 'Now, since this massacring act it hath been frequently spoken by the Rebells, that what they did was by Commission, which still they justifie.' He continued with a veiled criticism of Charles I: 'let all Christians stand here amazed to behold the Cessation of Armes to be granted to such Butcherly Hell-Hounds'.[124] Crant cited the cruelties committed in Ireland against Protestants as a means of discrediting the cessation of arms. He suggested that they would repeat their barbarous actions if they fought for the king in England.

From 1643 until 1647 news from Ireland did not focus on the 'bloody' nature of the war but became a further locus for royalists and parliamentarians to debate the merits of their respective war efforts. After parliamentarian accounts claimed that 154,000 Protestants had been killed (they had received this information from Temple and Parsons), the king responded with the argument that he had been forced to agree a ceasefire with Irish Catholics as he had been prevented from suppressing the rebellion by parliament and denied access to monies raised from the Adventurers' Act: 'It was evident that Men and Mony being raised, under pretence of quenching the Rebellion there, were both imployed in kindling and maintaining the Rebellion here.'[125] Parliamentary-leaning polemicists would later retort that those who refused to help them would be 'guilty' of the loss of Irish Protestant souls.[126] James Howell retorted by blaming parliament for interpreting the rebellion as a religious war, for their belligerence in executing Wentworth and for exacerbating tensions in Ireland by disbanding the Catholic army and 'consequently, it is easie to know upon the account of whose soules must be laid the blood of those hundred and odde thousands poore Christians, who perished in that war', i.e. parliament.[127] As the 1640s wore on, pamphlets

---

[122] Chidley Coote, *Irelands lamentation since the late cessation*, London 1644, 2–3.

[123] Thomas Crant, *The plott and progresse of the Irish rebellion*, London 1644, 1.

[124] Ibid. 7.

[125] *A declaration of the Commons assembled in parliament; concerning the rise and progresse of the grand rebellion in Ireland*, London 1643, 9–10; *The grovnds and motives inducing his maiesty to agree to a cessation of armes for one whole yeare, with the Roman Catholiques of Ireland*, Oxford 1643, at p. 2.

[126] *A true and exact relation of the most sad condition of Ireland, since the cessation, exprest in a ketter from Dublin, received the 16th of Novemb 1643*, London 1643, 5.

[127] *Mercurius hibernicus: or, A discourse of the late insurrection in Ireland*, Bristol 1644, 10.

then focused on the course of the war, provided military updates and the latest news on Irish and British politics. The first year or so of the rebellion, therefore, was exceptional in that it provided gory accounts that seemed less popular as the Wars of the Three Kingdoms raged across the Atlantic archipelago.

News of the 1641 rebellion in Ireland that appeared in pamphlets therefore stressed the desperate plight of the Protestant community in Ireland particularly when Ireland slipped down parliament's list of priorities. These bloody missives jeopardised the Adventurers' Act and directly contributed to the lack of confidence in it. Many of the details within contained vague information, but presented in highly formulaic language replete with suitable scenarios of gore and violence. A key theme to emerge from these publications was that of revenge. Throughout English colonies in the Atlantic world, when a massacre of settlers took place those who survived lobbied Englishmen to avenge their fallen comrades. As such the representation of the Irish rebellion conformed to cultural constructions of sectarian and colonial violence.

The 1641 rebellion in a New and Old World context

Sporadic tensions between England and Spain throughout the early modern period meant that many printers published accounts of the Spanish conquest of the Americas. At key moments in Anglo-Spanish relations pamphlets appeared that subscribed to the 'Black Legend' (that Spanish colonial forces were responsible for the deaths of 20 million Native Americans) to demonise their Spanish enemy. This adds another valuable perspective to the representation of the 1641 rebellion, that of Europe and the Atlantic world. Accounts of atrocities in the wider world had similarities to printed news from Ireland in the 1640s. This suggests that the 1641 rebellion was interpreted through English and Protestant lenses due to the complex constitutional relationship between Ireland and England and the fraught confessional atmosphere in Europe. Irish natives were similar to Native Americans in that they were colonised, yet representations of native Irish soldiers had more in common with Spanish Catholics. Paradoxically, Irish Protestants were depicted in a similar light to Native Americans who suffered at the hands of the Spanish empire.

Bartholomé de las Casas's 'Short account of the destruction of the Indies' provided the evidence for the 'Black Legend' and was a stinging indictment of Spanish involvement in the West Indies. As a representative of the Spanish colonial interest, de la Casas's account of the murder of twenty million Native Americans at the hands of Spanish (and Catholic) soldiers suited the objectives of Spain's European Protestant rivals who opposed their involvement in the Americas. This resulted in the reprinting of the tract in several European states, most notably in the Low Countries and England.[128] On several occasions, de las Casas noted how he had witnessed the massacres and assured his readers of the veracity of his account. Similarly, if he had not witnessed certain of the scenes that he described, de las Casas consulted reliable sources as a means of lending credence to his statements.[129] Writing his account out of a desire for justice and redress for the indigenous people, de las Casas called on Charles V, the Spanish king, to 'extirpate the causes of so many evils'.[130] Through focusing on the plight of the Native American victims and the brutality of Spanish soldiers de las Casas lobbied for a more benign approach to imperial rule. None the less, the ultimate goal was to portray the cruelty of the Spanish as extreme: Native Americans were murdered in their millions, and dogs were bred for the sole purpose of consuming native American bodies.[131] De las Casas lamented the perpetration of these atrocities, which, he felt, resulted from a distorted notion of 'divine will' on the part of the Spanish soldiers.[132]

The types of cruelty described by de las Casas were similar to those recounted of Germany and Ireland. For example, the 1656 edition of de las Casas's 'Short account', published as *The tears of the Indians*, described how Spanish soldiers ripped open the stomachs of pregnant women. They would then take Native Americans children 'by the feet and dash their innocent heads against the rocks'.[133] Women and children were seen as the main targets of Spanish agression.[134] Spanish soldiers, de las Casas argued, had laid waste to many of the regions and inflicted excessive torture on natives whom they encountered: 'Once it happened that they used eight hundred of the *Indians* in stead of a team to draw their carriages, as if they had been meer beasts and irational creatures ... And as for the country itself, they so far destroyed it.'[135] Honest, virtuous women feared being raped, although there is little mention of sexual violence in the tract.[136] In the end, de las Casas confessed that he had trouble condensing the extent of Spanish cruelties in the Americas: 'If I had decreed to reckon up the impieties, slaughters, cruelties, violences, rapines, murders, and iniquities, and other crimes committed by the Spaniards against God, the King, and these innocent Nations, I should

---

[128] 'Bartolomé de las Casas', in Nina Baym (ed.), *The Norton anthology of American literature*, New York 2003, vol. A, 38–9; Pagden, 'Introduction', pp. xiii–xli; Bartholomé de las Casas, *The tears of the Indians*, London 1656.
[129] De las Casas, *Tears of the Indians*, 64, 82, 84, 108.
[130] Ibid. 133–4.
[131] Ibid. 10. See also p. 63.
[132] Ibid. 13, 59, 75.
[133] Ibid. 8.
[134] Ibid. 8, 63, 64
[135] Ibid. 54. See also pp. 36, 40, 48, 59, 99, 106.
[136] Ibid. 57.

make too large a volume.'[137] Throughout the text de las Casas emphasised the bountiful nature of the soil of the West Indies and the willingness of the natives to assist Spanish colonists and partake in their colonial mission in an attempt to assure the king of the advantage of colonisation.

Similarly, after an attempted slave rebellion in Barbados in 1676, polemicists also described the colony as an opportunity for Englishmen to improve their social and economic lot. *Great newes from the Barbadoes* (1676) provides another Atlantic world comparison to the portrayal of the 1641 rebellion. Barbados was described as 'the most flouris[h]ing colony'. Barbadian produce surpassed English output: 'All Kitching Garden Herbs, and Fruits are much better and more fragrant than in *England* that are there at almost all times of the year to be had in their Excellency.'[138] Their plot was portrayed as a hidden conspiracy that threatened to murder all white people, and to spare the more attractive noble women to use as concubines.[139] The discovery of their design, and the prevention of the slaves' actions, however, meant that *Great newes from the Barbadoes* focused more on recounting how the English colonists had reasserted their authority, in a suitably excessive manner. Seventeen slaves were found guilty and were executed: 'Six burnt alive, and eleven beheaded, their dead bodies being dragged through the Streets ... and were afterwards burnt with those that were burned alive.'[140] The author happily concluded that Barbardos was 'the finest and worthiest I[s]land in the world'.[141] Thus, portrayals of attempted rebellions drew upon cultural constructions of violence that shaped victimhood and demonised enemies.

How were massacres in other European countries depicted in contemporary pamphlets? In 1655 the duke of Savoy, a vassal of the French king, ordered a group of evangelicals, the Waldensians, to conform to Catholicism. On 24 April 1655, having seen his proposal rejected, Savoy's troops moved into the Valltelline valley in Piedmont and began killing, torturing and expelling the Waldensians from their homes. One pamphlet, *The barbarous & inhumane proceedings ... of the duke of Savoy* (1655) blamed Irish, French and Savoyard Catholics and their clergy for perpetrating these massacres.[142] In fact, there are several resonances with the portrayal of the Irish rebellion. Women and children were portrayed as the main targets: 'In many corners they have shamefully abused and tormented many women with their young children, and after did cut off their heads; they dasht the children, even

---

137 Ibid. 72.
138 *Great newes from the Barbadoes*, London 1676, 5, 8.
139 Ibid. 10.
140 Ibid. 12.
141 Ibid. 14.
142 *The barbarous & inhumane proceedings against the professors of the reformed religion within the dominion of the duke of Savoy*, London 1655, 1, 3.

those of fifteen years old, that would not go to mass, against the Rocks.'[143] People were stripped of their clothes, stabbed, exposed to frost and snow, set on fire and old people were targeted for refusing to attend mass.[144] Giovanni Stoppa's digest history of Piedmont included a letter from a Waldensian who began his tale of woe claiming that 'our tears are no longer of water but of blood'.[145] Another letter from Lyon described the massacre as indiscriminate and aimed to rid the valleys of non-Catholics.[146] A final letter, written on 6/7 April 1655, provided greater, more gory, detail:

> The Mother hath lost her sucking Child, the Husband his Wife, the Brother his Brother, some have been barbarously massacred, whilst they were busy in saving their goods, others having fled to escape to the tops of the Mountains, were forced to cast themselves into the hollows of Rocks, and amongst the Snow, without fire, without nourishment.[147]

The letter continued to describe how the valleys were strewn with body parts and corpses of victims and exposed to the appetites of beasts that fed on the victims: 'Tears obscure my sight, and the violence of my sobbings hinders me from proceeding further.'[148]

The most relevant account for this discussion is a history of the Waldensian Church written by Samuel Morland, a trusted diplomat of Oliver Cromwell. Morland's *History of the evangelical Churches of the valleys of Piedmont* (1658) contained a massacre section substantiated by eyewitness accounts, much like John Temple's *Irish rebellion*. In his introduction to the reader Morland warned that what followed was particularly brutal: 'Some of their Women were ravisht, and afterwards staked down to the ground to their Privities; others strangley forced and then their Bellies rammed up with Stones and Rubbish; the Brains and breasts of others sodden and eaten by their Murderers.'[149] Much like Irish Protestant settlers, the Waldensians were completely outnumbered, and exposed to the cruel oppression of Catholic soldiers.[150] Using the examination of the Sieur de Petit Bourg, a captain in a local army, Morland used his generalisation of the nature of the conflict to argue that 'several men kill'd in cold bloud; as also women, aged persons,

---

[143] Ibid. 2.

[144] Ibid. 2–4.

[145] Giovanni Stoppa, *A collection or narrative sent to his highness the lord protector of the common-wealth of England, Scotland, & Ireland &c*, London 1655, 26.

[146] Ibid. 31–2.

[147] Ibid. 34.

[148] Ibid. 36.

[149] Samuel Morland, *The history of the evangelical Churches of the valleys of Piedmont*, London 1658, sig. Av.

[150] Ibid. 327.

and young children, miserably murdered'.[151] Petit Bourg claimed to have witnessed these crimes, yet provides no detail. A declaration by Thomas Buit and Francis Pra claimed that Savoy's soldiers ate the brains of 'several barbets', 'all of which we assure in words of truth, as having heard the same with our ears'.[152] Sara Rastignole recalled how her daughter-in-law witnessed the stabbing of a pregnant woman through the stomach and passed on this information.[153] Giovanni Michialin reported that three of his children were killed and a small baby was 'stript naked, and then its brains dasht out agianst the rocks'.[154] Most of the witness statements used by Morland contained gruesome stories of rape, children being attacked, attacks on pregnant women and their foetuses, much like atrocity stories from Ireland and the Americas. As with Temple's *Irish rebellion* no attempt was made by the author to corroborate what was being said or to evaluate the content that they described.

The main difference between accounts of atrocities that occurred in colonial contexts and those in Europe was that reports of colonial violence were quick to remind readers of the profitability of the land. Apart from this, the narratives contained similar atrocity stories, rooted in biblical imagery, and stressed how basic military codes of war were not being followed by Catholics (or Native Americans). Emerging military laws that protected women and children suggest that authors deliberately focused on their plight in times of war to evoke specific reader responses, perhaps sympathy, but perhaps something more proactive.

Reports on the 1641 rebellion in Ireland were only exceptional in the scale of what was published, not in their content. Avid followers of the Thirty Years' War, the burgeoning English empire, and later readers of events in Piedmont would no doubt have recognised similarities between such atrocities across the Old and New Worlds. All were concerned with the exercise of codes of conduct during the various military encounters and as a result paid more attention to cruelties enacted upon civilians, particularly women and children. There is another common feature to all these massacre accounts. All are written in the English language and are aimed at English audiences. This does not suggest that such types of violence may or may not have occurred, but this chapter has shown the representation of violent events across the world. These accounts drew upon cultural frameworks that shaped portrayals of assailants, victims and the range of cruelties that occurred. These cultural reference points derived from a range of sources – the Bible, classical texts – and were also inspired by real events. Many of the more

---

151 Ibid. 334.
152 Ibid. 337.
153 Ibid. 339.
154 Ibid. 346.

common brutal events were also described in the depositions. Another more substantial similarity exists. Massacre accounts were written to lobby for various political agendas. It is no coincidence that the more brutal accounts of the 1641 rebellion appeared at critical moments in Irish and British politics. The Ormond peace of 1646 prompted the publication of Temple's *Irish rebellion*, Rothwell's publications on the Thirty Years' War appeared when English authorities attempted to raise funds to donate to Protestant churches in Germany. Reports of the atrocities committed in Piedmont and South America appeared to urge Cromwell to pursue a variety of foreign policies. Later accounts and histories of the 1641 rebellion, in both an Irish and a British context, could be manipulated to justify a range of political initiatives.

5

Contesting the 1641 Rebellion

Throughout the course of the war, combatants referred back to the outbreak of rebellion and contested its nature. Accounts of rebel violence justified the use of excessive force by English and Scottish armies in Ireland in 1642 and again in 1649. After the successful conquest of Ireland by Oliver Cromwell, histories of 1641 appeared to remind authorities of what Irish Protestants had suffered during the previous decade. The establishment of the Cromwellian regime in Ireland provided an opportunity radically to alter the Irish political landscape. Histories of the 1641 rebellion played a key role in these debates: combatants in the Wars of the Three Kingdoms manipulated the past in order to defend their actions or to lobby Oliver Cromwell to pursue various policies in Ireland. This led to the confiscation of land and transplantation of entire communities, which drastically changed the social order in early modern Ireland. Recent work by Kevin McKenny has shown that over the course of the 1650s and 1660s the percentage of land held by Catholics fell from 66 per cent to 29 per cent, while Protestant land holdings increased from 30 per cent to 67 per cent.[1] Upon the restoration of Charles II in May 1660, many Catholics hoped that they would regain their lost estates as a reward for their loyalty to the Stuarts during the 1640s. Once again the spectre of 1641 reared its head and became a subtext to debates on whether Catholics should be restored to the lands that they had enjoyed prior to the rebellion. The purpose of this chapter is to investigate how the rebellion of 1641 came to be represented during the Cromwellian and Restoration eras and to show how pivotal initial interpretations of the rising were to subsequent histories of 1641.

The focus of this chapter will be the years from 1647 to 1662. For those interested in the influence of the memory of 1641 during the Popish Plot, scholars such as John Gibney, Michael Perceval Maxwell and Deana Rankin have covered this in detail.[2] This chapter, however, is more concerned with how participants in, and supporters of, the various sides in the Wars of the Three Kingdoms reflected on events in Ireland during the Cromwellian and

---

[1] Kevin McKenny, 'The Restoration land settlement in Ireland: a statistical interpretation', in Coleman A. Dennehy (ed.), *Restoration Ireland: always settling and never settled*, Aldershot 2008, 35–52.

[2] Gibney, *Ireland and the Popish Plot*, 99–114; Michael Perceval-Maxwell, 'Sir Robert Southwell and the duke of Ormond's reflections on the 1640's', in Ó Siochrú, *Kingdoms in crisis*, 229–47; Rankin, *Between Spenser and Swift*.

Restoration era. It traces how the initial interpretations advanced by political rivals in the 1640s shaped later accounts. In some cases these authors, or the polemicists who read their books, spoke to a popular audience; yet, the focus of most of this chapter will be on the political elites who passionately defended their actions in the 1640s and clarified their roles in the 1641 rebellion for the benefit of their peers.

The 'Protestant' version of events

This is problematic. First, there was no uniform 'Protestant' identity in early modern Ireland, particularly after the influx of Baptist, Independent and Quaker ministers and preachers that accompanied the Cromwellian armies into Ireland in the 1650s. Furthermore, Presbyterian recollections of the 1641 rebellion (which retrospectively imposed a Presbyterian identity on Scottish settlers) differed slightly in their interpretation of it.[3] Instead, the term 'Protestant' is used here to reflect the 'official' version of events first postulated by the lords justices, the deposition commission and their adherents in the years following the outbreak of the rebellion until the restoration of Charles II. The purpose of this section is to illustrate how the initial confusion that clouded the first intelligence of the rebellion, the trauma of deponents and the argument that the rebellion was religiously inspired laid the foundations for subsequent Protestant histories of the 1641 rebellion.

The legacy of the depositions and their effect on later scholarship on the rebellion can be measured in a number of ways. First, they provided evidence for the massacre of Protestant settlers. Secondly, they contain information on those who had been killed. The numbers controversy stems from the deposition of Robert Maxwell. He claimed that Catholic priests had recorded the names of 154,000 lost souls, which the deposition commission either believed or were willing to propagate as the official figure.[4] Maxwell's deposition came to the attention of both king and parliament in late March 1643 when the lords justices and council, buoyed by hard-liners such as Temple and Parsons, argued against the proposed ceasefire with the confederation of Kilkenny. They cited Maxwell's figure of 154,000 people killed since 23 October 1641 and argued that the Irish rebels

> Most barbarously in time of open and settled peace, (without any provocation or offence given) falling with armed force upon the unarmed and harm-

---

3   See, for example, W. D. Killen (ed.), *A true narrative of the rise and progress of the Presbyterian Church in Ireland, 1623–1670 by the Rev Patrick Adair minister of Belfast also The history of the Church in Ireland since the Scots were naturalized, by the Rev Andrew Stewart minister of Donaghadee*, Belfast 1866; Robert Armstrong, 'Ireland's Puritan revolution? The emergence of Ulster Presbyterianism reconsidered', *EHR* cxxi (2006), 1048–74.

4   Deposition of Robert Maxwell, 22 Aug. 1642, TCD, MS 809, fos 5r–12v at fo. 8v.

less British and Protestants, murdering, hanging, drowning, burying alive and starving them, men, women and children, of all ages and conditions, to the number of one hundred fifty four thousand before the end of March last.[5]

In July 1643 parliament, eager to discredit the ceasefire, published Maxwell's figure, which became the official death toll. Subsequent attempts to estimate the number of Protestant dead revolved around Maxwell's testimony.[6] Prosecutors borrowed the figure for the trial of Lord Conor Maguire although they misquoted it as 152,000.[7] Some simply copied Maxwell's figure.[8] Temple doubled it and claimed that 300,000 had died through violent death, starvation, disease or deprivation.[9] Others followed suit, calculating how many had perished using Maxwell's original deposition as a basis. Edward Bowles and Thomas Crant, presumably with Maxwell's figure in mind, argued that 200,000 Protestants were murdered in Ireland.[10] John Milton, then secretary for foreign tongues, originally argued that 154,000 Protestants had been massacred but later quadrupled this as 'the number of 154000 [refers to] the Province of *Ulster* onely ... which added to the other three [provinces], makes up the total summ of that slaughter in all likelyhood fowr times as great'.[11] Thus a single deposition provided the basis for the calculation of lost Protestant souls rather than any systematic trawl through the entire collection to ascertain an exact figure.

The establishment of the confederation of Kilkenny and the return from European theatres of war of Irish soldiers versed in military codes of conduct helped to end the butchery that characterised the early stages of the rebel-

---

5   Lords justices and council to the king, 16 Mar. 1643, HMC, *Ormond*, n.s. ii. 248.

6   Mary Hickson, *Ireland in the seventeenth century or The massacres of 1641–1642 their causes and results*, London 1884, i. 334; *A declaration of the Commons assembled in parliament; concerning the rise and progresse of the grand rebellion in Ireland*, 9–10.

7   *The last speeches and confession of the Lord Maguire*, London 1644. This figure was copied in 1649: John Cook, *King Charls his case*, London 1649, 28; William Prynne, *The subjection of all traytors, rebells, as well peers, as commons in Ireland, to the lawes, statutes, and trials by the juries of good and lawfull men of England, in the Kings Bench at Westminster*, London 1658. See Charlene Adair, 'The trial of Lord Maguire and "print culture"', in Darcy, Margey and Murphy, *The 1641 depositions*, 169–84.

8   Morley, *Remonstrance of barbarous cruelties*; *mercuvrivs hibernicvs, or The Irish mercurie*, n.p. 1645, 8; Thomas Waring, *A brief narration of the plotting, beginning and carrying on of that execrable rebellion and butcherie in Ireland: with the unheard of devilish-cruelties and massacres by the Irish-rebels, exercised upon Protestants and English there: faithfully collected out of depositions, taken by commissioners under the great seal of Ireland: hereunto are added observations, discovering the actions of the late king; and manifesting the concernemnt of the Protestant-army now imployed in Ireland*, London 1650; John Milton, *Eikonoklastes*, London 1649, 112.

9   Temple, *The Irish rebellion*, 6.

10   Crant, *Plott and progresse*, 7; Edward Bowles, *The mysterie of iniquitie*, London 1643, 32.

11   Milton, *Eikonklastes*, 115, and *Eikonklastes*, London 1650, 112.

lion.[12] Despite this, later accounts echoed claims made in early pamphlets that Irish rebels targeted noncombatants and ministers. Contemporaries could, therefore, draw ready comparison between Irish soldiers, Spanish colonists and Native Americans who killed civilian populations in times of war and rebellion. Initial discussions on the outbreak of the rebellion argued that the conduct of war was exceptionally violent. Such literary constructions shaped Henry Jones's *Remonstrance,* John Temple's *Irish rebellion* and other 'official' interpretations of the rebellion. These accounts demonised the native Irish and Old English but they also contained something unique: sworn testimonies from those living in Ireland and who had suffered at the hands of the Irish rebels. Both of these works could be consulted for detailed 'eye-witness' descriptions of the rebellion (that had been heavily edited). As a result many writers simply consulted these edited collections of depositions and constructed gory accounts of the Irish rebellion that originated from the traumatised memories of Irish deponents and the imaginations of a beleagured, bitter colonial administration in Ireland.

While the work of Jones and Temple may have been too expensive for members of the lower social orders, cheaper pamphlets contained information sourced from them. This meant that the 1641 depositions had the potential to reach a wide audience in England. Take, for example, the broadside *A prospect of bleeding Irelands miseries* (*see* frontispiece), published in 1647 by Joseph Hunscott. It contained fifty-four abstracts from Temple's section on the atrocities of 1641 and positioned them around a striking image of 'Lady Ireland' crying out for her Protestant dead, who had 'fal[le]n by the sword'.[13] Much like the description of the Apocalypse in the Book of Revelation, corpses are strewn across the ground being gorged upon by birds of prey. In a classic example of how atrocity accusations could be used to mobilise populations the broadside urged: 'Recompense unto them double what they have done unto others', which paraphrased another section in the Book of Revelation where vengeance is sought against Babylon.[14] Speech bubbles from Lady Ireland reveal her inner thoughts: 'myne eyes do fayle with teares', speaking to her audience, 'wee have sined', which must have struck a chord with contemporaries who understood the quotations from the Book of Lamentations. Through reflection on their own sins, readers would have identified with their fellow Protestants in Ireland, surrounded by Babylonian foes.

The positioning of the text surrounding the image meant that Hunscott provided readers with an interpretative framework within which to understand

---

12 Ó Siochrú, 'Atrocity', 55–86 at pp. 66–7.

13 *A prospect of bleeding Irelands miseries*, London 1647 (Wing P 3805[246]), dated 'Aprill 16th' by a contemporary hand.

14 Revelation xviii.6.

the significance of the broadside.[15] Following on from Lady Ireland's tears, the reader must empathise with the depiction, scan through the enumerated massacres and call for revenge. Readers were assured of the legitimacy of the massacres detailed, 'collected from the certain Intelligence', which described the deaths of 200,000 civilians in Ireland. 'Commiserating friends in England and Scotland', were to seek vengeance ('recompence unto them double') against the 'barbarous and blood-thirsty rebels'. A *prospect of bleeding Irelands miseries* argued that the Irish did not adhere to standard codes of conduct and targeted women and children. Unlike Temple, this broadside offered some hope to readers that 'dying Ireland may yet live'. Ireland's redeemer, parliament, in order 'to put an end to the bleeding miseries', was to send over two commanders, General Philip Skippon and General Edward Massey, to obtain 'victory over those inhumane blood-thirsty Rebels'. In truth, however, the decision to send Massey and Skippon to Ireland met with stern opposition from within the New Model Army and both remained in London.[16] Thus, this broadside following on from Temple's depiction (and the interpretation of the deponents themselves) of the Irish rebellion, showed a defenceless Protestant population pitted against an all-encompassing and voracious rebel force. Yet, Hunscott (prematurely) offered something new, a glimmer of hope through parliament and a conquering army hell-bent on vengeance.

The lords justices intended the depositions to serve a didactic purpose to future generations of politicians, to warn them of the Catholic menace in Ireland. Later histories of the rebellion appeared at opportune moments in an attempt to steer the course of Anglo-Irish relations. When it became clear, in May 1649, that Oliver Cromwell had been appointed lord lieutenant of Ireland and head of a large army to conquer the country and confiscate Irish lands, Temple and his colleagues were preparing to lobby for a full-scale confiscation of rebel/confederate landholdings and assets. Strategically, an expedition to Ireland made sense for Cromwell. English and Irish forces had rallied behind the royalist banner raised in Ireland by the hapless, idiotic and militarily unsuccessful James Butler, now marquis of Ormond. Politically, the decision to invade Ireland had its benefits, for it provided Cromwell with a chance to tackle his growing unpopularity in England. On his way to Chester to inspect his troops, Robert Lockyer led a mutiny against Cromwell for deposing the king and was subsequently executed. No doubt the huge crowds that turned out at Lockyer's funeral in London alarmed Cromwell who now had to address the concerns of the wider English public, many of whom were shocked at the thoughts of living in a polity without a monarch

---

[15] Christian Jouhaud, 'Readability and persuasion: political handbills', in Roger Chartier (ed.), *The culture of print: power and the uses of print in early modern Europe*, Oxford 1989, 235–60, esp. pp. 238–45.

[16] Andrew Warmington, 'Massey, Sir Edward (1604x9–1674)', *ODNB*: ww.oxforddnb.com/view/article/18297, accessed 23 Apr. 2009; Ian Gentles, 'Skippon, Philip (d. 1660)', *ODNB*: www.oxforddnb.com/view/article/25693, accessed 23 Apr. 2009.

as head of state. In the meantime, the council of state paid one of the clerks of the deposition commission, Thomas Waring, £100 to prepare copies of the depositions for publication. They also appointed John Milton as their main propagandist to oversee this process. Only a prefatory pamphlet emerged, however, and the plan for the larger work seems to have been shelved.[17] In 1649 Thomas Waring finalised his version of the depositions, taking roughly 992 copies and editing 691 for publication. Waring then allowed William Parsons to use his transcriptions of the depositions in his tract on the Irish rebellion, 'Examen Hibernicae'. Although it is unclear whether Parsons wrote the text himself, the council of state were happy to believe that he had and were confident that his text asserted 'English interest in Ireland, and discover[ed] the ingratitude and unworthy dealing of the Irish' and that it 'may be of public use'.[18]

Parsons's decision to prepare (or patronise) a history of the 1641 rebellion is noteworthy as prior to this his career had followed a similar trajectory to that of Sir John Temple. Both opposed the cessation of arms with the confederation of Kilkenny and were imprisoned as a result. The appointment of Lord Lisle as lord lieutenant in 1647 signalled their return to power. Parsons, then in London, rejected the opportunity to return to Ireland and instead lobbied his independent colleagues in parliament to pursue the conquest of Ireland. 'Examen Hibernicae' covered similar ground to Temple's *Irish rebellion* and both sang from the same hymn sheet. First, Parsons reaffirmed England's 'right' to govern Ireland. Second, 'Examen Hibernicae' answered accusations made by the confederation of Kilkenny against his political faction. Like Temple, Parsons defended the policies of his cohorts during the troublesome months of May–October 1641 and claimed that the 'gouernment of that kingdome was often committed to the lords and natiues of the ould English, which a wiseman would thinke had bene a proper orrdinacon to foster the peace'.[19] Those who tried to defend the colony were betrayed by the Old English who instead collaborated with the rebels in the defeat at Julianstown.[20] Parsons claimed that the Old English had degenerated into the habits of the native Irish, which prevented them from seeing the light of the Gospel. Together with the native Irish nobility, the Old English organised a 'conspiracie to extirpate ye Brittish and protestants, [which] was generally agreed & consented to by the Confederate Catholicques before the said 23th of October 1641'.[21] Most important, Parsons defended the veracity of the 1641 depositions, claiming that they only captured a small

[17] Council of state day proceedings, 9 May 1649; 8 Jan. 1650, *CSPD, 1649–1650*, 131–2, 474; Waring, *A brief narration*; David Lowenstein, *Representing revolution in Milton and his contemporaries*, Cambridge 2001, 194–5.

[18] William Parsons, 'Examen Hibernicae', NLI, MS 692, fo. 111; *CSPD, 1649–50*, 131–2.

[19] Parsons, 'Examen Hibernicae', fo. 21.

[20] Ibid. fo. 111.

[21] Ibid.

fraction of the cruelty experienced by Irish Protestants: 'The seuall tymes of all the murthers, spoiles and pillages comitted in theise seuerall counties, doe appeare in the examinacons taken, yet extant, but many other greate spoyles were then comitted in theise countries whereof the proprietors came not to be examined.'[22] Thus, Jones and Temple provided the framework for others to construct their polemical accounts of the 1641 rebellion and to use the depositions as evidence for the atrocities committed in Ireland. 'Examen Hibernicae' built upon early interpretations of the rebellion to lobby for the confiscation of Irish Catholic lands.

Cromwell had a number of issues to contend with at this time. First, he had to satisfy those who wished to reap their dividends from the Adventurers' Act. Second, major political figures across the three kingdoms called for a confusing mix of policy objectives to be pursued in Ireland. Finally, Cromwell had to take on a sizeable royalist army and a suspect local Irish population. His political skill can be evidenced by the fact that he altered his message, tone and stance on the native Irish, English royalists and Catholics depending on his audience. Take, for example, a speech supposedly given by Cromwell on 15 August 1649 in Dublin that was printed by the London-based newsbook, the *Perfect diurnall*. Cromwell swore vengeance against 'the barbarous and bloodthirsty Irish, and the rest of their adherents and confederates' and promised to propagate 'the Gospel of Christ, the establishing of truth and peace and restoring that bleeding nation to its former happiness and tranquility'.[23] To Irish audiences, however, Cromwell spoke of his plans to stimulate trade and encouraged Irish natives by saying that his army would adhere to established codes of conduct while in Ireland.[24] As time wore on, bloodthirsty audiences in England were fed a diet of salacious news from Ireland during Cromwell's time there, and the newly-appointed lord lieutenant of Ireland no doubt benefited from these propagandic accounts. As noted by Micheál Ó Siochrú, Cromwell's fledgling regime 'desperately needed military success to bolster flagging popularity on the domestic front'.[25] Pamphleteers called on Cromwell to avenge the deaths of thousands of Irish Protestants and delighted in the array of torture devices available to his army to use against the Irish. Now Cromwell's forces possessed a 'new engine of war for cutting off both legs and arms of any that shall oppose him'. A gruesome picture illustrated the full extent of the suffering that they could inflict.[26] When Cromwell captured the town of Drogheda

---

[22] Ibid. fo. 112.

[23] *The writings and speeches of Oliver Cromwell*, ed. W. C Abbott, Cambridge, MA 1937, ii. 107.

[24] Ó Siochrú, *God's executioner*, 79–80

[25] For more recent analysis on this see John Morrill, 'The Drogheda massacre in Cromwellian context', in Edwards, Lenihan and Tait, *Age of atrocity*, 242–65, 257–9; Ó Siochrú, *God's executioner*, 84–5.

[26] *Two great fights In Ireland*, London 1649.

in September 1649 a compendium of letters was published which described Cromwell's actions there (or how he wished his actions to be perceived in England). He claimed that his soldiers had killed 3,552 soldiers and inhabitants in arms. His justification for this atrocity was simple: he argued that he had finally imposed a just judgement on the perpetrators of the barbarities of 1641. His belief 'that this is a righteous judgement of God upon these barbarous wretches, who have imbrued their hands in so much innocent blood' has caused considerable debate among historians. John Morrill has argued that Cromwell referred to English royalists at the time, citing that many of those listed as killed in action were English royalists. Yet, this list of fallen soldiers appears to have been added to the letter in the original pamphlet. Furthermore, Cromwell's use of the term, 'imbrue their hands in the blood of the innocent' evoked massacre imagery that had been refined in the 1640s. Indeed this phrase was used repeatedly in contemporary pamphlet and manuscript literature on the Irish rebellion.[27]

Cromwell's rhetoric appealed to those who had read about the massacres of Protestant settlers in Ireland and were eager for revenge. Supporters of Cromwell waited tentatively for news of his success. One diarist mentioned that 'this day we kept a publicke thanksgiving for the successe against [Drogheda], and before we heard the great newes of the taking of Wexford, and putting the garrison, and some say the inhabitants to the sword'.[28] The massacres were therefore interpreted as a 'righteous' judgement on the 'barbarous' Irish rebels.[29] Other evidence supports the argument that Cromwell may have been referring explicitly to the Irish rebels of 1641. Describing his successful capture of Wexford, Cromwell told William Lenthall (again, in a letter printed for the benefit of the wider public) how his soldiers 'ran violently upon the Town with their ladders and stormed it: And when they were come into the Market place, the enemy making a stiff resistance, our forces brake them, and then put all to the sword that came in their way'. His dispatches from Ireland downplayed the casualties that his army suffered. In Wexford he claimed that 'I believe there was not lost of the Enemy not many less then two thousand, and I believe not Twenty of yours [i.e. parliament] killed, from first to last of the Siege.' Cromwell justified his sacking of the town by invoking divine providence:

> God ... in his Righteous Justice, brought a just Judgement upon them, causing them to become a prey to the Soldier, who in their Pyracies had made preys

---

[27] 'A treatise giving a representation of the grand rebellion in Ireland', MS Harleian 5999, fo. 20; Coote, Irelands lamentation, 7; Cranford, Teares of Ireland, 54.

[28] The diary of Ralph Josselin, 1616–1683, ed. Alan MacFarlane, London 1976, 183; Morrill, 'The Drogheda massacre', 242–65.

[29] John Morrill, 'Cromwell, Oliver (1599–1658)', ODNB: www.oxforddnb.com/view/article/6765, accessed 5 Mar. 2008. Morrill has subsequently changed his opinion on this: 'The Drogheda massacre', 257–9.

of so many families, and made with their bloods to answer the cruelties which they had exercised upon the lives of divers poor Protestants.

He defended this view by regaling his English audience with a story that he had heard from Wexford locals about the 1641 rebellion: 'About seven or eight score poor Protestants were by them [Irish rebels] put into an old Vessel, which being as some say bulged by them, the Vessel sunk, and they were all presently drowned in the Harbor.'[30] Allegedly in January 1642 a boat full of Protestant settlers who attempted to flee to England, sank. At the time, deponents estimated that between sixty and a hundred Protestants drowned on their way to England.[31] Only one account of this incident mentions that the refugees 'were wilfully cast away by the Irish owners or seamen'.[32] This reveals how the survivors and witnesses of this atrocity told others about this event and possibly related it on to Cromwell.

Furthermore, Cromwell was occasionally reminded during the 1650s of the massacres of 1641. In 1656 John Phillips's edition of de la Casas's account of Spanish cruelties in the Americas summoned the memory of 1641 to lobby Cromwell to pursue his failed Western Design: an integral part of the massacre genre was the desire for revenge. In this case Phillips claimed: 'Me-thinks I hear a sudden stillness among them [the Native Americans]; the cry of Blood ceasing at the noise of Your great Transactions, while you arm for their Revenge.'[33] As Cromwell avenged 1641, Phillips advanced the Protector's credentials in order to suggest that he would be similarly successful against Spain, although, 'the blood of Ireland spilt by the same Faction in comparison of these [in the Americas] was but as a drop to the Ocean'.[34] Evocations of the Black Legend were used to appeal for more stringent opposition to Spanish involvement in the Atlantic world. It also appears that the alleged massacres of 1641 had a personal effect on Cromwell. In 1655, in a bid to illustrate the extent of diplomatic unity between the Dutch Republic and England after the Piedmont massacre, the Dutch ambassador informed the States General that Cromwell 'told me, that above two hundred thousand souls were massacred [in Ireland]' and

---

[30] A letter from the lord lieutenant of Ireland: to the honorable William Lenthal esq; Speaker of the parliament of England: giving an acount of the proceedings of the army there under his lordships command; and several transactions between his lordship and the governor of Wexford, with the fort, haven and shipping there; and of several other garrisons of the enemy: as also the proposition tendred for the rendition of Wexford: and a copy of a censure, under the hand of Nicholas bishop of Ferns, against Talbot who dyed a Protestant, London 1649, 6–7.

[31] Examination of William Strafford, TCD MS 818, fos 269–70v; examination of Edward Sinott, fos 214r–215v; deposition of John Sims, fos 104r–105v; deposition of Thomas Lucas, fo. 77; deposition of Matthew Mudford, fos 75r–76v.

[32] Deposition of John Archer, ibid. fos 42r–43v.

[33] De las Casas, Tears of the Indians, [2], 'To the Lord Protector'.

[34] Ibid. [12–13], 'To all true-English men'.

had therefore promised full co-operation against the duke of Savoy.[35] It is important to note that Cromwell's justification of his actions at Drogheda may have been deliberately ambiguous. Readers may well have thought that he referred to royalists as 'barbarous wretches' as argued by John Morrill; however, his later views on 1641 clearly showed the effect of the atrocities on his thinking not just in relation to Ireland but also in international diplomacy.

English audiences were both thrilled and shocked at news of Cromwell's actions in Ireland. Rumours of the massacre underlined Cromwell's strength in Ireland and encouraged compliance from rival armies. The subsequent publication of Thomas Waring's *A brief narration of the plotting, beginning and carrying on of that execrable rebellion and butcherie in Ireland*, based on the 1641 depositions, within months (March 1650) of the events at Drogheda further justified Cromwell's actions there.[36] Waring claimed that the native Irish ('Irish rebels') had for eight years committed an 'execrable butchery' on 'English Protestants'.[37] Their aim was simply

> not to spare any of the English race, that were Protestants (as in severall Rebellions before they had likewise resolved to do). And that they would deprive of life all irrationall creatures of the English breed, as horses, cattell, sheep, swine, & even very cats and dogs.[38]

Irish rebels took arms in order to remove English legal and social customs, to 'deface and spoil all their Churches', to destroy all monuments and records of English rule and to 'deface' all English buildings, and any reminder of 'civility'.[39] Much like Jones and Temple, Waring believed that the conspiracy was organised by Irish Catholic priests and Catholics across Europe in a bid to conquer the three kingdoms.[40] Meanwhile, Irish Catholic nobles were duped into taking part.[41] Waring's section on the planning of the rising owed much to Jones's *Remonstrance* which carefully reconstructed meetings held among prominent Irish Catholics at Multyfarnham and the importation of seditious Catholic texts to rouse rebels to fight. In a bid to blame royalists for the rising, Waring skilfully brought Thomas Wentworth, the former lord lieutenant of Ireland, to the fore of the planning process and argued that Wentworth knew of the plot prior to his death.[42] Twenty-three pages of an

---

[35] Wilheim Niueport, the Dutch ambassador in England, to the States General, 4 June 1655, in *A collection of state papers of John Thurloe*, London 1742, iii. 476–7.

[36] Waring, *A brief narration*.

[37] Ibid. preface.

[38] Ibid. 18.

[39] Ibid. 19.

[40] Ibid. 1–7.

[41] Ibid. 17.

[42] Ibid. 8–11.

addendum, entitled 'observations', provided further proof of the role in the plot of the king, Wentworth and prominent Irish Catholics for those who did not believe him.[43]

In Waring's eyes, Catholic clerics made a vital contribution to the rebels' war effort. They promoted the rebellion and enlisted the wider population to support it. Prayers and sermons 'drew the common people into a unanimous expectation & strong resolution to prosecute the [rebellion]'.[44] The rage that followed meant that only one in forty managed to escape to Dublin and testify before the deposition commission while the rest were left to suffer at the hands of Irish Catholics.[45] Much like Temple, Waring argued that the Old English played a waiting game, hoping that the native Irish would score some initial 'success' which would allow them to enter the rebellion.[46] Once again Waring returned to the accusations made by the confederates during the tense negotiations for the 1643 cessation of arms. As argued by Temple and Parsons, A *brief narration* stated that the lords justices did not ignore the grievances of the Irish Catholics. In fact they had trusted the Old English to help defend the colony against the rebels' fury. Waring accused the Old English of betrayal when a relief force *en route* to Drogheda was routed by the rebels at Julianstown due to their treachery (as Parsons had argued in 'Examen Hibernicae').[47] Waring slightly modified Jones's argument regarding the national outbreak of the conspiracy. He claimed that this rebel victory encouraged all other Catholics across the country who had not yet taken arms to join the rebellion.[48] This slightly contradicted Jones's thesis and might reflect the fact that Waring, having read the entire collection of depositions, recognised the gradual spread of the rebellion from its epicentre in the north to the rest of the country in the months after October 1641 as captured by the original testimonies.

With all Catholics involved in the rebellion, Waring argued that Protestant settlers were subjected to sustained attacks that turned the social order on its head. Irish tenants attacked English landlords and servants betrayed their masters. Protestant corpses, English buildings and 'Christian' people were subjected to cruelty and destruction. Civilians were stabbed, and had their genitals cut off, although such acts, Waring claimed, were usually perpetrated by Irish children.[49] As in standard atrocity accounts of the era, Waring paid more attention to attacks upon women and children. Irish rebels ripped up pregnant women's stomachs and children's heads were

---

43 Ibid. 41–64.
44 Ibid. 17.
45 Ibid. 19–20.
46 Ibid. 20.
47 Ibid. 21.
48 Ibid. 21–2.
49 Ibid. 25–6.

dashed against stones, walls and rocks.[50] As in the *Remonstrance* and *The Irish rebellion*, the *Brief narration* contained detailed descriptions of how corpses were left exposed to the fowls of the air. For example, one unnamed minister, 'a good professour of Gods truth', was starved to death and then 'crows and ravens picked out his ey[e]s, and ravenous creatures devoured him'.[51] Unlike these other accounts Waring supplied a suitable biblical reference to help his readers to grasp the significance of this: 'The dead bodies of thy servants have they given to be meat for the fowls of Heaven, and the flesh of the Saints unto the beasts of the earth.'[52] This provides a clear example of the centrality of the Bible in shaping seventeenth-century accounts of atrocities.

According to Waring, the victims were targeted because they were 'British' and Protestant. There is no mention of Scottish victims in the text, Waring instead preferred to use terms such as 'Protestant', 'English' and 'Christian', while the ethnic term 'Irish' is only applied to the Irish rebels. The Old English, however, were labelled the 'Palle English' (as by Temple), but their actions exceeded the 'meer Irish' in their cruelty: 'the degenerated Palle English were most cruell amongst the British Protestants, never being satisfied with their bloud, untill they had in a manner seen the last drop therof', an allegation also made by Temple in *The Irish rebellion*.[53] Through calling the victims of the Irish rebellion 'English', God's 'servants' and 'saints', Waring hoped that English audiences would identify with Ireland's Protestant community. They were all part of the elect, and Cromwell's victories (according to Waring) comfirmed their place in the pantheon of true believers: 'In all which the wonderfull hand of God hath been remarkably seen in strengthning those his faithful instruments, [parliamentary and Cromwellian armies] to execute his just judgements against that bloody and deceitfull generation, in whose skirts are found much bloud of innocents.'[54] Waring clearly believed that Cromwell referred to Irish rebels as opposed to English royalists at Drogheda. A *Brief narration* informed the wider English population that Ireland and Irish land was now free in retribution for English investments of 'blood and treaure' over the preceding decade. For those who were interested in learning more about the nature of the rebellion, Waring urged his readers to await his edited collection of depositions which was due to appear in the following months (but never did). He finished with a call for a harsh execution of justice against the native Irish arguing that anything less would deny 'divine will'.[55]

---

[50] Ibid. 27.
[51] Ibid. 28.
[52] Jeremiah xxxiv.20; Waring, A *brief narration*, 29.
[53] Waring, A *brief narration*, 31.
[54] Ibid. 26.
[55] Ibid. 29–30.

Waring's *Brief narration* did not achieve the same success as Temple's *Irish rebellion*, which was the work most frequently consulted by other authors in their attempts to create their own histories of 1641, particularly in the eighteenth century. As shown by Raymond Gillespie, *The Irish rebellion* could be read in different ways: as a providential narrative or as a reference work. Samuel Clarke's *Generall martyrologie* survived as an example of how both renditions could become entwined.[56] Since Temple's narrative expressed more concern with the future of the colony, as opposed to the Church, Temple preferred to leave the religious overtones of his text to somebody else. While Temple reiterated the legitimacy of the Protestant faith, and reassured his readers with ghostly apparitions that illustrated God's support for the parliamentary war effort, he did not discuss the deaths of Protestant ministers to any great detail: 'But I shall not here touch any further upon those [ministers] who dyed thus gloriously this will be a worthy work for some more able pen to undertake, and indeed fit for a martyrology.'[57] It is therefore fitting to look at Samuel Clarke A *generall martyrologie* (1651) as it borrowed exclusively from Temple, and juxtaposed the troubles of the 1640s against the larger persecution of the 'true' Church from Old Testament times to the seventeenth century.[58] It appeared, albeit accidentally, as a logical successor to Temple's *Irish rebellion*. Clarke may have derived his entire argument from Temple, but, as is clear from a number of elements, he drew his own conclusions from the evidence in *The Irish rebellion*.

Clarke's narrative of the 1641 rebellion in A *generall martyrologie* comprised sixteen pages in an impressive 574-page history of persecutions committed against the 'Church of Christ' since Old Testament times.[59] While Clarke relied upon a godly network in Warwickshire for source materials for his other works it appears that his private library provided some of the information that he needed for his martyrology.[60] Authorities were not impressed by the fact that the *Generall martyrologie* printed verbatim abstracts from John Foxe's *Book of Martyrs*.[61] Clarke's reading of *The Irish rebellion* is revealed in telling textual differences between the two, which highlight how Temple's book could be used for reference material.[62] John Ball has incorrectly stated that this is an example of how stories of 1641 changed over the years from 1646 to 1651.[63] In truth, Clarke set these references in the context of the

[56] Gillespie, 'Temple's fate', 315–33 passim.

[57] Temple, *The Irish rebellion*, London 1646, 109.

[58] Samuel Clarke, A *generall martyrologie*, London 1651.

[59] Ibid. title page.

[60] Ann Hughes, 'Clarke, Samuel (1599–1682)', *ODNB*: www.oxforddnb.com/view/article/5528, accessed 6 June 2006.

[61] McKenzie and Bell, A *chronology and calendar*, i. 312.

[62] Temple, *The Irish rebellion*, 82–136.

[63] John Ball, 'Popular violence in the Irish uprising of 1641: the 1641 depositions, Irish

eternal and international struggle between God and the Catholic AntiChrist and paid little attention to the new political order established in England as argued by Ball. Kathleen Noonan has illustrated in greater detail the editorial changes made by Clarke to Temple's original commentary.[64] The purpose of this section, however, is to illustrate how Clarke emphasised the central tenets of Temple's discourse on the behaviour of the native Irish and his use of depositions that appeared in *The Irish rebellion*.

Whereas Temple preferred to term the events of the 1640s as a 'rebellion'[65] Clarke described them as a 'massacre'.[66] Indigenous Catholics, according to both works, heard the prayers of the local priests who gave 'free liberty to go out and take possession of all their lands, which they pretended to be unjustly detained from them by the *English*'.[67] Like Temple, Clarke maintained that members of the Catholic clergy urged their parishioners not to worry about any possible recriminations in heaven for 'the Protestants being, as they told them, worse then dogs, for they were devils, and served the devil, and therefore the killing of such was a meritorious act'.[68] Furthermore, orders were given to 'strip, rob and despoil' the settlers of their goods and chattels. Due to their barbaric nature, the rebels, 'having got what they could, they afterwards murthered them'.[69] Such examples of rebel cruelty were accompanied by descriptions of rebels boasting and rejoicing in their acts, according to Clarke, who placed more emphasis on this aspect of their behaviour than had Temple.

The nature of the argument behind *A generall martyrologie* meant that certain aspects of the rising as outlined in Temple's *Irish rebellion* had to be changed. Clarke moulded his account into a larger history of persecutions against the true faith. Any reference to the political grievances of Irish Catholics were deleted as Clarke stripped *The Irish rebellion* of Temple's defence of his colleagues. 1641 was another plot against true Christians: 'Their cruelties were exercised upon the Protestants ... neither were the *English* papists murthered, yea they joynd with the *Irish* in the murthering of their brethren.'[70] Unlike the 1646 edition of *The Irish rebellion*, Clarke's *Generall martyrologie* contained many fascinating illustrations and woodcuts that depicted various cruelties committed against those of the 'true' faith from biblical times to the present. In the section on the Irish rebellion the

---

resistance to English colonialism, and its representation in English sources', unpubl. DPhil diss. Johns Hopkins 2006, 203–5.

64 Noonan, '"Martyrs in flames"', 223–55.
65 Temple, *The Irish rebellion*, 87.
66 Clarke, *A generall martyrologie*, 348.
67 Ibid.
68 Ibid. The same phrase occurs in Temple, *The Irish rebellion*, 87.
69 Clarke, *A generall martyrologie*, 348.
70 Ibid. 347.

devouring of dead bodies by swine and dogs occurs frequently and such occurrences appear throughout the text.[71] Likewise, according to Clarke, Catholic adherents tore the intestines out of those who adopted Protestantism during the time of the Spanish Inquisition. This was also the subject of an illustration.[72] This meant that, even at a glance, contemporary readers were reminded that such callous acts were perpetrated against the Protestant tradition from the earliest times, adding credence to the arguments of Clarke and Temple that the Protestant settlers were the seventeenth-century equivalent of the Israelites.[73]

The constant revelling and rejoicing in the pain of Protestant victims recurred quite frequently in A generall martryologie and in some cases Clarke diverged from Temple's text to emphasise this fact. For example, as in Temple, Clarke warned that the Catholic clergy had granted a special dispensation claiming that the killing of a Protestant would spare one from the 'pains of Purgatory'.[74] While Temple provided the deposition of John Parry of Armagh to prove his point, Clarke combined this deposition with commentary in his own work. This indulgence 'caused some of these murtherous Cains to boast, after they had slain many of the English, that they knew that if they should die presently they should go strait to heaven'.[75] In another example, Temple referred to two rebels 'more merciful than the rest' who drowned Protestants on a regular basis.[76] According to Clarke, however, 'two boyes boasted that at several times they had murthered and drowned thirty-six women and children'.[77] Admittedly, Temple also published incidents of smug rebels satisfied with their various cruelties, but it is interesting to note that Clarke emphasised these incidents independently.

Clarke also interpreted The Irish rebellion as a godly narrative that warned of the dangers of tolerating popery. This is indicated by his condensed versions of the depositions published by Temple that described sightings of ghostly apparitions. These reports occupied the end of both works in their sections on the Irish rising. Temple provided extracts from seven depositions that referred to providential events. Two are by women, Katherine Coke and Elizabeth Price, and both appear in A generall martyrologie.[78] The difference in Clarke is that the author added his own commentary to this part of the text. He considered these spiritual experiences to be signs of 'Gods judge-

---

[71] Ibid. 100.

[72] Ibid. 230.

[73] Toby Barnard, 'The uses of 23 October 1641 and Irish Protestant celebrations', EHR cvi (1991), 889–920.

[74] Temple, The Irish rebellion, 87; Clarke, A generall martyrologie, 348.

[75] Clarke, A generall martyrologie, 348.

[76] Temple, The Irish rebellion, 106.

[77] Clarke, A generall martyrologie, 355.

[78] Temple, The Irish rebellion, 134–5; Clarke, A generall martyrologie, 362–3.

ments upon the *Irish*, whereby he hath not left the innocent blood of his servants to be altogether unrevenged', referring here to Cromwell's triumphs in Ireland.[79] At the end, bearing in mind that his commentary was about to finish and that the rest of the work was dedicated to the individual lives of Protestant martyrs, Clarke took the opportunity to reflect on the dire situation that faced the Church of Ireland in the 1650s: 'God is still fighting against [Catholics], and probably will continue their destruction, till they either shall truly be humbled for their horrid sins, or be utterly consumed from the face of the earth.'[80] Clarke's version of events in 1641 changed Temple's narrative into a recognisable persecution story; Clarke teased out an interpretation of the rebellion as a religiously-inspired assault on Irish Protestants. In this way 1641 became another chapter in the history of the plight of true believers when faced with their Babylonian enemies.

It is often stated that Temple's *Irish rebellion* provided a template for the demonisation of Catholics during later crises such as the Popish Plot (1678–81) and the Williamite wars (1688–91), both of which saw new editions of the book. Accounts that printed supposedly 'verbatim' accounts from *The Irish rebellion* were in fact lifted from Samuel Clarke's *Generall martyrologie*, not Temple work, largely because Clarke's portrayal was more suited to these contexts. For example, a pamphlet entitled A *looking-glass for England*, published in 1667, printed Clarke's version of events verbatim.[81] When the Popish Plot erupted in England and another anti-Catholic crisis gripped the English imaginations, a litany of publications appeared which provided reminders of the evil deeds committed by Catholics during the 1641 rebellion, but all were sourced from Clarke's *Generall martyrologie*, not Temple's *Irish rebellion*.[82] During the Williamite wars the spectre of a tyrannical Catholic king again loomed large. It is of no surprise that reprints of accounts from the 1640s emerged during moments of acute sectarian tensions, however the most prominent were sourced from Clarke, not Temple.[83] Richard Ansell is correct in his assertion that 'the reprinting of pamphlets from 1641 implied

---

[79] Clarke, A *generall martyrologie* 362.

[80] Ibid. 363.

[81] A *looking-glass for England: being an abstract of the bloody massacre in Ireland, by the instigation of the Jesuites, priests and friars, who were chief promoters of those horrible murthers, prodigious cruelties, barbarous villanies, and inhumane practices, executed by the Irish papists upon the English Protestants in the year 1642: as also a brief apology in the behalf of the Protestants in the walleys of Piedmont; with a narrative of the barbarous butcheries, inhumane cruelties, most execrable and unheard of villanies, perpetrated on them by the popish party during the heat of the late massacre in April 1655 stirred up by the malice and instigation of the devil acting in the popish clergie*, London 1667.

[82] An *account of the bloody massacre in Ireland: acted by the instigation of the Jesuites, priests, and friars*, London 1679.

[83] An *abstract of the unnatural rebellion and barbarous massacre of the Protestants in the kingdom of Ireland in the year 1641*, London 1689; A *relation of the bloody massacre in Ireland: acted by the instigation of the Jesuites, priests, and friars who were promoters of those*

that Irish Catholics would never change', yet the behaviour described of Irish people echoed descriptions of the Spanish in South America and drew upon cultural constructions of a demonic enemy.[84] In times of war the Irish could be readily portrayed as functioning outside codified military laws and thus easily demonised. In short, they fitted English cultural constructions of barbaric soldiers (usually Catholics) across Europe and the New World.

In 1691, for example, *The popish champion*, a vitriolic critique dressed up as a biography of the earl of Tyrconnell, linked the Catholic lord lieutenant of Ireland with the massacres of the 1641 rebellion. 'Irish papists' who engaged in the rebellion were frightened of pitched battle preferring guerrilla-type engagements. They were at their 'most cowardly when opposed in a manly way' by standing armies such as when they faced the Cromwellians.[85] In its brief narrative on the 1641 rebellion, *The popish champion* detailed attacks on non-combatants, women and children, and mentioned sexually motivated assaults: 'Virgins deflowred, Women ravished, Infants, as come into the World, cast out to Dogs and Swine to be devoured', while men were hung up by their genitals until they died. Overall 200,000 were killed, rivers 'swelled with blood', while the victims and survivors called for retribution: 'this blood did not fail to cry for vengeance'. *The popish champion* praised the Cromwellians for exacting revenge on the native Irish and for establishing English rule in Ireland. It finished with the hope that Williamite forces would do the same to Irish Catholics fighting for James II.[86] As time wore on it is clear that later accounts of the 1641 rebellion mimicked the atrocity stories contained as hearsay in the depositions or relied on the first reports printed about the rebellion in London during the 1640s.

It must be stressed that the appearance in print of the 1641 depositions, and the publication of histories of the rebellion, had mixed success in changing the course of Anglo-Irish relations or colonial policies in Ireland. During the 1650s Henry Jones, former head of the deposition commission and now scoutmaster-general in Ireland, compiled another history of the

---

horrible murders, prodigious cruelties, barbarous villanies, and inhuman practices executed by the Irish papists upon the English Protestants, London 1689.

[84] Richard Ansell, 'The 1688 Revolution and the memory of 1641', in Forrest and Williams, *Constructing the past*, 79.

[85] *The popish champion, or, A compleat history of the life and military actions of Richard earl of Tyrconnel, generalissimo of all the Irish forces now in arms wherein you have a true account of his birth and education, his advancement and honours, his treacherous disarming the Protestants* ... : [sic] *together with a relation of all the skirmishes, battels, sieges, and remarkable transactions which have happened under his government, with the particulars of the late bloody fight in the north* ... : *as also a brief description of the kingdom of Ireland* ... *the means how it came to be a conquer'd kingdom, with the sundry rebellions made by the natives against the crown of England, and by what means reduced / written for the present satisfaction of all good Protestants* ...; *to this treatise is added the life and memorable actions of Father Petre, &c*, London 1689, 7.

[86] Ibid. 6, 7, 9.

rebellion. This provided further evidence of Catholic barbarity gleaned from the depositions and appeared during a pivotal debate on Cromwellian policy in Ireland. While R.T. Dunlop's argument that the Cromwellians had forgotten about the 1641 depositions by May 1652 is nonsense, his most contentious claim is that the appearance of Henry Jones's *Abstract of some few of those barbarous, cruell massacres and murthers*, drastically altered Cromwellian intentions for Ireland. Dunlop argued that after the the appearance of Jones's *Abstract*, 'hardly a letter left Ireland without containing some reflexion on the blood-guiltiness of the nation and the necessity there was of propitiating the Divine wrath for the innocent blood spilt, by bringing the authors of the massacres to justice'.[87] According to Dunlop, the Act of Settlement subsequently expanded the net of people deemed guilty of the massacres of 1641 who now faced land confiscation. John Cunningham has recently argued that Dunlop over-stated his case and has claimed that the *Abstract* did not drastically alter Cromwellian policies toward former Irish confederates and royalists. In actual fact, the terms of the Act of Settlement had been drafted more than a year previously by Henry Ireton. As such the direct political impact of the *Abstract* was minimal: in fact many of its more moderate clauses were introduced into the act after its publication in May 1652.[88]

If one returns to the immediate military context in Ireland, however, one might be led to believe that Jones was concerned about how those who were 'blood-guilty' would face justice. There is little sense in the contemporary account which states that Jones's explosive presentation of the *Abstract* at a meeting of Cromwellian soldiers in Kilkenny in April 1652 was directed at the impending Act of Settlement. Those in attendance (various marshals and officials) were debating whether they should use excessive force against the native Irish. Divided between moderate and radical stances, Jones presented his *Abstract*, which described numerous massacres committed by Irish rebels and convinced those in attendance that greater clarity should be sought from England regarding whether those who committed these atrocities would be brought to justice. The unknown correspondent did reference the fact that parliament 'might shortly be in pursuance of a speedy settlement of this nation' but also lamented the fact that many of the victims of this violence were now dead. This meant that 'so ... few of the rebels can be particularly discriminated by any evidence now to be produced, as the usual course of justice doth require'. It seems to be more logical (particularly seeing how little influence the *Abstract* had in shaping the Act of Settlement) that the *Abstract* signalled the beginning of Jones's campaign to establish the High Court of Justice. In a matter of months, by August 1652, Jones was

---

[87] Robert Dunlop, *Ireland under the Commonwealth: being a selection of documents relating to the government of Ireland from 1651 to 1659*, Manchester 1913, i, p. cxxxi.

[88] John Cunningham, '1641 and the shaping of Cromwellian Ireland', in Darcy, Margey and Murphy, *The 1641 depositions*, 155–68 at pp. 161–4.

granted permission to head a High Court of Justice established to prosecute those guilty of the massacres of 1641.[89] Cunningham correctly identifies Florence Fitzpatrick as one of Jones's first targets in the court: Fitzpatrick was accused in the *Abstract* of murdering John Nicoloson and his wife in Queen's County and others to whom he had promised quarter.[90] One of the other more prominent rebels identified in Jones's *Abstract*, Sir Phelim O'Neill, was also brought before Jones's court.[91] In light of the limited impact of the *Abstract* on shaping the Act of Settlement, and its effect in establishing the High Court of Justice and dictating who was to be prosecuted, it appears that Jones skillfully used the depositions to lobby for the establishment of a court to prosecute suspected rebels of 1641.

Over the course of the seventeenth century histories of the 1641 rebellion appeared at key moments in Anglo-Irish politics and at times of potent anti-Catholic hysteria. With the restoration of Charles Stuart in May 1660, those who had been dispossessed by the Cromwellians and had fought for the Stuart cause in the 1640s had great hopes that their lands would be restored. This of course threatened the landholdings of a number of prominent Irish Protestant settlers who had enriched themselves at the expense of their Catholic neighbours. The spring and summer witnessed a period of intense printed petitioning from people across the religious spectrum in Ireland. Protestants of the established Church complained about the seditious influence of radical Protestant sects;[92] Catholics reminded the king of their loyalty during the 1640s and the oppression that they had suffered under the Cromwellians,[93] while vested Protestant interests took the opportunity to defend their new-

---

[89] Commissioners to the parliament, 5 May 1652, and commissioners of parliament to Henry Jones, 5 Aug. 1652, Dunlop, *Ireland under the Commonwealth*, i. 178–81, 242.

[90] Henry Jones, *An abstract of some few of those barbarous, cruell massacres and murthers, of the Protestants, and English in some parts of Ireland, committed since the 23 of October 1641: collected out of the examinations taken upon oath by persons of trust, in the beginning of the rebellion, by virtue of severall commissions under the great seal of Ireland: which particulars are singled out of a multitude of others of like nature: with the persons that acted those mrthers, and mssacres, with time, place, and other circumstances, are contained in the said examinations: sent over to the parliament in a letter from the commissioners of parliament in Ireland, and the generall and field officers there: and read in the parliament the 19 day of May 1652*, London 1652, 6–7; Cunningham, '1641', 164.

[91] TCD, MS 866, fo. 78

[92] *A faithfull representation of the state of Ireland: whose bleeding eye is on England for help: or The horrid conspiracy discovered and most humbly presented to the wisdom of parliament for timely prevention, if not impossible: wherein it appears the designe is laid at the root of all the parliaments interest there, the adventurers lands, and the new-English mens lives, (as they call them) as well as at the power of godliness, and of the present governmen: published by constant and cordial adherers to the parliament and common-wealth, on the behalf of themselves, and of thousands in Ireland*, London 1660.

[93] *To the king's most excellent majesty: the faithful protestation and humble remonstrance of the Roman Catholick nobility and gentry of Ireland*, [London 1660]; *A brief narrative how things were carried at the beginning of the troubles in the year 1641 in Ireland*, [London] 1660.

found wealth.[94] Prior to the proclamation of Charles II as king, Sir John Clot-worthy, who had amassed huge estates in Antrim and Down under dividends from the Adventurers' Act, warned the king that Catholics across Ireland were arming themselves and threatening rebellion. English MPs and lords believed him and presented a proclamation to Charles II 'to be signed against the Irish Papists, who were said to be actually in Rebellion, murdering his Majesties Protestant Subjects, violently intruding into other Mens posses-sions, with many other Characters of Infamy, rendring them odious to all Nations'.[95] Clotworthy's handiwork prompted Charles II to issue a proclama-tion in June 1660 urging all soldiers and justices of the peace to seek out these 'rebels' in Ireland who were guilty 'of the innocent bloud of so many thousands of Our English Protestant Subjects'.[96]

Memories of the 1641 rebellion or at least contesting accounts of it fed into discussions on the treatment of Catholics. Former confederates and royalists argued with Adventurers and Cromwellian soldiers who had legiti-mately (in their own eyes) come into possession of lands in Ireland. Debates intensified particularly in light of Charles II's attempt to reassess the land settlement in Ireland. Protestant commentators highlighted Irish Catholic treachery in 1641 and portrayed popish adherents as perfidious. Catholics responded by assuring Charles of their loyalty to the new monarchy.[97] Peter Walsh called for Catholic lands to be restored so that they could join Protes-

---

[94] *Ireland's declaration being a remonstrance of the generality of the good people of Ireland*, London 1660; *The state of the adventurers case which resolves it self I. into the nature of their title and the equity of it, consisting in these particulars*, London 1660.

[95] Nicholas French, *A narrative of the settlement and sale of Ireland: whereby the just English adventurer is much prejudiced, the antient proprietor destroyed, and publick faith violated; to the great discredit of the English Church, and government, (if not re-called and made void) as being against the principles of Christianity, and true Protestancy*, Louvain 1668, 3.

[96] *By the king: a proclamation against the rebels in Ireland*, London 1660.

[97] R. Caron, *Loyalty asserted and the late remonstrance or allegiance of the Irish clergy and layty confirmed and proved by the authority of Scriptures, fathers ... and by the evidences of several theological reasons: with a brief answer to Cardinal Peron's oration and objections / by R. Caron*, London 1662; *To the king's most excellent majesty the faithful protestation and humble remonstrance of the Roman Catholick nobility and gentry of Ireland*, London 1662; Peter Walsh, *To the king's most excellent majestie the humble remonstrance, acknoledgement, protestation, and petition of the Roman Catholick clergy of Ireland*, London 1662, and *The more ample accompt, the answers to the exceptions, the inducements, and invitation, promised in the advertisement annexed to the late printed remonstrance, protestation, &c. of the Roman Catholick clergy of Ireland: and (in conclusion of all) an humble earnest advise to the nobility, genrty, and other lay Catholicks of the three nations: moreover, and for the better information, and fuller satisfaction of the reader, the foresaid remonstrance, &c. and advertisment prefix'd: finally an appendix of censures and arrests against the uncatholick positions of some otherwise Catholick writers: by F. Peter Walsh, of St. Fran. ord. read. of div. procur. of the above clergy, both sec. and reg*, London 1662.

tants as 'his Majesty's most beautifull and approved subjects'.[98] The prospect of increased Catholic landowning prompted a further frenzy of Protestant accounts of the 1641 rebellion. Henry Jones, for example, reissued his 1652 *Abstract* once again in 1662, replete with the names of deponents, which were curiously absent from the original edition.[99] Members of the Protestant junta feared that Ormond's close kin and clan ties with prominent Irish Catholics such as the Butlers would lead him to overlook their collective guilt in the events of the 1640s.[100] Roger Boyle, first earl of Orrery, reminded Ormond that the Old English and the Irish had become part of a joint genetic 'stock' and were now in constant war with the 'English'.[101] No doubt aware of Ormond's fragile ego, Orrey buttered up the newly-appointed lord lieutenant and praised his 'glorious victories over them [the "Irish" in] the first two years of the Rebellion', a clear over-statement of Ormond's achievements and military ability.[102] It is significant that Orrery toed the party line that had originated from the pen of Henry Jones: 'Roman Catholique Nobles and Gentlemen' were all guilty of 'the last bloody Rebellion.'[103] It was unexpected 'like a sudden storm of lightning and thunder', and resulted in the deaths of 'above two hundred Thousand in the first two years'.[104]

Eager to preserve their status, the Parsons faction fanned the flames of 1641 to keep memories of Catholic barbarity alight. The 'Protestant' account of the 1641 rebellion depended not just upon Henry Jones's initial interpretation, but also upon the fears of deponents and the rumours that they recorded in their testimonies. Later commentators who perused the depositions or Jones's *Remonstrance* or Temple's *Irish rebellion*, neglected to consider that the depositions were a product of trauma, hearsay, rumour as well as eye-witness testimonies, and the inherent flaws and difficulties such a source could produce. One question remains, however: why did the restoration of Charles II produce such a vitriolic response from the 'Protestant' interest in Ireland?

[98] Peter Walsh, *A letter desiring a just and mercifull regard of the Roman Catholicks of Ireland, given about the end of October 1660 to the then marquess, now duke of Ormond, and the second time lord lieutenant of that kingdom*, [London 1662], one page proclamation.

[99] Jones, *Abstract*.

[100] Roger Boyle, *The Irish colours displayed, in a reply of an English Protestant to a late letter of an Irish Roman Catholique: both address'd to his grace the duke of Ormond lord lieutenant of his majesties kingdome of Ireland*, London 1662, 9.

[101] Ibid. 3–4.

[102] Ibid. 10.

[103] Ibid. 5.

[104] Ibid. 11–12.

The Catholic version of events

From the birth of the rising native Irish and Old English Catholics stressed the legitimacy of their actions. They blamed the lords justices for ignoring their grievances and alleged that colonial forces used excessive force against Ireland's Catholic population. Above all else, they denied that a widespread massacre of Protestant settlers had occurred, nor was it intended. In time, they questioned the validity of depositions as evidence for this. There was no uniform Catholic version of events. Put simply, there were two schools of thought: those who argued that the rebellion was a just cause conducted in a legitimate manner by men aggrieved by their loss of status. Alternatively, some gloried in the actions of Phelim O'Neill and celebrated events in Ulster as a plot to rid Ireland of heretics and foreigners. The official confederate party line on the rebellion, voiced in the 1640s, shaped the more moderate accounts of the 1641 rebellion written during the Restoration. To some extent recent work on the rebellion has followed their version of events. Aidan Clarke, for example, argued that the Old English reluctantly rebelled because they had been denied their traditional role as the crown's agents in such incidents.[105] More recent work, however, has suggested that the Old English were neither reluctant rebels nor reactionaries – rather they acquiesced in the actions of the native Irish.[106] A little discussed aspect of the Catholic version of the 1641 rebellion is the fact that some sections of Catholic society revelled in the deaths of Protestant settlers after years (in their opinion) of oppression from heretical monarchs and avaricious New English and Protestant settlers.

The first official confederate publication to outline the reasons why they had taken up arms appeared in December 1642 in the tract 'A discourse between two councillors of state'. This pamphlet has come to life due to the work of Aidan Clarke who transcribed available manuscript copies of the tract juxtaposed with Henry Jones's acerbic commentary on the narrative. Jones took a personal interest in this text for it critiqued the deposition commission on which he had staked his professional fortunes. The lords justices had portrayed the rebellion as a war of religion, much to the ire of the confederation of Kilkenny, which blamed rapacious New English settlers who had caused 'great impoverishment' to Catholics in Ireland and noted how 'martial law was executed amongst them with much severity, they began to murmur and repine, yet so that a man might see they were resolved to bear anything, if they might but enjoy their religion and lands'.[107] The confederates poured scorn on the lords justices' claims that Catholics were

105 Clarke, The Old English.
106 David Finnegan, 'The impact of the Counter-Reformation on the political thinking of Irish Catholics, c. 1540–c. 1640', unpubl. PhD diss. Cambridge 2006.
107 Aidan Clarke, 'A discourse between two councillors of state, the one of England, and the other of Ireland (1642)', Analecta Hibernica xxvi (1970), 159–75 at p. 163.

treated fairly by them and by the colonial administration in the years and months leading up to 23 October 1641: 'It hath been always the art of the governors there to keep this state ignorant of their doings, by engaging all men coming from thence to speak well of them here, by sending over some apt instruments successively to trumpet out the justice and candour of their proceedings.'[108] Addressing the lords justices' portrayal of the rebellion as a war of religion, the confederates retaliated by stating that their main grievances were the plantations and the forced selling of lands. The 'Discourse' thus began a series of exchanges between the confederates and the lords justices, Catholic and Protestant Ireland, which involved bouts of accusation and counter-accusation of atrocity.

Aware that their cause could be intepreted as a war of religion the 'Discourse' noted that much of the evidence rested on the testimonies gathered by 'clergymen' in Dublin. The sole purpose of these testimonies was to stoke 'up this nation [England] against the Irish to an implacable hatred ... as well to take away from the Irish all pretences of having any just provocation'.[109] They challenged the validity of the 1641 depositions as evidence for the arguments made in Jones's *Remonstrance* and the motivations of the authors: 'I give no credit to that remonstrance of the said ministers, who being over passionate in the cause and bent to please those from whom they expected both the vindication thereof, and present relief for themselves.'[110] In particular, they critiqued the lack of systematic analysis of the nature of the evidence contained within the depositions, through taking 'every hearsay for positive proof' and 'importing more than was delivered'.[111] With aspersions cast upon the 1641 depositions the confederates continued their offensive against the lords justices' version of events. Turning to Jones's cynical portrayal of the rebellion as a 'great slaughter of the English', the confederates argued that all rebels acted within contemporary codes of conduct: 'Doubtless they did in many places kill men resisting, and pillaging all protestants within their power, but the report of their killing women and children or men desireing quarter [and] such like inhumanities, they were inventions to draw the larger contributions from the people of this kingdom to maintain the war.'[112] They challenged the image of Protestant victimhood and argued that deaths occurred 'through mutual acts of hostility'.[113] This led to questions about the implementation of quarter. While rightly pointing out that 'there is no quarter due to rebels', the confederates stressed that they were not 'rebels, and surely are no more rebels than any other subjects who

108 Ibid. 165.
109 Ibid. 171.
110 Ibid. 172.
111 Ibid. 172, 173.
112 Ibid. 172.
113 Ibid.

took up arms against the king and yet had very good quarter'.[114] To make matters worse, 'English soldiers' treated women and children as legitimate targets, and those who had been granted quarter were none the less summarily executed.[115] The confederates claimed that Charles Coote, a commander based in Leinster, killed a poor labourer by forcing him to 'blow in his pistol, and gave fire when the muzzle was in the man's mouth'.[116] The 'Discourse' branded the lords justices 'monsters', who had 'hearts not only to destroy the innocent but even those that have no power to do harm, and might live to do good'.[117] Bearing in mind the excesses committed by the colonial forces the confederates called for the 'just revenge of the king'.[118] This illustrates the centrality of vengeance to massacre narratives and atrocity accusations in the early modern era.

The confederates alleged in a later publication that Coote and Parsons adopted a two-front offensive against Irish Catholics.[119] Parsons denied Catholics political access to diplomatic channels of communication with king and parliament, while Coote waged war against Catholic Ireland. In Wicklow 'he burnt, killed and destroyed, all in his way'.[120] The destruction of Santry, which housed a sizeable Old English community, proved, the confederates argued, that noncombatants were targeted by state forces: 'in that towne innocent husband-men, some of them being Catholicks, were murthered in their home, and their heads carried triumphant into Dublin; next morning complaint being made of this, no redress was obtained therein'.[121] As a result, they argued, all Catholics were forced to take up arms in self-defence particularly after the excessive use of force by Coote's soldiers and the directions given by the lords justices to Coote on his way into Clontarf: 'pillage, burne, kill, and destroy all that there was to bee found, which direction was readily and particularly observed'.[122] William St Leger, according to the *Remonstrance of grievances*, indulged in similar cruelties against the Catholics of Munster whether nobility, gentry or from the lower social orders. St Leger's troops 'burnt, preyed, and put to death Men, Women, and Children, without making any difference of quality, condition, age, or sex in severall parts of that Province'.[123] Those who were captured by state authorities faced prosecution in 'illegal courts'; thus, the confederates

---

114 Ibid. 173. See also Parker, 'Etiquette of atrocity', 143–68 at p. 149.
115 Clarke, 'A discourse', 173.
116 Ibid.
117 Ibid. 174.
118 Ibid. 175.
119 *Remonstrance of grievances*.
120 Ibid. 23
121 Ibid.
122 Ibid. 23–4.
123 Ibid. 25.

and Ireland's Catholics were exposed to an illegitimate government that exercised excessive military force against them.

As far as English-speaking audiences were concerned the Catholic version of events had to compete with an avalanche of material printed in London. To put this in perspective: by 1643 the confederates owned working presses at Kilkenny and Waterford which between them produced sixty-six works. The port at Waterford allowed the confederates to distribute their publications around Ireland, Britain and Europe.[124] This output, however, compared unfavourably with regional presses across the three kingdoms. During the 1640s, for example, presses at York, Edinburgh and Oxford produced 162, 426 and 884 titles respectively.[125] Between 1641 and 1653 a total of 20,767 works was printed in London.[126] Of these 921 related to Ireland specifically.[127] Confederate publications mainly consisted of proclamations and declarations (as shown in the surviving material). While they printed two devotional works and a play, they were primarily concerned with state affairs and to a lesser extent propaganda.[128] In total, the confederates published four 'news' pamphlets that described recent events in Ireland. These informed readers of the strong alliance forged by the confederation with the king. A *briefe relation of the most remarkeable feates and passages*, published in 1644, contained numerous printed letters to illustrate 'what his most Gracious Majesties Commanders hath done in England against the Rebells'. It was also an attempt to inform an Irish audience, albeit an English-speaking one, of events within the wider three kingdoms.[129] While the confederates' output was not to the same scale as parliamentarian or royalist publications, the fact that the lords justices responded to their allegations in print suggests that their polemics caused considerable consternation.

As the lords justices canvassed English politicians for aid through the medium of print, so the confederates turned to the Catholic powers of Europe for financial support. Apparently the confederates disseminated reports that spoke of English tyranny.[130] Temple criticised how 'with scandalous aspersions cast upon the present government' confederate diplomats used print 'to gain belief among foreign States abroad, as well as discontented persons at home; and so draw assistance and aide, to foment and strengthen their

124 *English short title catalogue online*, accessed 20 Nov. 2008; E. R. McClintock Dix, 'Printing in the city of Kilkenny in the seventeenth century', and 'Printing in the city of Waterford in the seventeenth century', *Proceedings of the Royal Irish Academy* xxxii (1914–16), 125–37, 333–44.

125 *English short title catalogue online*, accessed 9 Apr. 2009.

126 Ibid. accessed 6 Jan. 2009.

127 Ibid.

128 For more on confederate printing see Gillespie, *Reading Ireland*, 60–1.

129 *A briefe relation of the most remarkeable feates and passages of what his most gracious majesties commanders hath done in England against the rebels*, Waterford 1644.

130 Lords justices and council to Leicester, 27 Nov. 1641, HMC, *Ormond*, n.s. ii. 29–30.

rebellious party in Ireland'.[131] The diplomatic corps relied upon priests, particularly those who had trained in the many Irish colleges in Europe. Here they gained access to English-language accounts of the rebellion and also to news from Ireland. The confederation of Kilkenny, however, lacked a unified political goal as the group catered for a diverse mix of political agendas.[132] These political differences mirrored those of the wider Catholic society in Ireland at the time. Not all were loyal to Charles I, some wanted an Irish king, some wanted the establishment of the Catholic Church, others would be happy with limited toleration of Catholicism. While the confederates officially touted the more moderate line (loyalty to the king and some redress for their religious grievances) others lobbied their political leaders to adopt more radical courses.[133]

Perhaps the most controversial view is that of Conor O'Mahony, originally from Muskerry in Cork, who had by the 1640s been sent to Portugal as part of the Jesuit mission there. O'Mahony published his *Disputatio apologetica de iure regni Hiberniae pro catholicis hibernis adversys haereticos anglos* in Lisbon in 1645, a tract which argued that all 'Hiberni', that is Catholics of Ireland, should reject the authority of the heretical English monarchy in Ireland. O'Mahony denied the legality of *Laudabiliter*, the papal bull that had granted Henry II permission to invade Ireland. He read with avid interest English-language news reports on the rebellion and delighted in news that 'you have already killed one hundred and fifty thousand of (your) enemies'. He later exhorted his fellow 'Hiberni' to continue this work: 'It remains for you to kill the remaining heretics, or drive them from the boundaries of Ireland, lest they corrupt our Catholic homeland further with their heresies, and errors.'[134] O'Mahony's arguments contradicted the official confederate line and were roundly rejected by the confederate hierarchy. Even those sympathetic to O'Mahony's views, dubbed the clerical faction, dismissed his arguments regarding the deposing of a heretical king as out of hand. Tadhg Ó hAnnracháin has suggested that as the confederates had sworn allegiance to God, country and king they could not pursue so radical a position.[135] The supreme council subsequently ordered that the *Disputatio* should be burned

---

131 Temple, *The Irish rebellion*, preface.

132 Ó Siochrú, *Confederate Ireland*.

133 With the notable exception of Michelle O'Riordan, '"Political" poems in the mid seventeenth-century crisis', in Ohlmeyer, *Ireland from independence to occupation*, 112–27.

134 Conor O'Mahony, *Disputatio apologetica de iure regni Hiberniae pro catholicis hibernis adversys haereticos anglos*, Lisbon 1645, 125. I am very grateful to Julia Hofmann for providing me with a translation of this text. It is hoped that this will be published in a critical edition in the near future. For those who cannot wait there is another translation available: *Conor O'Mahony: an argument defending the right of the kingdom of Ireland* (1645), ed. John Minihane, Cork 2010, 200–1.

135 Tadhg Ó hAnnracháin, '"Though heretics and politicians should misinterpret their good zeale": political ideology and Catholicism in early modern Ireland', in Ohlmeyer, *Political thought*, 155–74, 166.

but the effect of O'Mahony's text is telling. His arguments appealed to Owen Roe O'Neill and the divisive papal legate Giovanni Rinuccini.[136]

O'Mahony's exhortation to his fellow Irish Catholics was not unusual. Bardic poets were inspired or paid to compose war poems encouraging popular participation in the rebellion. Uilliam Óg, the son of Uilliam Óg Mac Bhaird, composed 'Dia Libh, A Uaisle Éireann' (Bless you, people of Ireland) sometime after the beginning of the rebellion, but before the setting up of the confederation of Kilkenny. He urged the 'Gael' to take arms 'on behalf of the Christian faith' against 'the oppression of Ireland'.[137] Much like later confederate accounts of the events that led to the war, Uilliam Óg blamed the oppressive government of English rule: 'You have been in a state of great debility for a while, suffering hardship and tyranny that you were not thought likely to withstand.'[138] 'Dia Libh' called for all nobles to join in a nationwide effort to rid Ireland of foreigners who had 'the cream of your land' and channelled the 'anger' of the Irish: 'Stand up for one another! Let everyone understand your combined vehemence! Direct your bitterness at the Goill [the English]!'[139] As there is no mention of the English crown, or of Charles I, Uilliam Óg must have interpreted the 1641 rebellion as an attempt to rid Ireland of all Protestants and foreigners, a seemingly radical stance in light of arguments made by the confederates in the following years.[140] It must be noted, however, that Uilliam Óg's poetry reflected the grievances of some of those who attacked settler communities during the outbreak of popular violence in 1641. Many members of native Irish society were more vitriolic in their critique of their colonial overlords than were the confederates. Later writers lamented in their poetry the failure of this more radical element.

Other bardic poets discussed similar issues as Uilliam Óg. Poems such as 'The Gaill will not let us settle Ireland in peace' and 'This tops the trick: the law that's come overseas' claimed that the Irish suffered under the rod of religious, political, social, cultural and legal persecution at the hands of the 'foreigners' in Ireland.[141] 'The Irish were turned to seeming foreigners' expressed anger at the plantations and arrival of avaricious Englishmen such as Philip Perceval.[142] Paidraigín Haicéad's 'After the beginning of this war in Ireland' bitterly complained about how the Irish were 'yoked by cruel

---

136 Idem, 'Conor O'Mahony', DIB.

137 Eoin Mac Cárthaigh and Uilliam Og Mac Uilliam Oig Mheic an Bháird, 'Dia Libh, A Uaisle Éireann (1641)', Ériu lii (2002), 89–121 at p. 96. I am grateful to Marc Caball for providing me with this reference.

138 Ibid.

139 Ibid. 97, 98.

140 Ibid. 89–121.

141 John Minihane, The poems of Geoffrey O'Donoghue, Cork 2008, 20–3.

142 Ibid. 2–3.

desperation'.[143] He called for 'the revival of Gaelic glory'.[144] For Haicéad the rebellion had little to do with land, but 'to protect our clergymen' from 'crimes aimed at our clergy'.[145] His poem finished with a rousing call to arms:

> Rise up, Ireland, with the God of Grace!
> May her banner of the holy cross protect her race!
> May legions of God's angels watch over, as before,
> Her strong levied armies in war!
> May the edge of the sharp spears by hate honed,
> Wielded by our chivalry – our youths as their support –
> Deal deadly blows, piercing to the bone,
> Slashing and tearing, annihilate the foe![146]

Other bardic poets celebrated the wars of the 1640s as an attempt to restore honour to the Irish nobility and to 'defeat the heretics' villainy'.[147]

After the rebellion, and during the 1650s, some bardic poets reflected on what could have been, and appealed no doubt to the more radical element in Irish society. 'An Síogaí Rómhánach', or 'the Irish vision at Rome', composed by an Ulster poet, echoed similar sentiments.[148] Highly critical of Henry VIII and the persecution of the Catholic faith in Ireland under the Stuarts, the poet exclaimed: 'Every horror has been wrought upon Erin; A perpetual deadly curse is rained upon her.'[149] 'The Irish vision at Rome' also accused parliamentarian soldiers in Ireland of using excessive force and denigrated them as 'vile boors' who had beheaded the king 'with a keen sword'.[150] Facing more years of persecution under the Cromwellians ('the brood of Luther'), the poet called for the Irish to rally one final time and return Ireland to pre-English times:

> None shall league with the Saxon,
> Nor with the half naked Scot.
> Then shall Erin by freed from settlers,
> Then shall perish the Saxon tongue.
> The Gaels in arms shall triumph
> Over the crafty, thieving false sect of Calvin.[151]

---

[143] Michael Hartnett, *Haicéad*, Oldcastle 1993, 55.

[144] Ibid. 56.

[145] Ibid.

[146] Ibid. 59.

[147] *Conor O'Mahony*, 51–2.

[148] Cecile O'Rahilly (ed.), *Five seventeenth-century political poems*, Dublin 1952, 12–13.

[149] John T. Gilbert, 'The Irish vision at Rome', in *A contemporary history*, iii. 190–6

[150] Ibid. iii. 192.

[151] Ibid. iii. 195–6.

John O'Connell's *Ireland's dirge* or 'Tuireamh na hÉireann' echoed these sentiments. As the Reformation brought 'destruction on poor Erin's head' and the Stuarts persecuted Catholic priests, the rebels took arms against further English cultural, political and religious encroachment. Afterwards the arrival of Cromwell and his cohorts Charles Fleetwood, Henry Ireton and Edmund Ludlow 'Brought swarms hors'd – a most rapacious crew/ A sword or pistol seen in either hand, /And carbine too each has at his command'.[152] These poems were, to all intents and purposes, a call to rid Ireland of English people and the Protestant faith and to unite behind a faith and fatherland ideology. They all stressed Catholic persecution at the hands of Stuart and Cromwellian authorities. Much like the pamphlet literature that described the plight of Protestant survivors in the 1640s, Catholics who remained in Ireland were destitute and lacked a Church to support them.

These Irish-language poems did not reach a wide, three-kingdoms audience. There is little evidence to suggest the extent to which such sentiments occurred nationwide but they most likely reflected the desires of a range of Irish communities across the country. After the restoration of the Stuart monarchy Catholics adopted the medium of print to disseminate their version of events to the wider English-reading public and to petition the newly restored king, Charles II. Restoration interpretations of the 1641 rebellion drowned out Irish-language sources as the 1650s and 1660s witnessed the increasing use of English-language printing presses by Ireland's Catholics. The ready availability of these sources to subsequent historians shaped current historiography on the 1641 rebellion. Sadly, in some cases it is not clear who wrote these pamphlets yet they closely followed the party line set by the confederation of Kilkenny and merit further discussion. Take, for example, *A brief narrative [of] how things were carried at the beginning of the troubles in the year 1641 in Ireland* which spoke of the persecution that Irish Catholics had suffered under Sir William Parsons and Oliver Cromwell and accused colonial powers of engaging in a campaign of terror against Irish Catholics. Parsons allegedly 'at a publick Entertainment before many witnesses did positively declare, That within a twelve moneth no Catholique should be seen in Ireland' while 'thousands' signed a petition to introduce 'a severe persecution' against Catholics.[153] Much like confederate propaganda, *A brief narrative* pointed to the murders of innocent husbandmen in Santry, the burning of Clontarf and the racking of Sir John Read as examples of the cruelties suffered by Ireland's Catholics.[154] For the author of *A brief narrative* the imprisonment of the earl of Castlehaven, an Englishman and a Catholic who had offered his services to the lords justices, revealed the lords justices

---

[152] *Ireland's dirge: an historical peom, written in Irish by the right rev John O'Connell, bishop of Kerry*, trans Michael Clarke, Dublin 1827, 43–5.

[153] *A brief narrative*, 6.

[154] Ibid. 7–8.

'general distrust' towards 'the Nation'.[155] A *brief narrative* then claimed that the lords justices were responsible for the deaths of innocent settlers for they had prevented the nobility and gentry of the Pale from protecting the colony.[156] It was highly critical of how the memory of the 1641 massacres was trotted out to tar Ireland's Catholics as barbaric:

> These men amuse the world with the noise of Irish Barbarous Cruelties, but are far from doing us the Justice to let men know, that we are as desirous as they to see the Cruelties of all sides punisht. These men fill the ears of the people with their tenderness of the English Interest in *Ireland*, but conceal from them, that they themselves would destroy those who had their descent from *England*.[157]

In contrast, Catholic loyalty to the Stuarts was their trump card, which they hoped to play to win back lands lost under the Cromwellian settlement. Their arguments were aided by the apocryphal *Eikon basilike* attributed to Charles I who claimed that the lords justices were equally as guilty as those who began the rebellion for the bloodshed that followed.[158] The Parsons faction once again faced an onslaught from their confederate rivals from the 1640s.

In later years Catholic commentaries adopted a three-fold strategy to contest the Protestant version of events, closely following confederate propaganda of the 1640s. First, they blamed the lords justices, the avaricious New English and the vitrolic anti-Catholic 'Puritan' parliament in London for their recourse to arms. Secondly, they claimed that they were subjected to the frequent enforcement of martial law. Finally, more moderate accounts portrayed the rebellion as a two-tier revolt and blamed members of the lower social orders for all violence suffered by Protestant settlers. Peter Walsh, who had supported Ormond's peace of 1646, appealed to Ormond as his patron to address the grievances of Ireland's loyal Catholics. They had, in his words, been 'sufficiently punished', despite their loyalty, whereas, in contrast, the regicides and those who deserted the royal cause escaped censure.[159] As the confederates had done, James Tochet, earl of Castlehaven and former commander in the confederate army, blamed the lords justices, the plantations, Wentworth and the anti-Catholic rhetoric emanating from

---

155   Ibid. 9.

156   Ibid. 10.

157   Ibid. 11.

158   Charles I, *Eikon basilike: the pourtraictvre of his sacred maiestie in his solitudes and svfferings: together with his maiesties praiers delivered to Doctor Juxon immediately before his death: also his majesties reasons, against the pretended jurisdiction of the high court of justice, which he intended to deliver in writing on Munday January 22, 1648*, London 1649, 84; *A brief narrative*, 13.

159   Vincent Morley, 'Walsh, Peter', *DIB*; Walsh, *A letter desiring a just and mercifull regard of the Roman Catholicks of Ireland* (one page broadside).

Pym and his colleagues in parliament for exacerbating the fears of Ireland's Catholics and causing the rebellion.[160] The lords justices delighted in the outbreak of rebellion, according to Castlehaven, because they viewed it as a fine opportunity to seize more lands and advance their own political and economic interests. The lords justices 'were often heard to say that the more were in Rebellion, the more lands should be forfeit to them'.[161] As Nicholas French's *Narrative of the settlement and sale of Ireland* had earlier stated (and the *Remonstrance of grievances*) 'every man saw that the estates of Catholicks were first aymed at, and their lives next'.[162]

Catholic accusations that Irish Protestants had deserted the king in his moment of need provoked vitriolic responses from prominent figures in Protestant Ireland who fought to protect their reputations. Roger Boyle's *The Irish colours displayed* retaliated by claiming that Catholics complained of fabricated grievances which did not provide just cause for the 'the late unparallel'd Massacres'.[163] Despite this, Catholic authors continually accused Protestants of disloyalty and of massacring thousands of innocent Irish civilians. Castlehaven blamed the lords justices' excessive use of force and the harsh treatment of Catholics in Santry, the racking of Sir John Read and the burning of Clontarf for initiating the massacres of 1641. These incidents, however, were not on the same scale as those alleged by Protestant commentators to have occurred. The clearest public statement that Protestant cruelty toward Irish Catholics surpassed the supposed events of 1641 appeared during the debates that surrounded what would become the 1662 Act of Settlement. Once again questions over who should be punished for the events of the 1640s re-surfaced and political factions adopted the medium of print to forward their own claims. The reprinting of Jones's *Abstract* in 1662 prompted the vitriolic, pro-royalist and pro-Catholic account of the Irish rebellion entitled *A collection of some of the murthers and massacres committed on the Irish in Ireland*. As the author of the *Collection*, identified only by the initials R. S., argued:

> upon perusal of which Abstract I was satisfied that the design of Printing the same in a time when the settlement of that Kingdome was under his Majesties consideration, was for no other end then to render all Catholiques there (in all good mens opinion) blasted and unfit to partake of his Majesties grace and favour.[164]

---

160 James Touchet, *The earl of Castlehaven's review*, London 1684, 4–6.

161 Ibid. 34–5.

162 *Remonstrance of grievances*, 22; French, *A narrative of the settlement and sale of Ireland*, 2–3; Barnard, '"Parlour entertainment in an evening?"', 20–43 at p. 22.

163 Boyle, *The Irish colours displayed*, 4, 6.

164 R. S., *A collection of some of the murthers and massacres committed on the Irish in Ireland since the 23d of October 1641*, London 1662, 6, 'Preface to the reader'; Barnard, '"Parlour entertainment"', 20–43 at pp. 24–5.

Catholics were acutely aware of how 1641 could be used to bolster Protestant political and economic agendas.

The *Collection* followed the same layout as Jones's *Abstract* and the author took pains to illustrate to his audience the veracity of his account and the legitimacy of confederate objectives. R. S. took umbrage at 'scurilious and lying pamphlets' that portrayed the confederate wars as a massacre of thousands of settlers.[165] What Catholic histories of the 1640s lacked when compared to their Protestant counterparts emphasised the official nature of Protestant accounts of 1641. Jones's *Remonstrance* and Temple's *Irish rebellion* contained a plethora of governmental correspondence, state proclamations and examinations that underlined the truth of their narratives. In contrast, Catholic histories, devoid of any public documents to support their statements, resorted to counter accusations. For example, R. S. denied the evidence produced by the deposition commissions during the 1640s and 1650s and argued that

> it is publiquely known that Cromwels pretended High Court of Justice past through all parts of Ireland, and pickt out of the people all such as could be in any manner tainted with the spilling of English blood, with that rigour as may be esteemed rather *sumum jus* then moderate justice, that upon tryals in the said court and examinations taken in order to those tryals.[166]

R. S.'s task was difficult for all the 'scurilious and lying pamphlets' that 'took inhand the publishing of the murthers done upon the English, did raise the same to an immense number' and had a manifest effect on contemporary perceptions of the Irish and of Catholics.[167] This estimation was based largely on the fact that the massacre debate was largely one-sided, as Catholic writers 'have not until this time writ a syllable in vindication of themselves'.[168] As a result, R. S. decided 'to lay open the falsehood of the said printed pamphlet [the *Abstract*], and to publish a collection of some of the many murthers committed on the Irish hereafter' as proof that similar atrocities were committed on both sides.[169]

R. S.'s *Collection* owed much to the deposition publications that appeared in the 1640s and responded to attacks and accusations made against Irish Catholics. The treatment of the indigenous Irish at the hands of colonial forces was similar to the fate experienced by their Protestant counterparts. In Derry, for example, 'some 3000 men women and children of the Irish, having freely come under the protection of the garrison of London Derry were stript

---

165 R. S., *A collection*, 7, 'Preface to the reader'.
166 Ibid.
167 Ibid. 7–8.
168 Ibid. 10.
169 Ibid.

plundered and killed by the said garrison'.[170] In addition to this, R. S. accused Protestants of killing more than 500 Catholics in the river Bann.[171] Analogous to the fate of Captain Dergis, described by Morley in his *Remonstrance*, an old man murdered by Irish rebels, one Gerry FitzThibbot, who: 'aged about 70 years and in a burning Feavour, with his wife who was as old, were murthered in their beds [by English and Scots forces]'.[172] R. S. asserted 'that in this county of Gallway all the wartime several Protestant ministers viz. Dean Tork, Mr. Corroyn, Mr. Nelly and other ministers, had their Protestant flocks and meetings without interruption living amongst the Irish'.[173] The contested murders in Roscommon were also challenged and denied: 'no murthers were committed by any party in this County only five persons at Bellanfada by one Roger O'Connor; and no murther was committed at Bellalegue during the War, although in the Pamphlet [Jones's 1662 *Abstract*] the contrary is expressed.' The most barbaric behaviour witnessed in the theatre of war in the 1640s and 1650s was, more often than not, at the whim of Cromwell's soldiers. Due to the denial of quarter, inhabitants were 'cruelly massacred' or even deported. After a battle near Letterkenny, 'English Rebels adhering to Cromwel' took all the principal officers of the royalist and Irish armies and they 'were killed in cold blood, by order of Sir Charles Coote late lord of Mountrath, notwithstanding they had quarter from the Officers who took them Prisoners'.[174] Even children of prominent royalists were subject to the wrath of the Cromwellians:

> Capt. Hulet coming to Sir John Dongans house at Castle town, to search for a priest, tortured a child of Sir Johns of seven years of age with lighted matches to force a confession from him where the priest was, and the poor child not telling, or not knowing, hung him up with the Reins of his Bridle.[175]

The portrayal of 'English rebels' extended beyond the Cromwellians. In the eyes of R. S., publishers of tracts and pamphlets that sullied the name of Irish Catholics were also 'odious to their natural prince and fellow subjects of England'.[176] Thus the Catholic 'side' to the 1641 rebellion stressed how they had suffered similar violence as the 'lying' pamphlets and depositions had alleged Protestants had experienced. Furthermore, these accounts exaggerated the number of those killed, as argued by Walsh: 'The number of Two hundred thousand [Protestants slain] … is so exorbitantly vast.'[177]

---

[170] Ibid. 2.

[171] Ibid.

[172] Ibid. 6; Morley, *Remonstrance of the barbarous cruelties*, 3.

[173] R. S., *A collection*, 7.

[174] Ibid. 3.

[175] Ibid. 11.

[176] Ibid. 27.

[177] Peter Walsh, *The Irish colours folded*, London 1662, 3.

None the less, constant references to the atrocities of 1641 in Protestant pamphlets stained any attempts by Catholic writers to lobby for political favour under Charles II. Increasingly desperate voices began to curry favour for prominent individuals connected with the confederate cause.[178] Protestant writers, however, did not distinguish between the various groups that rebelled in 1641 and tarred them all with the same brush. As Henry Jones argued in 1643:

> It is a well grounded provision in the lawes of our Kingdome that whatsoever outrage or muther shall be in a rout or an unlawfull assembly committed by one or more in pursuance of the comon design though against or without the consent of the rest soe assembled shall be constructed as the act of the whole sect.[179]

The confederates and later Catholic writers attempted to challenge this portrayal of the rebellion as a united political and religious movement and emphasised its two-tier nature. Walsh distanced Irish Catholics from the alleged massacre of Irish Protestants: 'Your Grace knows with what horrour the *Irish* Nation looks upon those Massacres and Murders in the North, committed in the beginning of the Rebellion by the Raskal multitude upon their innocent, unwarned, and unprovided Neighbors.'[180] Other Catholic accounts of the 1641 rebellion would also blame the 'Raskal multitude' in order to exonerate the Catholic nobility and gentry of the murders of Protestant settlers. Similarly R. S.'s *Collection* blamed the lower social orders for the outbreak of popular violence. Rebels in Galway murdered 'about thirty Protestants', but this act was commited by 'irreligious prophane fellows'. In contrast, the Catholic gentry came to the rescue of the bishop of Killala, 'who by that pamphlet [Jones's 1662 *Abstract*] seems to have been murdered'.[181] Castlehaven would later perpetuate this interpretation: he argued that those who engaged in attacks on the settler community were part of the 'rabble' and operated as a separate movement to that of the main thrust of the rebellion organised by Sir Phelim O'Neill.[182]

Catholic commentators, therefore, contested the Protestant version of events espoused by Henry Jones and his colonist colleagues in a number of ways. First, they challenged the validity of the depositions as a source for the massacres of 1641. Secondly, they blamed the violent actions of the lords justices and claimed that they had been excluded from the political order. Finally, while they criticised the deposition commission for exaggerating the

---

178 Barnard, '"Parlour entertainment"', 20–1.

179 'A treatise giving a representation of the grand rebellion in Ireland', MS Harleian 5999, fo. 3.

180 Walsh, *The Irish colours folded*, 3.

181 R. S., *A collection*, 6–7.

182 Touchet, *The earl of Castlehaven's review*, 34–5.

number of killings that had occurred, Catholic elites blamed the lower social orders for the outbreak of popular violence and thereby exonerated themselves from blame for the alleged massacres.

In the fledgling years of the reign of Charles II, the re-emergence of questions over land ownership in Ireland meant that both sides returned to the events that had occurred in 1641 to bolster their own positions at court. The seventeenth-century land question maintained what contemporaries called 'the contention between the two Parties in Ireland'.[183] Through the use of the printing press they competed for the king's attention in a cacophony of petitions, pamphlets and protestations. Through print, the 'two parties' offered contrasting views on 1641, while others told of newly-discovered plots against the establishment in Ireland and the three kingdoms. *The horrid conspiracie of such impenitient traytors* alleged that Irish Catholics, 'after so long and various Rebellions', aimed at 'the Ruine and Destruction of all that love the Peace and Government of the three Nations' in 1663.[184] Polarised along sectarian lines, Protestants denied that the confederates were loyal to Charles I and his son Charles II. Catholic writers countered by reasserting their loyalty and called for their inclusion in contemporary politics as 'true' subjects. A petition from Irish Catholic priests to Charles II in 1662 professed that 'their Crimes are as numerous and divers as are the Inventions of their Adversaries: and because they cannot with freedom appear to justifie their Innocency, all the fictions and allegations against them are received as undoubted verities'.[185] The Catholic interpretation of 1641 was drowned out by Protestant printers which meant that they could not successfully contest the official version of events espoused by the remnants of Parson's party in Ireland. A distinction must be drawn between histories of the rebellion written to contribute to the conversation between adherents of the lords justices' and the confederate's political factions and more popular accounts of the rebellion that drew upon Clarke's *Generall martyrologie*. Each served various purposes, spoke to different audiences and influenced subsequent interpretations of the 1641 rebellion in different ways.

What is clear is that contesting interpretations of the rebellion emerged from its very beginning and have shaped the parameters of debate about 1641 to the present day. The 'Protestant' version of events closely followed the arguments of Jones and Temple which were constructed deliberately to portray the rebels in the most negative light possible. Later commentators followed this line of interpretation and could provide their own versions of depositions from Jones's and Temple's highly selective versions. Overall, they

---

183 Boyle, *The Irish colours displayed*, 2.

184 *The horrid conspiracie of such impenitent traytors as intended a nevv rebellion in the kingdom of Ireland*, London 1663, sig. A3.

185 *To the king's most excellent majestie the humble remonstrance, acknowledgement, protestation, and petition of the Roman Catholick clergy of Ireland*, [London 1662], no pagination.

argued that the 1641 rebellion was a desperate attempt by Irish Catholics to establish the Catholic Church and root out Protestantism and the English order in Ireland. The nobles and clerics of Ireland organised the plot, which aimed to massacre all the Protestant settlers on the island. In much the same manner the 'Catholic' version of 1641 followed the pattern established by the confederates during the 1640s. They had argued that the lords justices were to blame for the rebellion, that Catholics had legitimate grievances and that the lords justices exaggerated the cruelties committed against the settlers while at the same time waging a war of terror against Ireland's Catholics. More vitriolic accounts revelled in this slaughter, but more moderate ones, written by prominent members of the confederation, protected their reputations in this era of intense petitioning in restoration Ireland. As a result, more moderate Catholics promoted an interpretation that blamed the lower social orders for the outbreak of violence in October 1641 and distanced themselves from the early bloodshed. At the heart of the issue, therefore, was the question of who was to blame for the outbreak of rebellion and for the outbreak of popular violence. It comes as no surprise that the combatants in the Irish front in the Wars of the Three Kingdoms disagreed over these issues and blamed each other for the butchery that has dominated subsequent scholarship on the nature of the Irish rebellion of 1641.

Conclusion: The 1641 Rebellion in its British, European and Atlantic World Context

Writing in 1988, Hugh Trevor Roper, Emeritus Regius Professor of Modern History at Oxford, spoke of 'The lost moments of history'. Had certain events not occurred, he postulated, European and global history would have taken a radically different course. He pointed to numerous examples, such as the failed Pacification of Ghent in 1576, which might have brought about 'the historic unity of the Netherlands'. Instead, Belgium and Holland became two separate polities that 'remain apart today'. The purpose of Roper's article was to discuss moments that led to 'a long-term change of direction: a change, moreover which need not have occurred'. What would have happened had German forces won the First World War? What would have happened had early Christians not succeeded in converting Rome? Turning to one of his research areas, Roper delved into the nature of the English revolutions (the 'Puritan' Revolution in the 1640s and 1650s and the Glorious Revolution of the 1680s and 1690s) in the seventeenth century, which laid the foundations of England's famous parliamentary tradition. For Roper the pivotal moment was 1641 for it brought about lasting changes in England and Ireland: 'The heaviest price that we paid for certain undeniable liberties was in discrimination against Roman Catholics, excluded from public life for a century and a half, and in Ireland where the repercussions of a particularly repressive policy still haunt us today.' In Ireland it brought about an 'embittered civil war', which began with the 'Irish massacre', then 'the Cromwellian conquest of 1649–50 ... [that] paved the way for a continuing process of expropriation, discrimination, expulsion'. The lost moment for Irish history, according to Roper, was Francis Bacon's attempts to lobby Elizabeth I to pursue a peaceful policy in Ireland and to build a tolerant society that elided religious differences. Instead civil war, revolution and military conquest engulfed the 'three nations' of England, Ireland and Scotland.

Commenting on later historians' attempts to understand why the turmoil of the mid-seventeenth century erupted in England, Roper remarked that

> Historians, looking back, discover cause behind cause of our [English] civil war. Some of them seem to think it was foreordained in the previous century, others that it arose out of the accidents of high politics of the time. Since both of these opinions were advanced by contemporaries, we can hardly hope to settle the controversy. The views taken seem to depend, to some extent, on

political loyalties: Roundheads believe in ancient structural causes, Cavaliers in modern political accidents.[1]

Undoubtedly, the 1641 rebellion was a real turning-point in Irish history. Memories of the alleged massacres were evoked to label Irish Catholics as barbaric, perfidious or unfit for government. Much like the historiography of the English civil wars, Irish historians have taken sides over the causes and course of the 1641 rebellion that echo those first expressed by participants in the events themselves. This book has illustrated the key political and cultural contexts that shaped news, intelligence and the first histories of the 1641 rebellion.

From a political perspective, debates conducted about the nature, course and causes of the 1641 rebellion first took place in London. Politicians at Westminster, who read dispatches from the lords justices and other leading figures in Irish politics, perpetuated arguments that the rebellion was religiously motivated and that Protestants were massacred in their thousands. Printers and pamphleteers in the environs of St Paul's churchyard, the hub of printing in early modern Britain and Ireland, disseminated this version of events to the wider public. Instantly, English readers consumed salacious news of the 'barbarous massacres' of 'innocent' Protestant settlers. The Irish Catholic community was not the only victim of these accusations, however. After the publication of Henry Jones's *Remonstrance*, Charles I was implicated in the planning and execution of the rebellion. From the time of the calling of the Short and Long Parliaments in 1640 John Pym and his supporters feared that the king wished to reconvert the established Church to Catholicism. They looked on in envy at the Scottish covenanters, who had secured a considerable degree of independence to govern their Church, free from royal interference. The king's marriage to a Catholic, the 'popishly' inspired innovations in church services and sworn testimonies from Ireland claiming that Charles supported a Catholic uprising there against his Protestant opponents, further strengthened their resolve to lure the king into war. News from Ireland, therefore, was tailor-made by Irish politicians to suit the objectives of English politicians and English printers.

In England, Charles, much like other European monarchs, spent his entire reign trying to expand monarchical power, improve fiscal structures and impose religious 'uniformity' across the three kingdoms. These pressures, in terms of a religious settlement, convinced Irish confederates and Scottish covenanters to rebel. Nicholas Canny, Aidan Clarke and Michael Perceval-Maxwell have all argued that the 1641 rebellion must be seen within the wider context of 'Britain' and 'British politics'. Events in Scotland contributed to the outbreak of popular violence in Ireland. News of this, dissemi-

---

[1] All quotations in the preceding paragraphs are taken from Hugh Trevor Roper, 'The lost moments of history', *New York Review of Books*, 27 Oct. 1988. I am grateful to Dr John Gibney for bringing this article to my attention.

nated by the lords justices and council, contributed to the outbreak of the English front in the Wars of the Three Kingdoms. Key players in Ireland stage-managed news in their printed appeals to the wider British kingdoms. Sometimes this news made a significant contribution to the course of the Wars of the Three Kingdoms, as did the publication of Jones's *Remonstrance*, but often the propaganda of the lords justices and of the deposition commission had very little effect, particularly when attempting to derail the cessation of arms. Furthermore, gory news from Ireland jeopardised the Adventurers' Act and there is a marked change in the nature of reportage after May 1642 when it became clear that the projected investments were wide of the mark.

The lords justices and council paid little attention to the political and economic grievances of the native Irish in their very public protestations and justifications for taking to arms in the early stages of the rebellion. Initially, Phelim O'Neill spoke of an attack on Irish 'liberties' and did not overtly cite the lack of toleration for Catholicism as a cause for the rebellion. A rebellion requires rebels so the leaders of Catholic society in Ireland turned to the lower social orders and summoned an army that would take control of urban centres and fortifications. Theses recruits rallied to an anti-colonial and anti-Protestant banner as the rebel leadership cast its net far and wide to ensure success. In the highly charged confessional context of early modern Ireland it is no surprise that the authorities focused their attentions on religion as a motive for and cause of the rebellion. By portraying the rebellion as religiously inspired the lords justices hoped to grab the attention of the Long Parliament in a more effective manner and also believed that this would hasten supplies and men from England – supplies which the lords justices desperately needed. Their portrayal of the rebellion as a religious revolt rested on evidence contained in the 1641 depositions and the commissioners duly provided the information that they required. As it comprised Church of Ireland clergymen it is of no surprise that they viewed the rebellion as an attempt to rid Ireland of Protestantism, Protestant settlers and Protestant artefacts and buildings. A manuscript report sent to the newly constituted lords justices and council in the autumn of 1643 reminded them that the rebellion had 'a twofold end: first the extirpation of the English nation; and secondly the abolishment of the Protestant reformed Religion'.[2] While Europe attempted to move beyond these sectarian divisions, politicians in Britain and Ireland played the confessional card to tar their opponents and to rally people behind confederate, covenanter and parliamentarian war efforts respectively.

There is another important point to be made: pamphlet reports from Ireland did not simply portray the 'massacres' of Protestant settlers, they defended or besmirched the reputations of prominent politicians, which

[2] 'A treatise giving a representation of the grand rebellion in Ireland', MS Harleian 5999, fo. 2v.

reflects the growing use of print as a tool of statecraft in Ireland. Furthermore, particularly after the passing of the Adventurers' Act, pamphlets argued that the English and Scottish forces had successfully repelled the main thrust of the rebel assault, glorified the killing of Catholic civilians and assured investors of the inevitability of English military success. As the 1640s wore on, pamphlets then focused on the course of the war, providing military updates and the latest news on Irish and British politics. Keith Lindley's seminal analysis of the printed output from Ireland has provided subsequent generations of scholars with a detailed breakdown of the publications concerning Ireland that appeared in London and when they were printed.[3] These figures, however, do not account for the content of the news from Ireland; historians have assumed that all printed news from Ireland consisted of 'bloody' news after 'bloody' news. In fact the earliest accounts were exceptional in their portrayal of the rebellion as a wholesale massacre and a total war that engulfed the entire population of the island of Ireland. Later the lord justices and deposition commission, unhappy at wider events in the three kingdoms and the seeming lack of interest in Ireland, also clamoured for attention by evoking the plight of Protestant victims in Ireland who suffered at the hands of Catholic aggressors.

Historians of the English front in the Wars of the Three Kingdoms, or the English civil wars, have debated the importance of religion as a cause. Conrad Russell, with the wider European picture in mind, argued that religion was at the root of all problems in the Anglo-Irish relationship and John Morrill has supported this. Both are also fiercely critical of Charles I for exacerbating tensions across the three kingdoms and failing to understand the complexities of the polities that he governed.[4] John Adamson, however, argued that the key fomenters of civil war in England were members of the nobility, disillusioned with Charles's increasingly expansionist policies.[5] In reality the situation in Ireland was more complex. While religion mobilised the lower social orders, Catholic leaders actually downplayed their religious grievances to English audiences for fear of encouraging anti-popish sentiments. At the same time, confederate propaganda disseminated in Europe portrayed their struggle as one against a heretical parliament and appealed to the Catholic powers of Europe to support them. Some of the violence conducted by the Irish rebels was indeed religiously inspired. Deponents therefore understood what they witnessed through a biblical lens. What it suggested here, but not demonstrated on a national basis, is that members

[3] Keith Lindley, 'The impact of the 1641 rebellion upon England and Wales, 1641–5', *Irish Historical Studies* xviii (1972), 143–76.

[4] Conrad Russell, 'Composite monarchies in early modern Europe: the British and Irish example', in Alexander Grant and Keith Stringer (eds), *Uniting the kingdom? The making of British history*, London 1996, 133–46; John Morrill, *The nature of the English revolution: essays by John Morrill*, New York 1993, 45–86.

[5] John Adamson, *The noble revolt: the overthrow of Charles I*, London 2007.

of the nobility and gentry tolerated the use of violence against the settler community but (understandably) later denied their involvement.

It is necessary to consider the role of religion in the 1641 rebellion and the 1641 depositions in a number of ways. As popular rebellion broke out across the country a range of grievances directed the course of the violence. Those heavily in debt attacked their creditors; those aggrieved at the imposition of a foreign and English order burned English-style houses and buildings; those with personal vendettas seized the opportunity to avenge past wrongs. Although horrified at the scale of such attacks, the state authorities paid little attention to them simply because of the wider sectarian tensions that blighted early modern Irish society. In certain areas, such as Armagh, ministers were targeted, not simply because they were money-lenders as argued by Nicholas Canny, but because they were Protestant. Catholic clerics had suffered wave upon wave of persecution in the run up to the rebellion and a small minority encouraged their congregations to restore the Catholic order against the 'brood' of Calvin and Luther. Their exhortations were aided by the widely-held belief that the lords justices in Dublin and the 'Puritan' parliament in England would launch a full-scale military and political offensive against Catholics. Rumours that the queen's confessor had been executed added further fuel to the fire. Settlers alleged that the rebels were encouraged to attack them because of a papal indulgence absolving them of the sin of murder. The truth is that a range of strategies and rumours justified the outbreak of violence, from prophecies and fears of persecution to orders from community leaders. Verses, plays, meetings and gatherings in marketplaces were well attended by people across a range of social strata. Printed texts might not have been the main means adopted by the rebel readership to rally adherents to the cause, but the vibrant oral communication of information allowed for news of 'high' politics to be disseminated among the lower social orders thus enabling their mobilisation.

Much like the French wars of religion the outbreak of popular violence had a patterned meaning as rioters took to the streets driven by a range of economic, religious and social grievances.[6] This was not an indiscriminate slaughter of the settler community: the employment of a variety of excessive cruelties sought to control suspect populations. Such displays of power were witnessed and recounted by Catholics and Protestants alike. Rumours of violence and of news of the outbreak of rebellion deeply affected deponents. The targeting of prominent leaders of the settler community such as ministers, justices of the peace and sheriffs challenged traditional power structures.

---

[6] Perhaps the most famous of all articles on the course of violence in the French wars of religion is Natalie Zemon Davis, 'The rites of violence: religious riot in sixteenth-century France', P&P lix (May 1973), 51–91. Zemon Davis has been heavily criticised, however. For the most recent collection of essays on her work see Graeme Murdock, Penny Roberts and Andrew Spicer (eds), Ritual and violence: Natalie Zemon Davis and early modern France, Oxford 2012.

Threats made by rebels in Ulster led settlers and the colonial administration to believe that, by the end of October, a massacre of Protestants had taken place although nobody could verify or substantiate these claims. Many of the rumours of alleged atrocities were closely linked to biblical images of violence illustrating how, in times of conflict, frightened communities relied upon contemporary cultural constructions of war and conflict to describe their experiences. Attacks on pregnant women might not have occurred, but settlers believed that they had. Pioneering studies by John Horne, Donald Horowitz, Alan Kramer and Edgar Morin have all illustrated how rumours of terror shape fear in times of mass hysteria. During the German invasion of Belgium in the First World War, for example, refugees reported to French authorities that German soldiers chopped off the hands of Belgian children, but there is little evidence to prove that any such incidents occurred (it was a memory of an earlier war in the Congo).[7] As the 1641 depositions capture the memory and experience of clearly traumatised people, historians must tread carefully when attempting to investigate the course of violence. Both sides believed that they faced a demonic enemy capable of inflicting the most gruesome atrocities on civilians. These myth cycles of violence contributed to contemporaries' sense of terror and to the extreme butchery that Ireland witnessed during the rising. Both Catholics and Protestants believed that they would be targeted for their faith, or their ethnicity, revealing how tense inter-community relations were prior to 1641; a fact nobody would admit after the restoration of Charles II.

Deponents believed that the rebels were motivated by religious grievances and interpreted their plight through a providental lens. The other way in which religion shaped the legacy of the 1641 rebellion relates to the course of Irish history over the eighteenth, nineteenth and twentieth centuries. In a desire to move away from a sectarian interpretation of the rebellion, historians have stressed the social, economic and political grievances of the Irish rebels and the confederation of Kilkenny. Such interpretations neatly copy those of the confederates in the 1640s, eager, in light of wider British politics, to downplay religion as a cause of their actions, even though many of those who comprised the general assembly fought for toleration for Irish Catholics. By emphasising the religious grievances of the confederation the lords justices shaped English audiences' perceptions of the conflict in a number of ways. Printers, aware of the tense religious atmosphere in London, could easily portray the rebellion as another standard popish plot and demonise the native Irish as Catholic soldiers who target civilians in times of conflict. Such formulaic representations did not simply capture or reflect English-

---

[7] Edgar Morin, *Rumour in Orleans*, London 1971; John Horne and Alan Kramer, *German atrocities, 1914: a history of denial*, New Haven 2001, and 'War between soldiers and enemy civilians, 1914–1915', in Roger Chickering and Stig Forster (eds), *Great war, total war: combat and mobilization on the Western Front, 1914–1918*, Cambridge 2000, 153–68.

men's perception of violence. These pamphlets were the product of ambitious printers, booksellers and authors who aimed to make a profit. News,
particularly gory news, had to cater to the tastes of the market at which it
was aimed. Pamphleteers had to sell their tracts and needed to cater to their
readers. Historians have overlooked the fact that some publishers, such as
John Rothwell, traded on 'bloody' news in order to make a profit. Nicholas
French would later lament, 'how bloody and barbarous soever some are
pleased to print and paint it', suggesting that English printers portrayed the
conflict as bloodier than it actually was.[8] This might have been out of a fear
of international popery, but there could have been other considerations. As
Samuel Hinton put it, 'That there be 1000 English slain in Ireland, but with
a greater loss (for so it must be or the paper will not sell).'[9]

Cultural constructions of war shaped the primary source material; such
influences therefore need to be scrutinised closely. Publications that described
the Irish conflict conformed to the rhetoric of death and destruction prevalent in English constructions of violence. In an era which witnessed the St
Bartholomew's day massacre, the conquest of South America and the Thirty
Years' War in Germany, all of which were presented to English audiences
as examples of Catholic barbarity, news from Ireland had to contribute/
compete with/replicate or at least adhere to portrayals of other European
conflicts. These profitable atrocity accounts, regardless of context, shared
many characteristics. Enemies were demonised as barbaric, attacking women,
children and civilians; they denigrated either the colonial power or the rival
Church and committed a range of cruelties. Such narratives, however, served
a key function – they mobilised readers to support various war efforts in the
early modern period. *The lamentations of Germany* provided biblical allusions
which encouraged readers to reflect on their sins and to seek vengeance on
the Catholic aggressors. The portrayal of violence was rooted in biblical
imagery and many accounts, particularly during the 1640s, were loaded with
biblical citations that aided readers to interpret the text correctly. The fact
that these pamphlets paid considerable attention to the plight of civilians
suggests contemporary values invested in codes of conduct on the battlefield that emerged at this time. Biblical precedents and the principle of
reciprocity meant that when innocents were killed contemporaries called
for revenge. Colonists in Ireland used the victims of the 1641 rebellion to
call for revenge, a call answered by Oliver Cromwell. Similarly, the confederation of Kilkenny called on Charles I to avenge the atrocities committed
against Catholics by Charles Coote.

It is important to understand the common methods adopted to demonise
enemies. Cultural constructions of violence transcended oral and literate

---

[8]   French, *A narrative of the settlement and sale of Ireland*, 19.
[9]   Samuel Hinton to Sir Richard Leveson, 2 May 1642, HMC, *Fifth report*, London 1876,
182.

means of communication. Hearsay reports and printed news reports sourced from the imaginations of Cambridge students all followed the same format. First, they argued that women and children were the primary targets of the rebels' ire. Many accused rebels of murdering pregnant women and attacking their foetuses. Pregnant women may indeed have been killed but the lack of eye-witnesses testimonies on this matter would suggest that rumours of such incidents were part of the myth-cycle of violence that occurred in Ireland after the outbreak of rebellion. Furthermore, in other conflicts across the globe Englishmen were eager to believe that such attacks occurred and were a common threat/action meted out by Catholic soldiers or barbaric natives. Secondly, they argued (although evidence is scant on the issue) that Irish rebels raped English women. Accounts that described the Nine Years' War, the Thirty Years' War, and the 1641 rebellion all alleged that Catholic soldiers raped Protestant women. Finally, victims were portrayed as innocent and as true believers. They were pious and virtuous in contrast to the barbaric soldiers who attacked them without provocation. Much of the evidence that they relied upon for these arguments is either non-existant or the product of rumour and hearsay.

Irish Catholics were both 'papists' and 'natives'; news from Ireland during the 1640s therefore portrayed events as similar to other rebellions led by natives against their colonial overlords. This led to fears that the colonial project had been jeopardised. Reports of atrocities in colonial contexts thus tried to whip up support for the extension of the colony and the augmentation of English influence in foreign territories. Colonists had to assure readers and potential investors that the colony was in a territory ripe for exploitation. Ireland, like America, had fertile soil, plentiful game to hunt and the potential for people to prosper. Those who were more concerned about the conversion of native populations were assured that the conquest and colonisation of Ireland and North America were part of the God's divine plan for true believers. As these were territories governed by English colonists, however, another cultural construct came into play, that of civility. Civility provided a framework through which settlers could portray their government as fair and benign and political commentators wrote favourably about benign English governance. Any attack on a colony, particularly a rebellion, would suggest that natives were aggrieved at the policies of their overlords. Therefore, those who attempted to rebel or who attacked settlers were seen as particularly barbaric, and so stupid that they could not recognise the benefits of living under 'civil' Englishmen. Despite this, English colonists frequently imposed martial law to intimidate Native Americans and the native Irish throughout the early modern period. They were unwilling to admit this in their dispatches to London. To do so would mean that they admitted culpability and responsibility for the deaths of innocent colonists. The lords justices, therefore, refused to accept their role in the outbreak of 1641.

Politicians in Ireland and England stage-managed news from Ireland in order to manufacture consent among English audiences. The lords justices consistently refused to accept blame for the outbreak of the rebellion, even though the policies that they pursued clearly alienated and threatened Ireland's Catholic population which feared further persecution. Each side claimed that the other targeted innocent civilians in the early stages of the rising and the confederate wars. The record on this issue, contained in the state papers, official correspondence and in the Carte manuscripts, is one-sided. There is little mention of the excessive use of force by state armies (with the exception of Island Magee as recorded in the 1641 depositions), although confederate publications have provided some evidence on this point. None the less, the Protestant version of events closely followed the arguments made by Henry Jones in the *Remonstrance*. Jones, despite the fact that he had access to a huge body of evidence that suggested otherwise, contradicted early reports of the rebellion and claimed that Irish Catholic nobles and clerics plotted to massacre settler communities. His *Remonstrance* provided heavily edited proof that 23 October 1641 was the beginning of a nationwide wholesale massacre of Protestants. Jones skilfully linked the Catholic nobility and the Catholic powers of Europe into the plot and argued that the entire rebel force had been mobilised by either clerics or nobles hell-bent on ridding Ireland of supposed 'heretics'. As Jones led the deposition commission it is of no surprise that others who perused the depositions after him echoed his theses on the causes, course and nature of the 1641 rebellion. After the Cromwellian conquest of Ireland it became clear that adventurers, soldiers and loyal parliamentarians had to be paid. Cromwellian accounts of 1641, therefore, repeated the allegations made by the lords justices and the deposition commission against Catholic landowners. Catholic peers, many of whom had joined the confederation, saw their landholdings in Ireland reduced by 9 per cent as a result.[10] This created the subtext of Catholic guilt for 1641 and legitimated the confiscation of their lands.

In contrast, confederate propaganda blamed the oppressive policies of the lords justices for the rising and the eruption of popular violence. They alleged that William Parsons and others on the council viewed the outbreak of rebellion as an opportunity to advance their personal fortunes. Whether this is accurate is beyond the scope of this book. Without doubt, the lords justices and the deposition commission deliberately portrayed the rebellion as a religious war, implicated the nobility in the plot and argued that a wholesale massacre of Protestant settlers occurred. From the outset of the rebellion, even though extant intelligence contradicted their conclusions, the lords justices portrayed all Catholics as the enemy. Admittedly, they later apologised for this, but their sustained criticisms of the Catholic community in Ireland suggests that their apology was insincere. While the Protestant interpretation of the 1641 rebellion was largely consistent in the 1650s and 1660s, Catholic accounts oscillated between radical and moderate inter-

---

[10] Ohlmeyer, *Making Ireland English*, 88–9.

pretations. Some celebrated the deaths of settlers, while others distanced themselves from these killings. Moderate accounts that followed the official confederate line highlighted their loyalty to the Stuart monarchy, blamed the lords justices for the rebellion and denied that a wholesale massacre of the Protestant community had occurred. Their attempts were in vain as during the Restoration only a handful of Catholics were regranted their lands.[11] For the rest of the early modern period, the Protestant tradition on 1641 triumphed: much of the folklore on the massacres of 1641 turned into fact as the years went by. Catholic commentators faced an uphill struggle to change Protestant perceptions of what 'really' took place in 1641.

To understand why this happened it is essential to consider the cultural frameworks that Englishmen utilised to describe events during the rebellion. Eye-witnesses, polemicists and politicians alike drew upon the Bible, contemporary beliefs of war and English representations of barbaric peoples to demonise the native Irish. These shaped the primary source material which historians have used to describe events during the 1641 rebellion, yet little reference has been made to these crucial cultural and social contexts. At the heart of the matter were contemporary codes of conduct that were established to protect noncombatants. As English printers demonised the Catholics of Ireland claiming that they indiscriminately slaughtered Protestant settlers, they portrayed the conflict as a total war, much like other continental wars and colonial rebellions. In contrast, Catholics contested such formulaic portrayals of 1641 that were utilised to mobilise English and Irish Protestants to support the war efforts of the lords justices. They proclaimed allegiance to Charles I, blamed the belligerence of the lords justices for the outbreak of rebellion and accused members of the lower social orders of responsibility for the eruption of popular violence. There is a great irony here. Traditionally, the victor writes the historical record. By that standard it is hard to say who the victors were in 1641 for while the Protestant version gained acceptance for many years, the confederate narrative is currently enjoying ascendancy.

[11] Ibid. 280–300.

Bibliography

Unpublished primary sources

ENGLAND

Cambridge University Library
MSS *Additional*
MS 4246 Collection of letters related to the outbreak of the rebellion
MS 4345 An account of the Irish rebellion, 1641
MS 4353 'The rise and progress of the Irish rebellion begun in the year 1641'

London, British Library
MSS *Additional*
MS 4107 List of adventurers
MS 4107 Account of the rebellion in Co. Down
MS 4763 Miscellaneous papers relating to Ireland in the seventeenth century
MS 4777 Norman Pierpoint's account of the 1641 rebellion
MS 4786 Account of the 1641 rebellion in Connaught
MS 4816 Arthur Annesley, first earl of Anglesey: notes for his history of Ireland
MS 4819 Letters and papers relating to Ireland, 1641–9
MS 4821 James Ware's history of Ireland
MS 5754 Papers related to Ireland, 1578–1692
MS 6491 Oliver Cromwell's call for the surrender of Wexford
MS 6915 Historical and fabulous treatises relating to Ireland
MS 8883 Extracts of papers of the Irish council from 1641 to 1643
MS 11,721 Miscellaneous papers relating to Ireland
MS 15, 892 Miscellaneous correspondence
MS 18,730 Arthur Annesley, first earl of Anglesey: diary, 1675–84
MS 20,100 Narration on the outbreak of rebellion in Clare
MS 21,129 Reflections on Peter Walsh's account of the Irish rebellion
MS 21, 425 Letters from Thomas Morley to Lord Lambert and Captain [?] Baynes
MS 22,548 More Edmund Borlase correspondence
MS 34,253 Propositions of John Temple re. the rebellion from 1647
MS 34,770–1 James Butler, twelfth earl of Ormond: notes on Arthur Annesley, first earl of Anglesey, *Letter to the … earl of Castlehaven*
MS 37,207 Letter from Henry Jones to G. Lane
MS 37,772 Eight letters from Elizabeth Brabazon, countess of Meath, regarding family affairs in the 1650s
MS 40,860 Arthur Annesley, first earl of Anglesey: diary, 1667–75
MS 40,883 Nehemiah Wallington's diary of spiritual events, 1641–3

MSS *Egerton*

MS 78–9 Repertory of historical and state documents relating to Ireland
MS 80 Historical documents relating to Ireland, 1610–43
MS 917 Miscellaneous papers relating to Ireland, 1623–1728
MS 1,625 Edward Hyde, first earl of Clarendon, 'Short view'
MS 2,542 James Butler, marquis of Ormond: depiction of Oliver Cromwell's first months in Ireland
MS 2,646 Letter from John Temple to T. Barrington
MS 21,425 Letter of Thomas Morley
MS 46,929–31 Papers containing correspondence of Sir Philip Perceval

MSS *Harleian*

MS 5999 'A treatise giving a representation of the grand rebellion in Ireland'
MS 6865 Collection of state papers regarding the rebellion by H. Wanley

MSS *Sloane*

MS 1008 Edmund Borlase papers
MS 1015 Edmund Borlase's *Reflection* on the memoirs of James Touchet, third earl of Castlehaven
MS 3838 *A short view of the state ... of Ireland from 1640 ... with a vindication ... against the bishop of Ferns*

MSS *Stowe*

MSS 82–3 Contemporary copies of various histories on the rebellion
MSS 200–12 Correspondence of Robert Devereux, third earl of Essex
MS 744, fo. 127 Letter from Henry Jones to John Culpepper

Oxford, Bodleian Library
MSS *Carte*

MSS 2–29 James Butler's correspondence from the 1640s and 1650s
MSS 31–70 Papers relating to the rebellion
MS 103 Correspondence, 1641–60
MSS 109, 118, 130, 143, 199 James Butler's correspondence
MSS 213–15 Letters from James Butler on Irish affairs in the 1650s

MSS *Rawlinson*

MS A 258 Letters from parliament's Irish committee regarding affairs in Ireland.
MS B 482 'The case of the Catholics of Ireland'
MS B 507 Letters from Ireland, 1641–6
MS D 424 A history of the massacres of 1641 written to discredit the rule of James II
MS D 1321 'a breefe account of the lyfe and death of ... William Bedell'

IRELAND

City Library, Pearse Street, Dublin
MS 176 Friar Toirdhealbhach O'Mellan's journal of events in Ulster, 1641–7

MS 214 Treatise on the 1641 rebellion from the Plunkett manuscripts
MS 227 'Irish narrative'

National Library of Ireland, Dublin
MS 9 Edward Hyde, first earl of Clarendon, 'View of the state and condition of Ireland'
MSS 32–6 Papers of Roger Boyle, first earl of Orrery
MS 345 'Account of the war and rebellion in Ireland'
MS 692 William Parsons, 'Examen Hiberniae'
MS 693 Edmund Borlase's *History of the execrable Irish rebellion*
MS 856 Documents collated by J. T. Gilbert related to the Irish rebellion
MS 2257 Manuscript history of the Irish rebellion
MS 2504 Correspondence between James Butler and Robert Southwell
MS 2656/VII 'Mountjoy Fort'
MS 9900 Incomplete copy of the Edward, Hyde, first earl of Clarendon, 'Short view'
MS 31,882 'Narrative of outbreak of rebellion of 1641' (Mount Bellew papers)

Representative Church Body, Dublin
D7/1/1A Anthony Dopping, 'An account of the diocese of Meath'
GS 2/7/3/30 John Seymour's notes on the commonwealth papers
MS 25 Henry Jones's notebook on the diocese of Meath

Royal Irish Academy, Dublin
MS 4 A 45 Purcell family correspondence
MS 12 F 52 Charles Haliday's collection of manuscripts, seventeenth–nineteenth centuries
MS 12 W 20 Affairs in Ireland, 1640–51
MS 12 W 21 'An excellent vindication of Ormond 1646'
MS 14 B 11/7 Letter dated 25 October 1641
MS 14 E 2/30 Reports on the 1641 rebellion
MS 23 L 45 Short articles and speeches, sixteenth, seventeenth centuries
MS 24 Q 4 Letters on Irish political affairs in the seventeenth century
MS 24 Q 5 Roger Boyle's letters on the 1641 rising
MS H V I Manuscript on events in the 1640s
MS H VI 1 Confederate statutes
MS I IV 1 Edward Gibbon's 'Short survey of Ireland'

Trinity College, Dublin
MS 589 Edmund Spenser's 'View of Ireland'
MS 615 Journal of the Irish House of Lords, March 1639–May 1646
MS 650 State papers related to Orrery, Cromwell and Ormond
MS 652 Report on the Great Fire of London, 1667
MS 658 Edward Hyde, first earl of Clarendon, 'Short view'
MS 713 Roger Boyle, first earl of Orrery: commonplace book, 1640s
MS 747 Tract on the 1641 rebellion
MS 809–41 The depositions: MS 809–10 Dublin; MS 811 Wicklow; MS 812 Carlow

and Kilkenny; MS 813 Kildare; MS 814 Kings County; MS 815 Queens County; MS 816 Meath; MS 817 Longford and Westmeath; MS 818–19 Wexford; MS 820 Waterford; MS 821 Tipperary; MS 822–7 Cork; MS 828 Kerry; MS 829 Clare and Limerick; MS 830 Roscommon and Galway; MS 831 Leitrim, Sligo and Mayo; MS 832–3 Cavan; MS 834 Louth and Monaghan; MS 835 Fermanagh; MS 836 Armagh; MS 837 Down; MS 838 Antrim; MS 839 Tyrone, Derry and Donegal
MS 840–4 Documents and letters relating to the rebellion
MS 846 *Aphorismical discovery*
MS 866 Passages about the outbreak of the rebellion in Coleraine
MS 1178 'The treachery and disloyalty of parliament'
MS 1184 'State of Irish Catholic affairs', *c.* 1642
MS 1209/22 Map of Lifford, Dunalong and Derry

USA

San Marino, California, Huntington Library
Boxes 8–178 Irish correspondence, 1641–63

Hastings collection: miscellaneous
Box 1, folder 17 Notes on the history of Charles I published by William Senderson
Box 1, folder 20 Newspapers, 1674–1811

Hasting collection: literature
Box 1 literature from the seventeenth and eighteenth centuries

Hastings correspondence
HA boxes 16–23 Correspondence, 1640–63

Contemporary books and pamphlets

Anon., An *abstract of the unnatural rebellion and barbarous massacre of the Protestants in the kingdom of Ireland in the year 1641*, London 1689
—— *An account of the bloody massacre in Ireland: acted by the instigation of the Jesuits, priests, and friars*, London 1679
—— *An act for the speedie and effectuall reducing of the rebells in his majesties kingdom of Ireland to their due obedience to his majestie and the crown of England*, London 1642
—— *An alarvm to warre*, London 1642
—— *The apprentices of Londons petition presented to the honourable court of parliament: humbly shewing unto them the manifold abuses of their apprentiship, how the Frenchmen, Dutch, and Walloones, doe deprive them of their ancient customes, and former liberties in their trade*, London 1641
—— *The barbarous & inhumane proceedings against the professors of the reformed religion within the dominion of the duke of Savoy*, London 1655
—— *Bloody nevves from Ireland*, London 1641
—— *Bloody nevves from Ireland, or The barbarous crueltie by the papists used in that kingdome*, London 1641

—— *Bloody newes from Norwich: or, A true relation of a bloody attempt of the papists in Norwich, to consume the whole city by fire*, London 1641

—— *The bloody persecution of the Protestants in Ireland*, London 1641

—— *A brief of an act of parliament, humbly desired for the relief of the distressed Protestants of Ireland, who have left their estates by the present rebellion there, and to enlarge and explain these former acts already passed, for the more speedy and effectuall reducing of the rebells of Ireland to their due obedience to his majesty, and the crown of England*, London 1642

—— *A brief narrative [of] how things were carried at the beginning of the troubles in the year 1641 in Ireland*, [London] 1660

—— *Briefe relation of the most remarkeable feates and passages of what his most gracious majesties commanders hath done in England against the rebels*, Waterford 1644

—— *By the king; a proclamation against the rebels in Ireland*, London 1660

—— *By the lord lieutenant of Ireland, Henry Cromwell*, Dublin 1659

—— *Camilton's discoverie of the devilish designes and killing projects of the Society of Jesuites*, London 1641

—— *Certaine propositions, whereby the distressed Protestants of Ireland, who have lost their goods, and peronall estates there, by means of the present rebellion, may be relieved, if his majesty and both houses of parliament shall so think fit*, London 1642

—— *Confident newes from Ireland being a letter sent from Mr William Phillips, Merchant, dwelling in Dublin, to Mr William Barbar, a worthy friend of his, and one of the gentlemen of the Inner Temple*, London 1642

—— *The coppie of a letter sent from M Rider, deane of Saint Patricks, concerning the newes out of Ireland*, London 1601

—— *The coppy of a letter sent by the rebells in Ireland to the Lord Dillon, to declare to his maiestie the cause of their taking up armes*, London 1641

—— *A copy of a letter concerning the traiterovs conspiracy of the rebelliovs papists in Ireland*, London 1641

—— *The copy of a letter from Master Tristam Whitecomb, major of Kingsale in Ireland: dated the 21 of April 1642 to his brother Benjamin Whiecombe, merchant*, London 1642

—— *A copy of a letter vvhich Master Speaker is ordered by the Commons house of parliament, to send to the members of that house, that are now residing in their severall counties, to further the advancement of the adventure for Ireland*, London 1642

—— *A declaration of the Commons assembled in parliament; concerning the rise and progresse of the grand rebellion in Ireland*, London 1643

—— *A declaration of the Lords and Commons assembled in parliament, concerning the pressing necessities of this kingdome, caused by the traitorous and bloody counsels and attempts of those pernicious and desperate councellors, still about the king, and protected by him, while they more and more manifest their implacable enmity to our religion, the parliament, and peace of all his majesties good subjects and dominions; endeavouring with fire and sword to root out our religion, and all that professe it here, as they still proceed to do in Ireland*, London 1643

—— *The distressed estate of the city of Dvblin in Ireland at this present*, London 1641

—— *Dolefull nevves from Ireland sent in a letter*, London 1642

—— An elegie upon the death of the most illustrious and victorious Prince Gustavus Adolphus King of Swethland, London 1633

—— The exact and trve relation of that bloody battell fought betweene his royall majestie of Swethland, and the imperiall army the 5 and 6 of November 1632, Edinburgh 1633

—— Exceeding good newes from the Neweries in Ireland being, the true copie of a letter sent from Dublin the 20 of April 1642 to Sir William Adderton, now resident in London, from Mr Stephen Johnson merchant, London 1642

—— Exceeding happy newes from Ireland: being a true relation of many passages of great consequence very joyfull and delectable to all true hearted Protestants, London 1642

—— Exceeding happy nevvs from Ireland: declaring the proceedings of the Protestants army in Kildare, against the castle of Ithlone, the castle of Knock and Mores Castle Ogle, London 1642

—— Exceeding joyfull newes from Ireland or a true relation of a great and happy victorie, obtained by a Colonell David Douglasse and Sir James Carr, two Scottish commanders, with the helpe of the Scots planted in the north of Ireland, against the arch-rebels Philemy Oneale, London 164[2]

—— A faithfull remonstrance, of all the chiefe matters of note which have happened in and about Dublin, and other parts of Ireland, from the 26 of January, to this present, being the I of March, 1642, London 1642

—— A faithfull representation of the state of Ireland: whose bleeding eye is on England for help: or The horrid conspiracy discovered and most humbly presented to the wisdom of parliament for timely prevention, if not impossible: wherein it appears the designe is laid at the root of all the parliaments interest there, the adventurers lands, and the new-English mens lives, (as they call them) as well as at the power of godliness, and of the present government: published by constant and cordial adherers to the parliament and common-wealth, on the behalf of themselves, and of thousands in Ireland, London 1660

—— A general remonstrance or declaration of the Catholickes of Ireland, received of George Wentworth, London 1641

—— A geographicall description of the kingdom of Ireland, London 1642

—— Good newes from Alsasia and the Palatinate, the fift of Iune, London 1622

—— A great conspiracy by the papists in the kingdome of Ireland discovered by the lords, juistices, and counsell at Dvblin, and proclamed there October 23 1641, London [1641]

—— That great expedition for Ireland by way of underwriting proposed, by both houses of parliament, and graciously assented vnto by his majesty is heere vindicated as pious charitable, Iust, politice, profitable and obiections to the contrary clearely answered, by one who heartily wisheth the speedy promotion of this proposition of underwriting, as almost the onely remedy, London 1642, 6.

—— The great and famovs battel of Lvtzen, fought betweene the renowned king of Sweeden, and Walstein, London 1633

—— Great newes from the Barbadoes, London 1676

—— The grovnds and motives inducing his maiesty to agree to a cessation of armes for one whole yeare, with the Roman Catholiques of Ireland, Oxford 1643

—— The happiest newes from Ireland that ever came to England, London 1641

—— His maiesties answer to a petition presented to him at Yorke, Aprill 18 1642, London 1642

—— *The horrid conspiracie of such impenitent traytors as intended a nevv rebellion in the kingdom of Ireland*, London 1663

—— *The hvmble petition of the Lords and Commons assembled in parliament, unto his majesty (with the reasons moving them, to advise his majesty) to decline his intended journey into Ireland*, London 1642

—— *The invasions of Germanie*, London 1638

—— *Ireland's declaration being a remonstrance of the generality of the good people of Ireland*, London 1660

—— *Irelands advocate: or, A sermon preched at a publicke fast held by authoritie, July the 27 in behalfe of bleeding Ireland*, London 1642

—— *Irelands complaint, and Englands pitie*, London 1641

—— *Irelands misery since the late cessation*, London 1644

—— *Irelands tragical tyrannie*, London 1643

—— *Irelands trve divrnall, or A continved relation of the cheife passages that have happened there since the 11th of January unto this present*, London 1642

—— *Joyfull news from Ireland, being a relation of a battell which was fought between the Protestants, and the rebels of Ireland*, London 1641

—— *The kings maiesties speech on the 2 day of December, 1641 to the honourable house of parliament*, London 1641

—— *Lacrymae Germaniae: or, The tears of Germany*, London 1638

—— *A lamentable list, of certaine hidious, frightfull, and prodifious signes, which have bin seene in the aire, earth and waters, at severall times*, London 1638

—— *Lancasters massacre or The new way of advancing the Protestant religion, and expressing loyaltie to the king and queene*, London 1643

—— *A lanthorne for landlords*, London 1630

—— *The last and best newes from Ireland: declaring first the warlike and cruell proceeding of the rebels who are all papists and Jesuits of that kingdome burnt up*, London 1641

—— *The last nevves from Ireland being a relation of the hostile and bloody proceedings of the rebellious papists there at this present*, London 1641

—— *The last nevves from Ireland; or A trve relation of the sad estate and feares of Dublin, and of the siege of Tredavgh by the rebels*, London 1641

—— *The last speeches and confession of the Lord Maguire*, London 1644

—— *Late and lamentable news from Ireland, wherein are truly related, the rebellious, and cruell proceedings of the papists there, at this present, extracted out of the last letters from Dublin*, London 1641

—— *A late and trve relation from Ireland: of the vvarlike and bloody proceedings of the rebellious papists in that kingdome, from Novemb 1 to this present, 1641*, London 1641

—— *Later newes from Ireland concerning the late treacherous action, and rebellion, of Sir Carey Adoughertie, and Felli Me Reeah Mack Davy*, London 1608

—— *A letter from the lord lieutenant of Ireland, to the honorable William Lenthal esq; Speaker of the parliament of England: giving an acount of the proceedings of the army there under his lordships command; and several transactions between his lordship and the governor of Wexford, with the fort, haven and shipping there; and of several other garrisons of the enemy, as also the proposition tendred for the rendition of Wexford: and a copy of a censure, under the hand of Nicholas bishop of Ferns, against Talbot who dyed a Protestant*, London 1649

—— *Londons teares, vpon the never too much to be lamented death of our late worthie* member of the House of Commons, Sr Richard Wiseman knight and baronet, London 1642

—— A looking-glass for England: being an abstract of the bloody massacre in Ireland, by the instigation of the Jesuites, priests and friars, who were chief promoters of those horrible murthers, prodigious cruelties, barbarous villanies, and inhumane practices, executed by the Irish papists upon the English Protestants in the year 1642: as also a brief apology in the behalf of the Protestants in the walleys of Piedmont; with a narrative of the barbarous butcheries, inhumane cruelties, most execrable and unheard of villanies, perpetrated on them by the popish party during the heat of the late massacre in April 1655 stirred up by the malice and instigation of the devil acting in the popish clergie, London 1667

—— Mercurius hibernicus: or, A discourse of the late insurrection in Ireland, Bristol 1644

—— Mercuvrivs hibernicvs, or The Irish mercurie, n.p., 1645

—— A merry ballad of a rich maid that had 18 severall suitors of severall countries, London 1620

—— More happy newes from Ireland of a battell fought betwixt the Scottish volunteers against the Irish rebels, London 1641

—— More nevves from the Palatinate; and more comfort to every true Christian, that either favoureth the cause of religion, or wisheth well to the king of Bohemia's proceedings, London 1622

—— More newes from Ireland: or The bloody practices and proceedings of the papists in that kingdome at this present, London 1641

—— The most blessed and truest newes from Ireland, shewing the fortunate successe of the Protestants, and Gods just vengance on the rebels, London 1642

—— The names of such members of the Commons house of parliament, as have already subscribed in pursuance of the act of parliament, for the speedy reducing of the rebels, and the future peace and safety of this kingdome (a worke tending much to the glory of Almighty God, and the succour and reliefe of our distressed brethren in Ireland) together with the summes they have severally underwritten, London 1642

—— The new starr of the north, shining vpon the victorious king of Sweden, London 1631

—— No pamphlet, bvt a detestation against all such pamphlets as are printed, concerning the Irish rebellion, London 1642

—— An order made by both houses of parliament, to prevent the going over of popish commanders into Ireland, and also to hinder the transportation of arms, ammunition, money, corne, victuals, and al other provision to the rebels, and for the sending back of the Irish papists lately come over, London 1642

—— The petition of both houses of parliament to his majestie, concerning his intended going to Ireland, London 1642

—— The poets knavery discouered, in all their lying pamphlets, London [1642?]

—— The popish champion, or, A compleat history of the life and military actions of Richard earl of Tyrconnel, generalissimo of all the Irish forces now in arms wherein you have a true account of his birth and education, his advancement and honours, his treacherous disarming the Protestants ... : [sic] together with a relation of all the skirmishes, battels, sieges, and remarkable transactions which have happened under his government, with the particulars of the late bloody fight in the north ...: as also a brief description of the kingdom of Ireland ... the means how it came to be a conquer'd kingdom, with the sundry rebellions made by the natives against the crown of England, and by what means reduced / written for the present satisfaction of all good Protestants ... ; to this treatise is added the life and memorable actions of Father Petre, &c, London 1689

—— The prisoners of New Gates condemnation declaring every verdict of the whole bench at the Sessions House in the Old Bayly April 22 with the Jesuits and freyers being censured by the parliament, five fryers being examined by a committee in the Court of Wards, with their confessions at the same time, also those 18 that were suspected to adjoin with the Irish rebels, with a pilgrim, and four more Irish souldiers, London 1642

—— Propositions made to the Lords and Commons in parliament: for the speedie and effectuall reducing of the kingdom of Ireland: and the votes thereupon, by both houses presented unto the kings majestie: with his majesties gracious answer and royal assent thereunto, London 1642

—— A prospect of bleeding Irelands miseries, London 1647

—— The protestation of the archbishops and bishops of Ireland against the toleration of popery agreed upon, and subscribed by them at Dublin, the 26 of November, London 1641

—— The rebels of Irelands wicked conspiracie against Kingsaile in the province of Munstearre, and County of Corke, London 1641

—— A relation of the bloody massacre in Ireland: acted by the instigation of the Jesuits, priests, and friars who were promoters of those horrible murders, prodigious cruelties, barbarous villanies, and inhuman practices executed by the Irish papists upon the English Protestants, London 1689

—— A relation of the king of Svveden, his happie and incomparable successe and victories, against the forces of the emperour, London 1631

—— A remonstrance of grievances presented to his most excellent majestie, in the behalfe of the Catholicks of Ireland, Waterford 1643

—— The Spaniards perpetvall designes to an vniversall monarchie: translated according to the French, London 1624

—— A speech made in the House of Peeres: by the right honorable the earle of Monmouth, on Thursday the thirteenth of Ianuary 1641, London 1642

—— The state of the Adventurers case which resolves it self I. into the nature of their title and the equity of it, consisting in these particulars, London 1660

—— Still worse newes from Ireland, shewing in what a miserable estate the cittie of Dublin is, at this present time, London 1641

—— That great expedition for Ireland by way of underwriting proposed, by both houses of parliament, and graciously assented vnto by his majesty is heere vindicated as pious charitable, Iust, politice, profitable and obiections to the contrary clearely answered, by one who heartily wisheth the speedy promotion of this proposition of underwriting, as almost the onely remedy, London 1642

—— Timely advice, or Motives to incite all men of ability to subscribe to the propositions for Ireland, London 1642

—— Tiomna nuadh ar dTighearnia agus ar Slanaightheora Íosa Criosd, Dublin 1602

—— To the king's most excellent majesty: the faithful protestation and humble remonstrance of the Roman Catholick nobility and gentry of Ireland, [London 1660]

—— To the king's most excellent majesty the faithful protestation and humble remonstrance of the Roman Catholick nobility and gentry of Ireland, London 1662

—— To the king's most excellent majestie the humble remonstrance, acknowledgement, protestation, and petition of the Roman Catholick clergy of Ireland, [London 1662]

—— A treacherous plot of a confederacie in Ireland, with the rebels at Calway, with the furniture of guns and ammunition for warre, London 1641

—— A true coppie of the lawes and rules of government, agreed upon and established by the nobles of the severall counties of Ireland, London 1641

—— A true and credible relation of the barbarous crueltie and bloudy massacres of the English Protestants that lived in the kingdome of Ireland, anno dom 1641, London 1642

—— A true declaration of the last affaires in Ireland, shewing the late overthrowes given to the Irish rebels, London 1642

—— A true and exact relation of the chiefe passages in Ireland, since the first rising of the rebels, London 1642

—— A true and exact relation of the most sad condition of Ireland, since the cessation, exprest in a letter from Dublin, received the 16th of Novemb 1643, London 1643

—— A true and perfect relation of all the severall skirmishes, brave exploits, and glorious victories obtained by the English Protestants, over the Irish rebels, when they raised the siege of Tredagh, London 1641

—— A trve relation of the proceedings of the Bauarian and Spanish forces before the City Heydelburgh, London 1622

—— The true reporte of the prosperous successe which God gaue vnto our English souldiours against the forraine bands of our Romaine enemies lately ariued, (but soone inough to theyr cost) in Ireland, in the yeare 1580, London 1581

—— The truest intelligence from the province of Munster, London 1642

—— The truest, most happy and joyfull newes that ever came from Ireland, London 1641

—— The tvvo famous pitcht battels of Lypsich, and Lutzen wherein the ever-renowned Prince Gustavus the Great lived and died a conquerour, London 1634

—— Two famous and victorious battells fovght in Ireland, London 1642

—— Two great fights In Ireland, London 1649

—— Two speeches by Sir Beniamin Rudyard concerning the Palatinate, London 1641

—— Two very lamentable relations, London 1620

—— The victorious proceedings of the Protestants in Ireland; from the beginning of March to this present, being the 22 of the same month, London 1642

—— Warnings of Germany, London 1638

—— Worse and worse nevves from Ireland being the coppy of a letter read in the house of parliament, the 14 of this instant moneth of December, 1641, London 1642

Barclay, John, The mirrour of mindes, or, Barclay's Icon animorum, Englished by T.M., London 1631

Barrow, Henry, Mr Henry Barrowes platform, London 1611

Blenerhasset, Thomas, A direction for the plantation in Vlster: contayning in it, sixe principall thinges, viz 1 the securing of that wilde countrye to the crowne of England; 2 The withdrawing of all the charge of the garrison and men of warre; 3 The rewarding of olde seruitors to their good content; 4 The means how to increase the reuenue to the crowne, with a yearely very great somme; 5 How to establish the puritie of religion there; 6 And how the vndertakers may with securitie be inriched, London 1610

Botero, Giovanni, Relations of the most famous kingdomes and common-wealths thorowout the world, London 1630

Bowles, Edward, *The mysterie of iniquitie*, London 1643

Boyle, Roger, *The Irish colours displayed, in a reply of an English Protestant to a late letter of an Irish Roman Catholique: both address'd to his grace the duke of Ormond lord lieutenant of his majesties kingdome of Ireland*, London 1662

Brinsley, John, *A consolation for our grammar schooles*, London 1622

Camden, William, *Annales the true and royall history of the famous empresse Elizabeth queene of England France and Ireland*, London 1625

—— *Britain, or A chorographicall description of the most flourishing kingdomes, England, Scotland, and Ireland*, London 1637

Caron, R., *Loyalty asserted and the late remonstrance or allegiance of the Irish clergy and layty confirmed and proved by the authority of Scriptures, fathers … and by the evidences of several theological reasons: with a brief answer to Cardinal Peron's oration and objections / by R. Caron*, London 1662

Casas, Bartholomé de las, *The tears of the Indians*, London 1656

—— *The Spanish colonie, or Briefe chronicle of the acts and gestes of the Spaniardes in the West Indies, called the newe world, for the space of xl. yeeres: written in the Castilian tongue by the reuerend Bishop Bartholomew de las Cases or Casaus, a friar of the order of S. Dominicke: and nowe first translated into english, by M.M.S*, London 1583

Charles I, *Eikon basilike: the pourtraictvre of his sacred maiestie in his solitudes and svfferings: together with his maiesties praiers delivered to Doctor Juxon immediately before his death: also his majesties reasons, against the pretended jurisdiction of the high court of justice, which he intended to deliver in writing on Munday January 22, 1648*, London 1649

Clarke, Samuel, *A generall martyrologie*, London 1651

Cook, John, *King Charls his case*, London 1649

Coote, Chidley, *Irelands lamentation since the late cessation*, London 1644

Cox, Richard, *Hibernia anglicana, or, The history of Ireland, from the conquest thereof by the English*, London 1689

Cranford, James, *The teares of Ireland wherein is lively presented as a map, a list of the unheard off cruelties and perfidious treacheries of bloud-thirsty Jesuits and the popish faction: as a warning piece to her sister nations to prevent the like miseries, as are now acted on the stage of this fresh bleeding nation: reported by gentlemen of good credit living there, but forced to flie for their lives, as Iobs messengers, to tell us what they have heard and seene with their eyes, illustrated by pictures: fit to be reserved by all true Protestants as a monument of their perpetuall reproach and ignominy, and to animate the spiris of Protestants against such bloudy villains*, London 1642

Crant, Thomas, *The plott and progresse of the Irish rebellion*, London 1644

D'Ewes, Simonds, *A speech delivered In the House of Commons, July 7th 1641*, London 1641

Davies, John, *A discoverie of the state of Ireland: with the true causes why that kingdom was neuer entirely subdued, nor brought vnder obedience of the crowne of England, vntill the beginning of his maiesties most happie raigne*, London 1613

Derricke, John, *The image of Irelande*, London 1581

Duigenan, Patrick, *The nature and extent of the demands of the Irish Roman Catholics fully explained*, London 1810

Emitie, Thomas, *A new remonstrance from Ireland*, London 1642

189

Farewell, Christopher, *An East-India colation; or a discourse of travels set forth in sundry obseruations, briefe and delightfull*, London 1633

French, Nicholas, *A narrative of the settlement and sale of Ireland: whereby the just English adventurer is much prejudiced, the antient proprietor destroyed, and publick faith violated; to the great discredit of the English Church, and government, (if not re-called and made void) as being against the principles of Christianity, and true Protestancy*, Louvain 1668

Gainsford, Thomas, *The glory of England*, London 1618

Gordon, John, *Enotikon or A sermon of the vnion of Great Brittanie*, London 1604

Gray, Robert, *A good speed to Virginia*, London 1609

Hakluyt, Richard, *The principal nauigations, voyages, traffiques and discoueries of the English nation*, London 1599–1600

Herring, Francis, *Mischeefes mysterie: or, Treasons master-peece*, London 1617

Heylyn, Peter, *Mikrokosmos: a little description of the great world: augmented and reuised*, Oxford 1625

Holinshed, Raphael, *The second volume of chronicles: conteining the description, conquest, inhabitation, and troblesome estate of Ireland*, London 1586

James VI, *Basilikon doron*, London 1682

Jones, Henry, *A remonstrance of divers remarkeable passages concerning the Church and kingdome of Ireland recommended by letters from the right honourable the lords justices and counsell of Ireland, and presented by Henry Jones doctor in divinity, and agent for the ministers of the Gospel in that kingdom, to the honourable House of Commons in England*, London 1642

—— *An abstract of some few of those barbarous, cruell massacres and murthers, of the Protestants, and English in some parts of Ireland, committed since the 23 of October 1641: collected out of the examinations taken upon oath by persons of trust, in the beginning of the rebellion, by virtue of severall commissions under the great seal of Ireland: which particulars are singled out of a multitude of others of like nature: with the persons that acted those murthers, and massacres, with time, place, and other circumstances, are contained in the said examinations: sent over to the parliament in a letter from the commissioners of parliament in Ireland, and the generall and field officers there: and read in the parliament the 19 day of May 1652*, London 1652

Kearney, John, *Aibidil Gaoidheilge & caiticiosma*, Dublin 1571

Meredith, Adam, *Ormond's cvrtain drawn*, London 1646

Milton, John, *Eikonoklastes*, London 1649, 1650

Montaigne, Michel de, *Essays of Michael, seigneur de Montaigne in three books, with marginal notes and quotations of the cited authors, and an account of the author's life*, London 1685

Morland, Samuel, *The history of the evangelical Churches of the valleys of Piedmont*, London 1658

Morley, Thomas, *Remonstrance of the barbarous cruelties and bloody murders committed by the Irish rebels against the Protestants in Ireland both before and since the cessation*, London 1644

Norden, John, *A prayer for the prosperovs proceedings and good successe of the earle of Essex*, London 1599

O'Mahony, Conor, *Disputatio apologetica de iure regni Hiberniae pro catholicis hibernis adversys haereticos anglos*, Lisbon 1645

Payne, Robert, *A briefe description of Ireland: made in this yeare, 1589 by Robert*

Payne, vnto xxv of his partners for whome he is vndertaker there: truly published verbatim, according to his letters, by Nich Gorsan one of the sayd partners, for that he would his countreymen should be partakers of the many good notes therein contained, London 1589

Prynne, William, *The subjection of all traytors, rebells, as well peers, as commons in Ireland, to the laws, statutes, and trials by the juries of good and lawfull men of England, in the Kings Bench at Westminster*, London 1658

Purchas, Samuel, *Purchas his pilgrimage*, London 1613

—— *Purchas his pilgrimes in fiue bookes*, London 1625

[Puttocke, Roger], *An abstract of certain depositions*, London 1642

Rich, Barnaby, *A souldiers vvishe to Britons welfare: or A discourse, fit to be read of all gentlemen and souldiers*, London 1604

—— *A short svrvey of Ireland*, London 1609

—— *A nevv description of Ireland: wherein is described the disposition of the Irish wherevnto they are inclined: no lesse admirable to be perused then credible to be beleeued: neither vnprofitable nor vnpleasant to bee read and vnderstood, by those worty cittizens of London that be now vndertakers in Ireland*, London 1610

—— *The Irish hubbub*, Dublin 1618

G. S., *A briefe declaration of the barbarous and inhumane dealings of the northerne Irish rebels, and many others in severall counties uprising against the English, that dwelt both lovingly and securely among them*, London 1641

R. S., *A collection of some of the murthers and massacres committed on the Irish in Ireland since the 23d of October 1641*, London 1662

Salmon, James, *Bloody nevves from Ireland*, London 1641

Smith, John, *New Englands trials*, London 1622

—— *The true travels, adventures*, London 1630

Speed, John, *The theatre of the empire of Great Britaine: presenting an exact geography of the kingdoms of England, Scotland and Ireland*, London 1611

—— *A prospect of the most famous parts of the vvorld*, London 1646

Stoppa, Giovanni, *A collection or narrative sent to his highness the lord protector of the common-wealth of England, Scotland, & Ireland &c*, London 1655

Strachey, William, *For the colony in Virginea Britannia*, London 1612

Temple, John, *The Irish rebellion: or, An history of the beginnings and first progresse of the generall rebellion raised within the kingdom of Ireland, upon the three and twentieth day of October, in the year 1641: together with the barbarous cruelties and bloody massacres which ensued thereupon: by Sir John Temple knight: Master of the Rolles, and one of his majesties most honourable privie councell within the kingdom of Ireland*, London 1646

Touchet, James, *The earl of Castlehaven's review*, London 1684

Vincent, Philip, *Lamentations of Germany*, London 1638

Walsh, Peter, *The Irish colours folded*, London 1662

—— *To the king's most excellent majestie the humble remonstrance, acknoledgement, protestation, and petition of the Roman Catholick clergy of Ireland*, London 1662

—— *A letter desiring a just and mercifull regard of the Roman Catholicks of Ireland, given about the end of October 1660 to the then marquess, now duke of Ormond, and the second time lord lieutenant of that kingdom*, [London 1662]

—— *The more ample accompt, the answers to the exceptions, the inducements, and invitation, promised in the advertisement annexed to the late printed remonstrance, protestation, &c. of the Roman Catholick clergy of Ireland: and (in conclusion of all) an humble earnest advise to the nobility, genrty, and other lay Catholicks of the three nations: moreover, and for the better information, and fuller satisfaction of the reader, the foresaid remonstrance, &c. and advertisment prefix'd: finally an appendix of censures and arrests against the uncatholick positions of some otherwise Catholick writers: by F. Peter Walsh, of St. Fran. ord. read. of div. procur. of the above clergy, both sec. and reg,* London 1662.

Waring, Thomas, *A brief narration of the plotting, beginning and carrying on of that execrable rebellion and butcherie in Ireland: with the unheard of devilish-cruelties and massacres by the Irish-Rebels, exercised upon Protestants and English there: faithfully collected out of depositions, taken by commissioners under the great seal of Ireland: hereunto are added observations, discovering the actions of the late king; and manifesting the concernemnt of the Protestant-army now imployed in Ireland,* London 1650

Waterhouse, Edward, *A declaration of the state of the colony and affaires of Virgina,* London 1622

Wharton, George, *Bellum hybernicale or Irelands vvarre,* [Oxford] 1647

Whetcombe, Tristam, *The rebels Turkish tyranny, in their march Decem. 24. 1641,* London 1641

Published primary sources

'Bartolomé de las Casas', in Nina Baym (ed.), *The Norton anthology of American literature,* New York 2003, 38–42

Brooke, Christopher, 'A poem on the late massacre in Virginia', *Virginia Magazine of History and Bibliography* lxxii (July 1964), 259–92

Calendar of state papers, domestic series, 2nd ser. London 1858–97

Calendar of state papers relating to Ireland, London 1860–1911

Carpenter, Andrew (ed.), *Verse in English from Tudor and Stuart Ireland,* Cork 2003

Carte, Thomas, *A collection of letters, written by the Kings Charles I and II the duke of Ormonde, the secretaries of state, the marques of Clanricarde, and toerh great men, during the troubles of Great Britain and Ireland serving to verify and clear up matters related in the history of the life and times of James the first duke of Ormonde, and published by way of appendix to that History, whereof it makes,* London 1735

Clarke, Aidan, 'A discourse between two councillors of state, the one of England, and the other of Ireland (1642)', *Analecta Hibernica* xxvi (1970), 159–75

Clarke, Andrew, *The Shirburn ballads, 1585–1616,* Oxford 1907

Clayton, Margaret Curtis, *The council book for the province of Munster, c. 1599–1641,* Dublin 2008

Cobbett's parliamentary history of England: from the Norman Conquest in 1066 to the year 1803: from which last-mentioned epoch is continued downwards in the work entitled, 'Cobbett's parliamentary debates, London 1807

A collection of the state letters of ... Orrery, Dublin 1743

A collection of state papers of John Thurloe, London 1742

Conor O'Mahony: an argument defending the right of the kingdom of Ireland (1645), ed. John Minihane, Cork 2010

A contemporary history of affairs in Ireland from 1641–1652, ed. J. T. Gilbert, Dublin 1879

The diary of Ralph Josselin, 1616–1683, ed. Alan MacFarlane, London 1976

Dunlop, Robert, *Ireland under the Commonwealth: being a selection of documents relating to the government of Ireland from 1651 to 1659*, Manchester 1913

The embassy in Ireland of Monsignor G. B. Rinuccini, archbishop of Fermo, in the years 1645–1649 published from the original mss in the Rinuccini library tr. by Annie Hutton, ed. Guiseppe Aiazza, Dublin 1873

Fasti ecclesiae hibernicae: the succession of the prelates and members of the cathedral bodies of Ireland, ed. Henry Cotton, Dublin 1878

Graham, John, *Annals of Ireland, ecclesiastical, civil and military*, London 1817

Hartnett, Michael, *Haicéad*, Oldcastle 1993

Hickson, Mary, *Ireland in the seventeenth century or The massacres of 1641–1642 their causes and results*, London 1884

Hindley, Charles, *The Roxburghe ballads*, London 1873

Hinton, Edward, 'Rych's anothomy of Ireland, with an account of the author', *PMLA*, lv (Mar. 1940), 73–101

Historical catalogue of the printed editions of Holy Scripture in the Library of the British and Foreign Bible Society, London 1903

Historical Manuscripts Commission, *Second report*, London 1874

—— *Fourth report*, pt I, London 1874

—— *Fifth report*, London 1876

—— *Seventh report*, pt I, London 1879

—— *Eighth report*, part I, London 1881

—— *The manuscripts of the Earl Cowper, K.G., preserved at Melbourne Hall, Derbyshire*, London 1889

—— *The manuscripts of his grace the duke of Portland, preserved at Welbeck Abbey*, London 1891

—— *Calendar of the manuscripts of the marquess of Ormonde, K.P. preserved at Kilkenny Castle* n.s. ii, London 1903

—— *Report on the manuscripts of the earl of Egmont*, London 1905–9

—— *Report of the manuscripts of the late Reginald Rawdon Hastings, esq. of the Manor House, Ashby-de-la-Zouche* edited by Francis Bickley, London 1930

—— *Report on the manuscripts of the right honorable Viscount De L'Isle, V.C. preserved at Penshurst Place Kent*, London 1966

The historical works ... of Nicholas French, ed. S. H. Bindon, Dublin 1846

History of the Irish confederation and the war in Ireland, 1641–1649, ed. J. T. Gilbert, Dublin 1882

Ireland's dirge, an historical peom, written in Irish by the right rev John O'Connell, bishop of Kerry, trans. Michael Clarke, Dublin 1827

Journals of the House of Commons of the kingdom of Ireland ... 1613–1791, Dublin 1753–91

Journals of the House of Lords [of Ireland] ... 1634–1800, Dublin 1779–1800

Leslie, James, *Armagh clergy and parishes: being an account of the clergy of the Church of Ireland in the diocese of Armagh, from the earliest period, with historical notices of the severall parishes, churches &c*, Dundalk 1911

Lindley, Keith, *The English civil war and revolutions: a sourcebook*, London 1998

The Lismore papers, ed. Alexander Grosart, London 1886–8

The Lismore papers (second series), viz Selections from the private and public (or state) correspondence of Sir Richard Boyle, first and 'great' earl of Cork, never before printed: edited, with introductions and notes and illustrations, London 1888

Mac Cárthaigh, Eoin and Uilliam Og Mac Uilliam Oig Mheic an Bháird, 'Dia Libh, A Uaisle Éireann (1641)', Ériu lii (2002), 89–121

McGuire, James and James Quinn (eds), Dictionary of Irish biography: from the earliest times to the year 2002, Cambridge 2009: dib.cambridge.org

McKenzie, D. F. and Maureen Bell (eds), A chronology and calendar of documents relating to the London book trade, 1641–1700, Oxford 2005

Maley, Willy, 'The supplication of blood of the English most lamentably murdered in Ireland, cryeng out of the yearth for revenge (1598)', Analecta Hibernica xxxvi (1995), 1, 3–77

Minihane, John, The poems of Geoffrey O'Donoghue, Cork 2008

O'Rahilly, Cecile (ed.), Five seventeenth-century political poems, Dublin 1952

Plomer, Henry, A dictionary of the booksellers and printers who were at work in England, Scotland and Ireland from 1641 to 1667, London 1907

The private journals of the Long Parliament 7 March to 1 June 1642, ed. Vernon Snow and Anne Steele Young, Yale 1987

Rushworth, John, Historicall collections of private passages of state, London 1721

The statutes at large, passed in the parliaments held in Ireland: from the third year of Edward the Second, A. D. 1310, to the first year of George the Third, A.D. 1761 inclusive, Dublin 1765

A true narrative of the rise and progress of the Presbyterian Church in Ireland, 1623–1670 by the Rev Patrick Adair minister of Belfast also The history of the Church in Ireland since the Scots were naturalized, by the Rev Andrew Stewart minister of Donaghadee, ed. W. D. Killen Belfast 1866

'A true relation of the life and death of the right reverend Father in God William Bedell, lord bishop of Kilmore in Ireland', in Thomas Wharton Jones (ed.), Camden Miscellany civ, London 1872

The writings and speeches of Oliver Cromwell, ed. W. C. Abbott, Cambridge, MA 1937

Secondary sources

Adair, Charlene, 'The trial of Lord Maguire and "print culture"', in Darcy, Margey and Murphy, The 1641 depositions, 169–84

Adamson, John, 'Strafford's ghost: the British context of Viscount Lisle's lieutenancy of Ireland', in Ohlmeyer, Ireland from independence to occupation, 128–59

—— The noble revolt: the overthrow of Charles I, London 2007

Ansell, Richard, 'The 1688 Revolution and the memory of 1641', in Forrest and Williams, Constructing the past, 73–93

Armstrong, Robert, Protestant war: the 'British' of Ireland and the Wars of the Three Kingdoms, Manchester 2005

—— 'Ireland's Puritan revolution? The emergence of Ulster Presbyterianism reconsidered', EHR cxxi (2006), 1048–74

Barnard, Toby, 'The uses of 23 October 1641 and Irish Protestant celebrations', EHR cvi (1991), 889–920

—— Cromwellian Ireland: English government and reform in Ireland, 1649–1660, Oxford 2000

—— '"Parlour entertainment in an evening?" Histories of the 1640s', in Ó Siochrú, *Kingdoms in crisis*, 20–43

Benjamin, Thomas, *The Atlantic world: Europeans, Africans, Indians and their shared history, 1400–1900*, Cambridge 2009

Braddick, Michael and John Walter, 'Introduction: grids of power: order, hierarchy and subordination in early modern society', in Michael Braddick and John Walter (eds), *Negotiating power in early modern society: order, hierarchy, and subordination in Britain and Ireland*, Cambridge 2001, 1–42

Brady, Ciaran and Raymond Gillespie (eds), *Natives and newcomers: essays on the making of Irish colonial society, 1534–1641*, Woodbridge 1986

Caball, Marc, *Poets and politics: continuity and reaction in Irish poetry, 1558–1625*, Cork 1998

Canny, Nicholas, *Kingdom and colony: Ireland in the Atlantic world, 1560–1800*, Baltimore 1988

—— 'The 1641 depositons as a source for the writing of social history: County Cork as a case study', in P. O'Flanaghan and C. Buttimer (eds), *Cork history and society: interdisciplinary approaches to the history of an Irish county*, Cork 1993, 249–308

—— 'What really happened in Ireland in 1641?', in Ohlmeyer, *Ireland from independence to occupation*, 24–42

—— 'Religion, politics, and the Irish uprising of 1641', in Judith Delvin and Ronan Fanning (eds), *Religion and rebellion: the proceedings of the Twenty Second Irish Conference of Historians*, Dublin 1997, 40–70

—— *Making Ireland British, 1580–1650*, Oxford 2001

—— and Philip Morgan (eds), *The Oxford handbook of the Atlantic world, 1450–1850*, Oxford 2011

Clarke, Aidan, 'Ireland and the general crisis', *P&P* xlviii (1970), 79–99

—— 'The 1641 depositions', in Peter Fox (ed.), *Treasures of the Library, Trinity College Dublin*, Dublin 1986, 111–22

—— 'Bishop William Bedell, 1571–1642 and the Irish Reformation', in Ciaran Brady (ed.), *Worsted in the game: losers in Irish history*, Dublin 1989, 61–70

—— *The Old English in Ireland, 1625–1642*, Dublin 2000

—— 'The Commission for the Despoiled Subject, 1641–7', in Brian Mac Cuarta (ed.), *Reshaping Ireland, 1550–1700: colonization and its consequences*, Dublin 2011, 241–60

Clifton, Robin, '"An indiscriminate blackness"? Massacre, counter-massacre, and ethnic cleansing in Ireland, 1640–1660', in Michael Levene and Penny Roberts (eds), *The massacre in history*, Oxford 1999, 107–26

Cope, Joseph, 'The experience of survival during the 1641 Irish rebellion', *HJ* xlvi (2003), 295–316

—— *England and the 1641 rebellion*, Woodbridge 2009

Cunningham, Bernadette, *The world of Geoffrey Keating: history, myth and religion in seventeenth-century Ireland*, Dublin 2007

—— 'Seventeenth-century constructions of the historical kingdom of Ireland', in Forrest and Williams, *Constructing the past*, 9–26

Cunningham, John, '1641 and the shaping of Cromwellian Ireland', in Darcy, Margey and Murphy, *The 1641 depositions*, 155–68

Darcy, Eamon, 'The social order of the 1641 rebellion', in Darcy, Margey and Murphy, *The 1641 depositions*, 97–112

—— 'The three kingdoms', in Laura Knoppers (ed.), *The Oxford handbook of literature on the English rebellion*, Oxford 2013, 44–64

—— Annaleigh Margey and Elaine Murphy (eds), *The 1641 depositions and the Irish rebellion*, London 2012

Davis, Natalie Zemon, 'The rites of violence: religious riot in sixteenth-century France', *P&P* lix (May 1973), 51–91

Donagan, Barbara, 'Codes and conduct in the English civil war', *P&P* cxviii (Feb. 1988), 65–96

Donnelly, Colm, 'The archaeology of the Ulster plantation', in Audrey Horning and others (eds), *The post-medieval archaeology of Ireland, 1550–1850*, Dublin 2007, 37–50

Duffy, Charles Gavan, 'Books for the Irish people', in *The revival of Irish literature*, London 1896

Edwards, David, 'Ideology and experience: Spenser's *View* and martial law in Ireland', in Morgan, *Political ideology*, 127–57

—— 'The escalation of violence in sixteenth-century Ireland', in Edwards, Lenihan and Tait, *Age of atrocity*, 34–78.

—— 'The plight of the earls: Tyrone and Tyrconnell's "grievances" and crown coercion in Ulster, 1603–7', in Thomas O'Connor and Mary Ann Lyons (eds), *The Ulster earls and baroque Europe: refashioning Irish identities, 1600–1800*, Dublin 2010, 53–76

—— Padraig Lenihan and Clodagh Tait, 'Early modern Ireland: a history of violence', in Edwards, Lenihan and Tait, *Age of atrocity*, 9–33

—— Pádraig Lenihan and Clodagh Tait (eds), *Age of atrocity: violence and political conflict in early modern Ireland*, Dublin 2007

Elliott, J. H., *Empires of the Atlantic world: Britain and Spain in America, 1492–1830*, New Haven 2007

Finnegan, David, Éamonn Ó Ciardha and Marie-Claire Peters (eds), *The flight of the earls: Imeacht na nIarlaí*, Derry 2010

Flanagan, Eugene, 'The anatomy of Jacobean Ireland: Captain Barnaby Rich, Sir John Davies and the failure of reform, 1609–22', in Morgan, *Political ideology*, 158–80

Ford, Alan, *The Protestant Reformation in Ireland, 1590–1641*, Frankfurt 1987

—— 'Who went to Trinity? The early students of Dublin University', in Helga Robinson-Hammerstein (ed.), *European universities in the age of Reformation and Counter-Reformation*, Dublin 1998, 53–74

—— 'Living together, living apart: sectarianism in early modern Ireland', in Ford and McCafferty, *Origins of sectarianism*, 1–23

—— and John McCafferty (eds), *The origins of sectarianism in early modern Ireland*, Cambridge 2005

Forrest, Stephen and Mark Williams (eds), *Constructing the past: writing Irish history, 1600–1800*, Woodbridge 2010

Fox, Adam, *Oral and literate culture in England, 1500–1700*, Oxford 2000

Gentles, Ian, *The English revolution and the Wars in the Three Kingdoms, 1638–1652*, London 2007

Gibney, John, *Ireland and the Popish Plot*, Basingstoke 2009

Gillespie, Raymond, 'Harvest crises in early seventeenth-century Ireland', *Irish Economic and Social History* xi (1984), 5–18

—— 'The end of an era: Ulster and the outbreak of the 1641 rising', in Brady and Gillespie, *Natives and newcomers*, 191–213

—— *Conspiracy: Ulster plots and plotters in 1615*, Belfast 1987

—— 'The murder of Arthur Champion and the 1641 rising in Fermanagh', *Clogher Record: Journal of the Clogher Historical Society* xiv/3 (1993), 54–66

—— 'The circulation of print in seventeenth-century Ireland', *Studia Hibernica* xxix (1995–7), 31–58

—— *Devoted people: belief and religion in early modern Ireland*, Manchester 1997

—— *Reading Ireland: print, reading and social change in early modern Ireland*, Manchester 2005

—— 'Temple's fate: reading *The Irish rebellion* in late seventeenth-century Ireland', in Ciaran Brady and Jane Ohlmeyer (eds), *British interventions in early modern Ireland*, Cambridge 2005, 315–33

—— 'Print culture, 1550–1700', in Gillespie and Hadfield, *The Oxford history of the Irish book*, iii. 17–33

—— 'The problems of plantations: material culture and social change in early modern Ireland', in James Lyttleton and Colin Rynne (eds), *Plantation Ireland: settlement and material culture, c. 1550–c. 1700*, Dublin 2009, 43–60

—— and Andrew Hadfield (eds), *The Oxford history of the Irish book: the Irish book in English, 1550–1800*, Oxford 2006

Gillingham, John, 'From civilitas to civility: codes of manners in medieval and early-modern England', *Transactions of the Royal Historical Society* 6th ser. xii (2002), 267–89

Hadfield, Andrew, 'Historical writing, 1550–1660', in Gillespie and Hadfield, *The Oxford history of the Irish book*, iii. 250–63

—— *Literature, travel, and colonial writing in the English Renaissance, 1545–1625*, Oxford 2007

Harding, David, 'Objects of English colonial discourse: the Irish and Native Americans', *Nordic Irish Studies* iv (2005), 37–60

Herron, Thomas, 'Early modern Ireland and the new English epic: connecting Edmund Spenser and Sir George Carew', *Eolas: The Journal of the American Society of Irish Medieval Studies* i (2006), 27–52

Hill, Jacqueline, 'Politics and the writing of history: the impact of the 1690s and 1790s on Irish historiography', in D. G. Boyce, R. Eccleshall and V. Geohegan (eds), *Political discourse in seventeenth- and eighteenth-century Ireland*, New York 2001, 222–39

Horne, John and Alan Kramer, 'War between soldiers and enemy civilians, 1914–1915', in Roger Chickering and Stig Forster (eds), *Great War, total war: combat and mobilization on the Western Front, 1914–1918*, Cambridge 2000, 153–68

—— *German atrocities, 1914: a history of denial*, New Haven 2001

Horowitz, Donald, *The deadly ethnic riot*, London 2001

Houston, Rab, *Literacy in early modern Europe: culture and education, 1500–1800*, London 2002

Jouhaud, Christian, 'Readability and persuasion: political handbills', in Roger Chartier (ed.), *The culture of print: power and the uses of print in early modern Europe*, Oxford 1989, 235–60

Kalyvas, Stathis N., *The logic of violence in civil war*, Cambridge 2005

Kane, Brendan, 'A dynastic nation? Re-thinking national consciousness in early seventeenth-century Ireland', in Finnegan, Ó Ciardha and Peters, *The flight of the earls*, 124–31

Lake, Peter, 'Deeds against nature: cheap print, Protestantism and murder in early seventeenth-century England', in Peter Lake and Kevin Sharpe (eds), *Culture and politics in early Stuart England*, London 1994, 257–84

Lecky, William, *Historical and political essays*, London 1908

Lenman, Bruce P., *England's colonial wars, 1550–1688: conflicts, empire and national identity*, London 2001

Lennon, Colm, 'The Counter Reformation in Ireland, 1542–1641', in Brady and Gillespie, *Natives and newcomers*, 75–92

—— 'The print trade, 1550–1700', in Gillespie and Hadfield, *The Oxford history of the Irish book*, iii. 61–73

Lindley, Keith, 'The impact of the 1641 rebellion upon England and Wales, 1641–5', *Irish Historical Studies* xviii (1972), 143–76

Loeber, Rolf and Geoffrey Parker, 'The military revolution in seventeenth century Ireland', in Ohlmeyer, *Ireland from independence to occupation*, 66–88

Lotz-Heumann, Ute, 'Confessionalisation in Ireland: periodisation and character, 1534–1649', in Ford and McCafferty, *Origins of sectarianism*, 24–53

Love, Walter, 'Civil war in Ireland: appearances in three centuries of historical writing', *Emory University Quarterly* xxii (1966), 57–72

Lowenstein, David, *Representing revolution in Milton and his contemporaries*, Cambridge 2001

McCavitt, John, *Sir Arthur Chichester: lord deputy of Ireland, 1605–1616*, Belfast 1998

McClintock Dix, E. R., 'Printing in the city of Kilkenny in the seventeenth century', *Proceedings of the Royal Irish Academy* xxxii (1914–16), 125–37

—— 'Printing in the city of Waterford in the seventeenth century', *Proceedings of the Royal Irish Academy* xxxii (1914–16), 333–44

Mac Cuarta, Brian, *Catholic revival in the north of Ireland, 1603–41*, Dublin 2007

McGurk, John, 'The pacification of Ulster, 1600–3', in Edwards, Lenihan and Tait, *Age of atrocity*, 119–29

Macinnes, Allan, *The British revolution, 1629–1660*, Houndsmills 2005

McKenny, Kevin, 'The Restoration land settlement in Ireland: a statistical interpretation', in Coleman A. Dennehy (ed.), *Restoration Ireland: always settling and never settled*, Aldershot 2008, 35–52

Margey, Annaleigh, 'Representing plantation landscapes: the mapping of Ulster, c. 1560–1640', in James Lyttleton and Colin Rynne (eds), *Plantation Ireland: settlement and material culture, c. 1550–c. 1700*, Dublin 2009, 140–64

Masschaele, James, 'The public space of the marketplace in medieval England', *Speculum* lxxvii (2002), 383–421

Morales, Óscar Recio, *Ireland and the Spanish empire, 1600–1825*, Dublin 2010

Morgan, Hiram, 'Hugh O'Neill and the Nine Years War in Tudor Ireland', *HJ* xxxvi (1993), 21–37

—— 'Giraldus Cambrensis and the Tudor conquest of Ireland', in Morgan, *Political ideology*, 22–44

—— (ed.), *Political ideology in Ireland, 1541–1641*, Dublin 1999

Morin, Edgar, *Rumour in Orleans*, London 1971

Morrill, John, *The nature of the English revolution: essays by John Morrill*, New York 1993

—— 'The Drogheda massacre in Cromwellian context', in Edwards, Lenihan and Tait, *Age of atrocity*, 242–65

Murdock, Graeme, Penny Roberts and Andrew Spicer (eds), *Ritual and violence: Natalie Zemon Davis and early modern France*, Oxford 2012.

Murphy, Andrew, *But the Irish sea betwixt us: Ireland, colonialism, and Renaissance literature*, Lexington 1999

Netzloff, Mark, *England's internal colonies: class, capital, and the literature of early modern English colonialism*, London 2003

Neyts, Ciska, 'Mapping the outbreak of the rebellion: robberies in County Cavan (October 1641)', in Darcy, Margey and Murphy, *The 1641 depositions*, 35–50

Noonan, Kathleen, '"Martyrs in flames": Sir John Temple and the conception of the Irish in English martyrologies', *Albion* xxxvi (Summer 2004), 223–55

O'Connor, Thomas and Mary Ann Lyons (eds), *Strangers to citizens: the Irish in Europe, 1600–1800*, Dublin 2008

—— *The Ulster earls and baroque Europe: refashioning Irish identities, 1600–1800*, Dublin 2010

Ó Cuív, Brian, 'The Irish language in the early modern period', in T. W. Moody, F. X. Martin and F. J. Byrne (eds), *A new history of Ireland*, III: *Early modern Ireland, 1534–1691*, Oxford 1976, 509–45

O'Dowd, Mary, 'Women and war in Ireland in the 1640s', in Mary Mac Curtain and Mary O'Dowd (eds), *Women in early modern Ireland*, Edinburgh 1991, 91–111

Ó hAnnracháin, Tadhg, '"Though heretics and politicians should misinterpret their good zeale": political ideology and Catholicism in early modern Ireland', in Ohlmeyer, *Political thought*, 155–74

—— *Catholic Reformation in Ireland: the mission of Rinuccini, 1645–1649*, Oxford 2002

—— 'The survival of the Catholic Church in Ulster in the era of the flight of the earls and the Ulster plantation', in Finnegan, Ó Ciardha and Peters, *The flight of the earls*, 221–6

O'Riordan, Michelle, *The Gaelic mind and the collapse of the Gaelic world*, Cork 1990

—— '"Political" poems in the mid seventeenth-century crisis', in Ohlmeyer, *Ireland from independence to occupation*, 112–27

Ó Siochrú, Micheál, *Confederate Ireland, 1642–1649: a constitutional and political analysis*, Dublin 1999

—— 'Atrocity, codes of conduct and the Irish in the British civil wars, 1641–1653', *P&P* clxxxxv (May 2007), 55–86

—— *God's executioner: Oliver Cromwell and the conquest of Ireland*, Dublin 2008, 18–21

—— (ed.), *Kingdoms in crisis: Ireland in the 1640s: essays in honour of Donal Cregan*, Dublin 2001

Ohlmeyer, Jane, 'Ireland independent: confederate foreign policy and international relations during the mid–seventeenth century', in Ohlmeyer, *Ireland from independence to occupation*, 89–111

—— 'Strafford, "the Londonderry business" and the "new British histories"', in Julia Merritt (ed.), *The political world of Thomas Wentworth, the earl of Strafford, 1621–1641*, Cambridge 1996, 209–29

—— '"Civilisinge of those rude partes": colonization within Britain and Ireland,

1580s–1640s', in Nicholas Canny (ed.), *The origins of empire: British overseas enterprise to the close of the seventeenth century*, Oxford 1998, 124–47

—— 'A laboratory for empire? Early modern Ireland and English imperialism', in Kevin Kenny (ed.), *Ireland and the British Empire*, Oxford 2004, 26–60

—— *Making Ireland English: the Irish aristocracy in the seventeenth century*, New Haven 2012

—— (ed.), *Ireland from independence to occupation, 1641–1660*, Cambridge 1995

—— (ed.), *Political thought in seventeenth-century Ireland: kingdom or colony?*, Cambridge 2000

Ordahl Kupperman, Karen, 'English perceptions of treachery, 1583–1640: the case of the American "savages"', *HJ* xx (1977), 263–87

—— *Settling with the Indians: the meeting of English and Indian cultures in America, 1580–1640*, London 1980

Pagden, Anthony, 'Introduction', in Nigel Griffin (ed.), *Bartolomé de las Casas: a short account of the destruction of the Indies*, London 2004, pp. xiii–xlii

Parker, Geoffrey, 'The etiquette of atrocity: the laws of war in early modern Europe', in Geoffrey Parker (ed.), *Empire, war and faith in early modern Europe*, London 2002, 143–68

—— and Lesley Smith (eds), *The general crisis of the seventeenth century*, London 1997

Peacey, Jason, *Politicians and pamphleteers: propaganda during the English civil wars and interregnum*, Aldershot 2004

Perceval-Maxwell, Michael, *The outbreak of the Irish rebellion of 1641*, London 1994

—— 'Sir Robert Southwell and the duke of Ormond's reflections on the 1640s', in Ó Siochrú, *Kingdoms in crisis*, 229–47

Perez Tostado, Igor, *Irish influence at the court of Spain in the seventeenth century*, Dublin 2008

Pocock, J. G. A., 'Two kingdoms and three histories? Political thought in British contexts', in Roger Mason (ed.), *Scots and Britons: Scottish political thought and the union of 1603*, Cambridge 1994, 293–312

Ranelagh, John, *A short history of Ireland*, Dublin 1999

Rankin, Deana, *Between Spenser and Swift: English writings in seventeenth-century Ireland*, Cambridge 2005

Robinson, Philip, *The plantation of Ulster*, Dublin 1994

Robinson-Hammerstein, Helga, 'Royal policy and civic pride: founding a university in Dublin', in David Scott (ed.), *Treasures of the mind: a Trinity College Dublin quatercentenary exhibition catalogue*, London 1992, 1–15

Ruff, Julius, *Violence in early modern Europe*, Cambridge 2001

Russell, Conrad, 'Composite monarchies in early modern Europe: the British and Irish example', in Alexander Grant and Keith Stringer (eds), *Uniting the kingdom? The making of British history*, London 1996, 133–46

Seaver, Paul, *Wallington's world: a Puritan artisan in seventeenth-century London*, Stanford 1985

Shagan, Ethan, 'Constructing discord: ideology, propaganda, and English response to the Irish rebellion of 1641', *JBS* xxxvi (1997), 4–34.

—— 'Rumours and popular politics in the reign of Henry VIII', in Tim Harris (ed.), *The politics of the excluded*, Basingstoke 2001, 30–66

—— *The rule of moderation: violence, religion and the politics of restraint in early modern England*, Cambridge 2011

Sheehan, Bernard, *Savagism and civility: Indians and Englishmen in colonial Virginia*, Cambridge 1980

Simms, Hillary, 'Violence in County Armagh, 1641', in Brian Mac Cuarta (ed.), *Ulster 1641: aspects of the rising*, Belfast 1993, 123–38

Smith, David, 'Sir Benjamin Rudyerd and England's "wars of religion"', in Michael Braddick and David Smith (eds), *The experience of revolution in Stuart Britain and Ireland: essays for John Morrill*, Cambridge 2011, 52–73

Smyth, William, *Map-making, landscapes and memory: a geography of colonial and early modern Ireland, c. 1530–1750*, Cork 2006

Sommerville, Johann, *King James VI and I: political writings*, Cambridge 1994

Spufford, Margaret, *Small books and pleasant histories: popular fiction and its readership in seventeenth-century England*, London 1981

Tait, Clodagh, 'Riots, rescues and "Grene Bowes": Catholics and protest in Ireland', in Robert Armstrong and Tadhg Ó hAnnracháin (eds), *Insular Christianity: alternative models of the Church in Britain and Ireland, c. 1570–c. 1700*, Manchester 2012, 67–87

Theibault, John, 'The rhetoric of death and destruction in the Thirty Years War', *Journal of Social History* xxvii (Winter 1993), 271–90

Treadwell, Victor, *Buckingham and Ireland, 1616–1628: a study in Anglo-Irish politics*, Dublin 1998

Trevor Roper, Hugh, 'The lost moments of history', *New York Review of Books*, 27 Oct. 1988

Walsham, Alexandra, *Providence in early modern England*, Oxford 2001

Walter, John, *Understanding popular violence in the English revolution*, Cambridge 1999

—— *Crowds and popular politics in early modern England*, Manchester 2006

—— 'Performative violence: patterns of political violence in the 1641 depositions', in Jane Ohlmeyer and Micheál Ó Siochrú (eds), *Ireland 1641: contexts and reactions*, Manchester 2013, forthcoming

Woolrych, Austin, *Britain in revolution*, Oxford 2002

Unpublished theses

Ball, John, 'Popular violence in the Irish uprising of 1641: the 1641 depositions, Irish resistance to English colonialism, and its representation in English sources', DPhil. Johns Hopkins 2006

Donovan, Iain, '"Bloody news from Ireland": the pamphlet literature of the Irish massacres of the 1640s', M.Litt. Dublin 1995

Finnegan, David, 'The impact of the Counter-Reformation on the political thinking of Irish Catholics, c. 1540–c. 1640', PhD, Cambridge 2006

Index

Gray, Robert, 17, 22, 23
Green, Elizabeth, 98
Green, Thomas, 69, 70, 98
Greensmith, John, 114, 116, 119; fabricated pamphlets, 114, 118–19. *See also* print.
Greg, Alice, 69, 70
Grissell, John, 98
Gunpowder Plot (1605), 109

Haicéad, Paidraigín, 158–9
Hanmer, Meredith, 56; 'Chronicle of Ireland', 56
Harcourt, Sir Simon, 121
Hayward, Thomas, 109
Henrietta Maria, queen of England, Ireland and Scotland, 87, 90, 169; confessor hanged, 75, 172
Herbert, Sir Jasper, 64
Herbert, Thomas, 114
Henry II, king of England, 10, 157
Henry VIII, king of England and Ireland, 159
Hill, Anne, 98
Hill, Thomas, 97
Holland, Roger, 69
Hovenden, Alexander, 3
Hovenden, Katherine, 3, 4
Hovenden, Robert, 1
Howell, James, 125
Hudson, Fretum, 26
Hunscott, Joseph, 84, 135, 136
Hyde, Edward, first earl of Clarendon, 44

Ireland, *passim*, and 6, 10, 43, 148, 168; anglicisation, 41–2, 57; Church of Ireland, 5, 7, 88, 150, 169; colonial writings on, 11–12, 17, 28–40, 46; Davies's views on, 35–6; English language, 42–4; Irish language, 41–2, 62; kingdom or colony?, 18; laboratory for empire, 8, 11–12, 28; news from, 14, 15, 77–99, 103, 107–8, 109–24, 130–1, 135–7, 143, 147, 156, 169, 170, 171, 174, 177; parliament, 5, 50, 79; peerage, 5, 6; sectarian tensions in, 4, 5, 7, 29, 30, 44, 45, 51, 53, 100, 101, 158; Stuart rule in, 7, 20, 23, 48, 49; Tudor rule in, 4, 20, 31; violence against natives, 4–5, 30–1, 39, 61
Ireton, Henry, 149, 160
Irish colleges on the continent, 6, 157

Irish Rebellion of 1641, *passim*; causes, 2, 7, 44, 47, 48, 51–2; death toll, 2, 54, 95, 148; definition, 1; historiography, 1, 3, 15–16, 52–3, 171, 177; 'indiscriminate blackness'?, 53–67; memory of, 15–6, 132–67; outbreak, 52–67
Ironmonger, Thomas, 109, 112
Island Magee, 176

James II, king of England, Ireland and Scotland, 148
James VI and I, king of England, Ireland and Scotland, 5, 9, 10, 19, 20, 22, 23, 38; bardic poetry on, 10; *Basilikon Doron*, 20, 22–3; views on the Highlands, 22–3
Johnson, Julian, 98
Jones, Henry, 57, 58, 117–18, 120, 122, 123, 138, 141; *Abstract* (1652), 148–50, 163, republished in 1662, 152, 162, 164, 165; commentary on 'A discourse of two councillors of state', 153; *Remonstrance*, 99, 123, 135, 138, 141, 152, 154, 163, 166, criticisms of 92–3, 154, publication, 85–91, 169, 170, response to, 92–3, similarities in later publications, 95, 100, 107, 141, 143, 176
Justice, High Court of, 149–50, 163

Keating, Geoffrey, 6; 'Foras Feasa ar Éirinn', 6
Kerdiff, John, 56, 58, 69–70
Kildare, George Fitzgerald, sixteenth earl of, *see* Fitzgerald, George
Kildare, county, 43, 56, 66; Naas, 66; reconsecration of the church, 66
Kilkenny, county, 66, 67, 73, 149
Kilkenny, town, 66, 149; printing press in, 156; severed heads displayed in marketplace, 66–7
Kinde, Joyce, 69
King, George, *see* Dublin, Clontarf
King, Robert, 42
King's County, 64; Philipstown, 64

A lanthorne for landlords, 40
Laois, 36, 41, 42, 124
Laud, William, 49; reactions to his 'innovations', 50
Le Strange, Thomas, 72
Lecky, William, 15–16

Leicester, Robert Sidney, second earl of,
see Sidney, Robert
Lenthall, William, 87, 139
Lisle, Philip Sidney, Viscount, see Sidney,
Philip
Littlefield, George, 44
Lockyer, Robert, 136
London, 72, 111, 136, 137, 169, 173, 175;
anti-Catholicism in, 51, 61, 63, 83,
124, 161; Irish people in, 113, 123;
print trade, 8, 13, 14, 84, 85, 86, 100,
105, 108, 109, 114, 116, 118, 119,
138, 148, 156. See also print
Lone, Martha, 63
lords justices (John Borlase and William
Parsons), 61, 62, 91, 98, 101, 113,
136, 156, 166, 171, 172; actions
prior to 1641, 50–1; angered by
Remonstrance of grievances, 94, 156;
appointment, 50–1; blamed for the
rebellion, 56, 94, 153, 154, 155, 156,
160–1, 162, 165, 167, 177; criticised
by Castlehaven, 161–2; defended by
Temple, 97; defended by Waring, 142;
dissemination of news from Ireland,
77, 86, 87, 109, 133, 169, 170; initial
interpretations of the rebellion,
77–85, 87, 93, 100, 154, 173, 175–6;
suppressing the rebellion, 119, 122, 155
Low Countries, 58, 127, 140–1, 168;
Dutch Revolt, 21
Louth, county, 43; Drogheda, 43, 59,
86, 95, 113, 120, 122, 138, 142, 143,
sacked by Cromwell, 138–9, 141;
Dundalk, 70
Lucas, William, 67
Ludlow, Edmund, 160
Lynch, Brian, 65

McAuley, Tibbott, 64
Mac Bhaird, Uilliam Óg, 158
McCann, Toole, 72
McCarthy, Donnell, 64
McCarthy, Florence, 64
MacDonnell, Randal, third earl of
Antrim, 2, 50; ill-fated 'Irish' army, 50;
implicated in the Rising, 87
McGeoghegan, Ross, 66
MacMahon, Hugh Óg, 51, 78, 79
Madison, Katherine, 98
Maguire, clan, 54, 55, 72
Maguire, Conor, second baron
Enniskillen, 54, 79, 99, 112, 134

Maguire, Don Carrage, 54
marketplace, 39, 60, 63–4, 65, 66, 67,
139, 172; displays of violence, 64,
66–7; venue for communication, 60,
172
Massey, Edward, 100, 136
Mawe, Nathaniell, 98
Maxwell, James, 56
Maxwell, Robert, 1–4, 41, 43, 71, 95, 96,
133, 134
Maynes, James, 112
Mayo, county, 63
Meath, county, 43, 66, 111; Crufty, 86;
Julianstown, 137, 141, 142; Kells, 111;
Trim, 94
Meredith, Adam, 96; Ormond's cvrtain
drawn, 96–8
Meredith, Robert, 95
Milton, John, 134, 137
Monaghan, county, 43, 51, 66, 69, 79,
90, 112; Carrickmacross, 66; Castle
Blaney, 78
Monaghan, town, 51, 79
Monro, Robert, 93
Montgomery, Sir James, 83
Morland, Samuel, 129–30; History of the
evangelical Churches of the valleys of
Piedmont, 129
Morley, Thomas, 95; Remonstrance of the
barbarous cruelties, 95–6, 134, 164
Moryson, Fynes, 11
Mountgarret, Richard Butler, third
Viscount, see Butler, Richard

Native Americans, 9, 14, 22, 24, 27,
126, 127, 130, 135, 140; literary
representations, 12, 17, 18, 19–20, 21,
27, 40, 126; massacre at Jamestown,
Virginia, 24–8
native Irish, passim, 62, 64, 68, 70, 77, 79,
87, 99, 124, 138, 149; chieftains seen
as violent, 20, 24, 36; definition, 10;
fears of Protestant anti-popish plot, 50,
75; grievances pre-1641, 52–8, 83, 84,
170; literary representations pre-1641,
9, 11, 12, 17, 29–40, 46; New English
views on, 5, 11, 17, 29, 37, 38–40,
45, 51; portrayal of native Irish rebels,
88, 100, 111–13, 117, 126, 135,
137, 141–3, 145, 148, 173, 175, 177;
relations with New English, 4, 5, 40–7,
80–2; relations with Old English, 2, 4,
6, 7, 10, 59, 153; response to the wider

INDEX

Wicklow, town, 65, 74, 82, 115; Arklow, 112; burned by Coote, 155; Carnew, 65; Kilmouth, 115; O'Byrne rebels in, 74

Wisedom, John, 69

Wrixon, Steven, 112

York, 156

Lightning Source UK Ltd.
Milton Keynes UK
UKHW021448040219
336726UK00003B/494/P